FOOTBALL COACH'S SURVIVAL GUIDE

Michael D. Koehler

PARKER PUBLISHING COMPANY
West Nyack, New York 10995

Library of Congress Cataloging-in-Publication Data

Koehler, Mike,
    Football coach's survival guide : practical techniques and materials
for building an effective program and a winning team /
Michael D. Koehler.
      p. cm.
     ISBN 0-13-324187-4 (spiral)   ISBN 0-13-570011-6 (paper)
     1. Football—United States—Coaching.   2. Motivation (Psychology)
I. Title.
GV954.4K64   1992   92-2937
796.332'07—dc20   CIP

Printed in the United States of America

10 9 8 7 6 5 4 3 2 1

ISBN: 0-13-324187-4(S)   ISBN: 0-13-570011-6(P)

PARKER PUBLISHING COMPANY
West Nyack, NY 10994

A Simon & Schuster Company

On the World Wide Web at http://www.phdirect.com

Prentice-Hall International (UK) Limited, *London*
Prentice-Hall of Australia Pty. Limited, *Sydney*
Prentice-Hall Canada Inc., *Toronto*
Prentice-Hall Hispanoamericana, S.A., *Mexico*
Prentice-Hall of India Private Limited, *New Delhi*
Prentice-Hall of Japan, Inc., *Tokyo*
Simon & Schuster Asia Pte. Ltd., *Singapore*
Editora Prentice-Hall do Brasil, Ltda., *Rio de Janeiro*

ACKNOWLEDGMENTS

The author would like to extend a special note of appreciation to Neil Wiawolowski and Shari Mueller for providing so much information on nutrition and conditioning, to Mike Penrod for his help with the materials on weightlifting, to Paul Adams for his assistance with all the nitty gritty, to Kevin Lefevre for the equipment checklist in Section 8, and to Pat Koehler for her continuing association with the word processor. This book would not have been the same without them.

DEDICATION

To Pat for helping me find the way.

To Kathleen, Carrie, and Peggy for being
   one of my life's greatest accomplishments.

And to 29 years of football players for allowing
   me to touch their lives—and for touching mine.

ABOUT THE AUTHOR

Mike Koehler has been a counselor and football coach at Deerfield High School for 27 years, and an adjunct professor of educational administration and supervision at Northeastern Illinois University for 18 years. He played fullback for the universities of Marquette and Nebraska and has been involved in football for almost 40 years. He has written four books on the subject, all published by Prentice Hall. He has also developed a videotape for the College Board entitled "The ABCs of Eligibility for the College-Bound Student Athlete." The grandson of Jim Thorpe, Mike has written a biography of his grandfather for a university press, has co-authored *Commitment of Champions* with former NFL standout Bill Glass, and has recently published *America's Greatest Coaches*. A Ph.D. in administration, he has written scores of articles for educational journals, a newspaper column, a nationally syndicated radio show for John Doremus, and the *Dial Santa* and *Cinnamon Bear* episodes for Bell Telephone. Dr. Koehler has been happily married to wife Pat for 29 years and is the father of three lovely daughters: Kathleen, Carrie, and Peggy.

FOREWORD

It doesn't take a young football coach long to realize that coaching is a whole lot more than Xs and Os and inspirational pep talks. It also involves team discipline, motivation, scouting, game day preparation, academic advisement, even budgeting and recordkeeping. Coaches must have an awareness of drugs, particularly steroids, and of their negative effects on the minds and bodies of athletes.

They must be familiar with many of the bylaws of the NCAA, particularly those governing eligibility and recruiting. The problems confronting athletes and coaches at the interscholastic and intercollegiate levels are important issues. The NCAA is one of the nation's primary organizations trying to do something about them. Obviously, therefore, coaches have responsibilities extending well beyond the practice and game fields.

That's why I recommend Mike's book. It takes a good look at fundamentals, scouting, and the development of solid offensive and defensive programs. But it does more. It considers the academic as well as the athletic needs of players. It discusses discipline and motivation, and it addresses organizational needs such as budgeting, fundraising, and recordkeeping that are so important to the development and maintenance of a successful football program.

I discovered a long time ago that effective organization is accompanied by a lot of good luck. The two go hand-in-hand. This book provides solid principles of offensive and defensive football; it outlines materials and processes for scouting and practice; and, most importantly, it addresses the personal and educational needs of athletes—the primary reason why you and I went into coaching in the first place.

George Kelly
Assistant Football Coach and
Assistant Athletic Director
University of Notre Dame

For those of us who still savor the smells of analgesic balm and musty shoulder pads, high school football represents one of this country's few remaining havens for amateurism. It is a corner in the sports world where the search for personal excellence transcends money and win-loss records, where the coach is the head of a family which takes pride in the personal as well as the physical accomplishments of each of its members. Unfortunately, however, high school coaches encounter problems along the way.

Their jobs have become increasingly complicated by community expectations to win, legal issues, drug use by athletes, financial limitations, time constraints, declining student enrollments, and a range of pressures that reflect the unique character of their schools. Add to these such intangibles as society's growing preoccupation with self-indulgence over self-sacrifice, and a "me-first" philosophy that compromises attempts at team commitment, and the challenges facing to-day's football coaches become disturbingly obvious.

In addition, such challenges sometimes turn into conflicts and, occasionally, into all-out war. This book will help; it will help you survive *and* win. Most importantly, it will help your players think and behave like winners, regardless of the number of games they win each year. And it will help you survive that ever-widening range of critical and often unpredictable situations that confront every high school football coach.

Consider the following topics:

- Motivation is one of the most important factors. Great coaches are great teachers. They use the same principles on the playing field and in the locker room that teachers use in the classroom. They want their athletes to be motivated to learn and, once they've learned, to perform to the best of their ability. Motivation is the key. Great coaches have complete repertoires of motivational strategies. Like great teachers, coaches don't fill buckets; they light fires.

  Section 2 helps light those fires by identifying motivation as a needs-based system and by discussing ways to influence the conditions and circumstances that affect player and team motivation. It distinguishes between motivation and inspiration and incorporates the most recent thinking on visualization as a technique to enhance player performance.

- Once the players are actualizing their potential, a few will be identified by you and others as "college material." As important, most will not. These two facts require early and continuing communication with parents and players to align their expectations with the "real world" of athletic scholarships. The college-bound student-athlete warrants one kind of treatment. It will be dealt with extensively in a later section. The college-bound student *non*-athlete warrants another.

  Section 10, therefore, provides a well-documented look at the whole question of college athletics: the availability of scholarships, "walk-on" opportunities, and the unlikelihood of ever playing professionally. All football coaches, particularly those who are successful, are inconvenienced each year by a surprisingly large number of players and parents who simply don't understand college football well enough to evaluate their son's performance realistically. This section will help you provide that information for them—and reaffirm your relationship with them in the process.

• Section 1 addresses a related issue by looking at athletics and academics. Most of the concerns expressed in the media are based in reality. Many athletes are sacrificing their educational development for a few fast years in the "sports spotlight." As tragically, a few unprincipled college coaches are helping them. Any chance of reversing this situation depends on the willingness and the ability of high school coaches to intervene.

This section emphasizes, therefore, a process for building a coalition among coaches, counselors, teachers, and parents to assure the academic as well as the athletic achievement of football players. It even outlines ways to work with feeder schools to help establish appropriate academic programs for prospective high school athletes. The NCAA's By-law 14.3 (Proposition 48) is discussed, along with processes for receiving information from teachers regarding the classroom performance of players. The procedure accomplishes two important things. It constitutes good PR for you and the football program, and it provides the information parents need to plan within the changing framework of NCAA rules.

• Game preparation is one of the most important tasks facing any high school football coach. Scouting your opponents is a time-consuming task but can be accomplished with a minimum of hassle with the right format. Section 5 provides one of the best formats in the country. It provides the forms and the processes needed to determine not only your opponent's offensive and defensive tendencies but your own as well. Self-scouting is essential for the coach who wants to break his own offensive tendencies in big games. This section also provides a formation-calling system that makes scouting relatively simple and that can be integrated within your own offensive system.

• Section 8 provides a detailed look at game-day activities, including pre-game preparations, sideline control, halftime activities, post-game wrap-ups, and even media coverage.
  −How can the selection of game captains be used as a motivational factor each week?
  −When is the right time to "climb on them" or "back off" at halftime?
  −When should you "peak" a team during the week or before a game?
  −How do you deal with losses, victories, final-game letdown?

• Schools across the country are realizing the benefits of audio-visual technology in a variety of ways. Scores of universities videotape their entire practice sessions as teaching tools for team meetings. High school coaches can do the same thing, using AV equipment to provide mirrors for team and individual performance during practice and in games. Section 7 discusses several ways that videotapes can be used by coaches to complement explanations of both fundamental and strategic player skills.

- The day steroids found their way into high school football programs was the day coaches should have taken a real, hard look at their own values and priorities. Society's preoccupation with "winning at all costs" should remain the province of the benighted masses that will never understand the fundamental purposes of high school sports programs. Such a philosophy and its potential for abuses of all kinds has no place in high schools.

  Section 12, therefore, provides a detailed process, including relevant statistics, for informing parents and students of the dangers of drug use and for establishing a pre-season dialogue among coaches, players, and parents to explain the program's position regarding drug use and other training violations. A sample agenda is provided, along with copies of presentation materials that can be made into transparencies.

- The highly recruited athlete and his parents can become nervous wrecks well before the time to sign a National Letter of Intent. NCAA guidelines, as restrictive as they may try to be regarding phone calls and visits from coaches, are still generous enough to provide substantial interference to a family's normal home and school routine. Coaches must often, therefore, run interference for their players.

  Section 11 outlines a process for working with the families and a series of questions that must be asked of recruiters before, during, and after the athlete actually visits the school. Selection of the right school involves appropriate program of study and optimal levels of academic and athletic competition. That the word "student" comes first in the term "student-athlete" is an important consideration for players and their parents. Coaches often have to help sustain the focus.

- The most visible criterion for the success of a football coach and his program is his win-loss record. This book emphasizes the fact that it is not the only criterion; it is, however, among the most important. Section 4, therefore, discusses a process for developing and organizing a strong offense and defense. Specifics include a professional growth package for assistant coaches, methods for refining the offense and the defense, and sample agendas for meeting with the staff to coordinate what is to be taught from the freshman through the varsity levels.

- Remaining sections emphasize in and off-season conditioning and weightlifting, individual and team discipline, the recruitment of players, fundraising activities and procedures, communication with the parent community, and legal issues.

Finally, reproducible copies of all forms and letters are provided in each section to simplify the tasks and processes outlined in the book. Coaches soon discover that their associations with students and parents are among their most satisfying professional responsibilities. They can also be among the most frustrating. Such experiences affirm the adage that the recipe for winning unfortunately is almost the same as for a nervous breakdown.

This book will enable you to distinguish between the two.

Michael Koehler

====== CONTENTS ======

Section 4   OFFENSIVE AND DEFENSIVE FOOTBALL: GUIDING PRINCIPLES 61

The Three Essentials (62) ● Sequence (63) ● Integration (73) ● Passing Offense (80) ● Continuity (80) ● Sequence (81) ● Integration (82) ● Examples (82) ● Defense (86) ● Continuity (86) ● Sequence (88) ● Integration (90) ● Teachability (92) ● Personnel Considerations (94) ● Adaptability (95) ● Let's Wrap It Up (96)

Section 5   GAME PREPARATION 97

Know Your Opponent (97) • The Scouting Format (104)
• Bringing Things into Focus (110) • The Who and
When of Scouting (113) • About Films and Tapes (116) •
Coaches' Meeting (118) • *Perfect* Practice Makes Perfect
(121) • Practicing the Game Plan (121) • A Final Word:
Take a Good Look at Yourself (132)

Section 6   PRACTICING TO WIN 133

Practice in General (134) • More About Drill (135) • A
Few Specifics (141) • The Scouting Report (142) •
Scrimmaging (146) • When to Scrimmage (146) • When
Not to Scrimmage (147) • Let's Wrap It Up (148)

Section 10   ATHLETIC SCHOLARSHIPS

A Look at the Past (205) ● A Look at the Present (206) ●
Athletic Scholarships: Fact and Fantasy (207) ● What
About the Pros? (209) ● More About the Meeting (209) ●
Additional Specifics (212) ● More to Share in the
Meeting—or Elsewhere (212) ● Let's Wrap It Up (220)

Section 10 Figures:

Section 11   PLAYER RECRUITMENT

The Need for Bodies (221) ● Supply Lines (222) ●
Coordinating Experiences (225) ● Working Together
(226) ● Attracting Parents (228) ● Attracting Athletes
(228) ● A Word About "The Specialist" (233) ● Let's
Wrap It Up (234)

Section 11 Figures:

Section 16 RECORDKEEPING

The "How" (289) ● The "What" (290) ● The Intermediate File (291) ● The Indeterminate File (299) ● Let's Wrap It Up (304)

SECTION 1

Athletics and Academics

Remember the time during your football career when "abuse" was something you did to your body to stay in shape? Well, maybe "abuse" isn't the right word, although some of those workouts came close. It is the right word, however, for what some coaches and players are doing today to standards of integrity and fair play—*some* coaches. Fortunately, most of us still play by the rules. That's what this book is all about, a much-needed reassertion that "class" is still more than a room on campus. Within most football programs, class still represents conviction and strength of character.

But let's admit it. We coaches do have our problems, particularly since society has created such a wide range of temptations to entice kids away from self-sacrifice and hard work. Self-gratification has replaced self-sacrifice and hard drugs have replaced hard work. Remember, for example, when a dumbbell was the only "muscle enhancer" you could find? Today, dumbbells *use* muscle enhancers, and a few of them become NFL rookies with 4.3 forties and 1.3 GPAs.

What bothers me most is that they think a "poor sport" is an educated old-timer like me who never landed a million-dollar contract. Our job as coaches is to do something about that, to teach kids that drugs are killers and a pay-off is the satisfaction of a game well-played—not well-paid—that even great athletes should not expect to go from the cradle of knowledge to the lap of luxury. You and I know that such expectations often introduce some of life's greatest disappointments.

I have been involved in organized football for 40 years, and it has never disappointed me, primarily because—to paraphrase Jack Kennedy—I was interested in what I could do for the game, not what the game could do for me. I expected from it only the day-by-day opportunity to find a challenge that ultimately fulfilled me as a person. The bonuses it provided were post-season awards, not pre-season checks.

I capped my teeth, not business deals—and paydirt was always the end zone. Power plays, quarterback sneaks, and end runs were nothing more than

1

offensive strategies—not contract maneuvers and recruiting tactics. For that matter, "offensive" players were defined by their play *on* the field, instead of their behavior *off* the field. And fortunately, my experiences in high school football saved me from dealing with strikes; we had wide-outs, not hold outs.

Remember when doctored transcripts were restricted to the players in pre-med, and graduation rates were cap and gown fees? In some schools today they are statistics coaches try to hide. Fortunately, the NCAA has done something about that by requiring member institutions to publicize the graduation rates of their athletes. High school football coaches can help by expecting recruiters to share such information with kids who are good enough to play in college. That, too, is the focus of this section.

The primary focus, however, is to put the "student" back into "student-athlete." It outlines a process for assuring a complementary relationship between academics and athletics and for safeguarding each athlete's right and responsibility to get an education. It reminds coaches that "crossing the line" is scoring a touchdown, not violating traditional principles of decency and fair play. And it suggests ways to teach abusers that winning at all costs is too high a price to pay.

UNITED WE STAND

Abusers will never have to pay the price until the people who have the power decide to use it. American education's romance with the hierarchy reaches into every aspect of our relationships, especially into athletics. Head coaches in some universities are nothing short of emperors, their immediate power virtually unlimited. Even their assistants share the power. They represent it with players and others inside and outside the university.

Wise college coaches realize, however, that the source of their power is well outside the castle gates. The folks at the lower levels of the hierarchy, the high school coaches and the parents of the athletes, are the wellsprings of the college coach's power. If they don't give it, the college coach doesn't have it. Major college coaches (most of whom are not abusers) may enjoy widespread popularity and recurring moments in the spotlight, but the ultimate power they exercise is a reflection of the athletes they recruit. They need the help of high school coaches to recruit great athletes.

Recent NCAA legislation has limited the amount of time an athlete may devote to his or her sport and has sought to publicize the graduation rates of athletes. Abuses in college sports, however, will not be significantly reduced until the people with the power, parents and high school coaches, start sending kids to the right schools for the right reasons.

Anyone who has put the pads on, survived the workouts, and bumped into his fellow-man for more than a few hours, realizes that a college coach isn't doing you a favor when he awards you an athletic scholarship to play football. The physical commitment can be health-threatening, and the time commitment can be grade-threatening. Without athletes who are willing to make such commitments, coaches soon lose their jobs.

We're in this together. High school and college coaches need each other, and both need dedicated and talented athletes to maintain their programs. Most important, the athletes need high school and college experiences that not only showcase their athletic talents but develop their intellectual and social gifts as well. It's obvious that only one element in the equation is more important than the others—the athletes.

So forget the hierarchy. The traditional perception that college coaches are more important or better than high school coaches and their athletes has resulted in a concession of power that leads inevitably to abuse—by some. Power must not be conceded to all college coaches because of their perceived status in the sports hierarchy. It must be given selectively to those college coaches who use it to develop upstanding football programs that operate in the best interests of themselves, their schools, and their athletes.

THE NEED FOR A COALITION

If all those theorists who told about "synergy" are correct—if combined actions are stronger than the sum of their individual actions, then a high school coalition of coach, counselor, parent, administrator, and student-athlete carries the potential not only to curb the power of abusers, but to provide the process for student-athletes to select schools for the right reasons. When the right people seek the right information and, by their involvement, underscore the importance of such variables as program of study and likelihood of graduation, then the personal charisma of coaches and their win-loss records become less important reasons for selecting certain schools.

QUESTIONS OF POWER

As illustrated in Figure 1–1, the coalition working with the student-athlete generates the power that ultimately flows only to those college coaches who seek to educate as well as train their athletes. Power is abused when it is unearned and unrestrained. Appropriate coalitions at the high school level, can withhold power from certain coaches and encourage others to recruit and to train student-

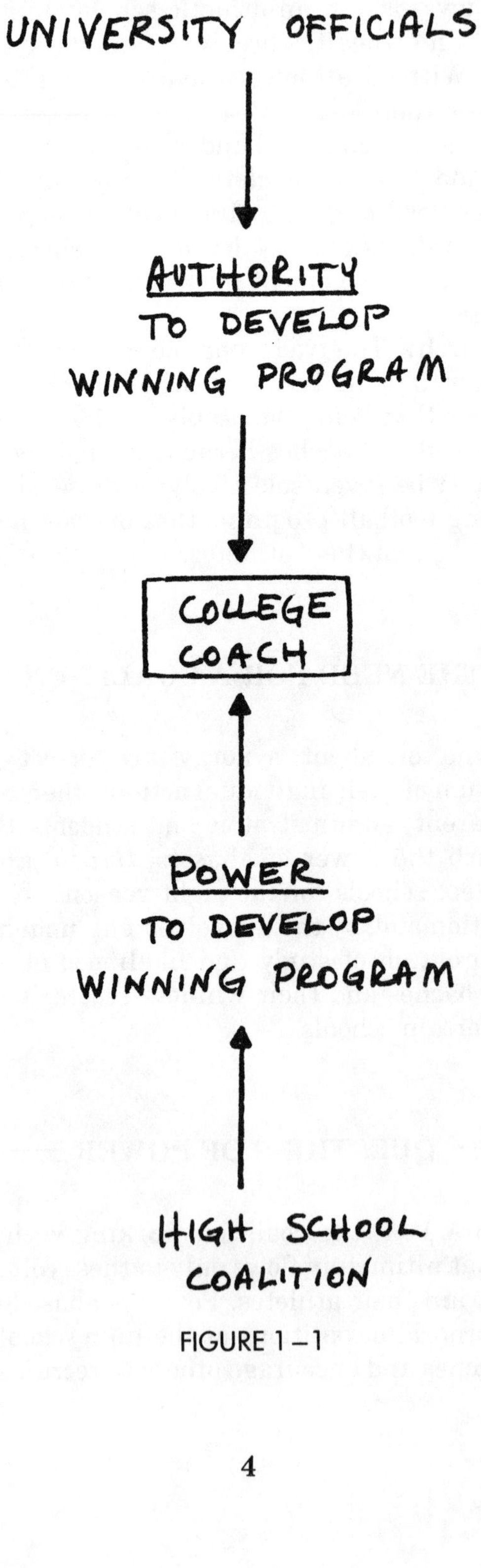

UNIVERSITY OFFICIALS

$\downarrow$

<u>AUTHORITY</u>
TO DEVELOP
WINNING PROGRAM

$\downarrow$

```
COLLEGE
COACH
```

$\uparrow$

<u>POWER</u>
TO DEVELOP
WINNING PROGRAM

$\uparrow$

HIGH SCHOOL
COALITION

FIGURE 1-1

4

athletes. Remember—college coaches have the authority to grant scholarships; the high school coalition has the power to direct the futures of these athletes who ultimately receive them.

Parents are more inclined to enter into an eventual coalition with school personnel if their earliest experiences with the school have been rewarding. One of those early experiences should involve freshman athletes and their parents in an informational meeting with representatives of the athletic and guidance departments. The purpose of this meeting is to identify and discuss all the variables that affect the young athlete's participation in high school athletics and his or her future involvement on the college level. See Figures 1–2, 1–3, 1–4, and 1–5, for reproducible ideas to use in such a meeting.

The primary emphasis should involve academics and the process and programs available in the school to assist students with their learning. The eligibility requirements of state associations and of the high school should be discussed and reinforced by appropriate passouts. The School Code should be highlighted, particularly as it relates to training rules and their violations. Given society's current battles with drugs, special mention should be made of the school's position regarding drug use, including alcohol, tobacco, and steroids. Some schools go so far as to require students and their parents to attend informational meetings and to sign agreements before the student is permitted to participate in athletics. See Figure 1–6.

THE MEETING IS THE THING

Exactly how these meetings are offered is less important than when they are offered. Too few high schools across the country routinely meet with freshman athletes and their parents to emphasize the importance of academics, to outline the expectations of such regulating bodies as the NCAA, and to initiate that necessary first meeting that can result in a crucial coalition of parents and school personnel.

The meeting is a first attempt to create the synergy that results from people working together. Most high schools within the past several years have been characterized by a diffusion of power that ultimately concedes control to college coaches—all college coaches, even those who are inclined to abuse that control. The high school coalition can curb such abuse, and the informational meeting is the beginning of the coalition.

To make the meeting worthwhile for everyone, parents require the kind of information that enhances academic planning throughout high school and that identifies school personnel who can assist them with such planning. When the coach is one of these school people and is seen this soon in the athlete's high school career as an academic helpmate as well as an athletic taskmaster, parents are more inclined to enter into a coalition with him when and if college athletics becomes an issue.

Use the following checklist to remind yourself of your coalition tasks.

PRE-SEASON

Did I:

_____ Meet with counselor in spring of junior year to discuss college?

_____ Establish calendar with student to assure completion of career inventories?

_____ Discuss senior year registration with counselor to assure completion of NCAA requirements?

_____ Discuss with student a list of colleges developed with counselor?

_____ Visit selected college campuses?

IN-SEASON

Did I:

_____ See that student gains admission to at least one school?

_____ Check with counselor to assure completion of NCAA requirements?

_____ Check with teachers to assure good academic progress?

_____ Meet with coach to deal with persistent recruiters?

POST-SEASON

Did I:

_____ Revise list of schools to reflect possible scholarship offers?

_____ Meet with coach to assess student's athletic skills?

_____ Meet with coach to deal with persistent recruiters?

_____ Accompany student on all college visitations?

_____ Sustain contact with coalition?

FIGURE 1–2

COALITION CHECKLIST—COUNSELOR

Use the following checklist to remind yourself of your coalition tasks.

PRE-SEASON

Did I:

_____ Meet with athlete to administer career inventories?

_____ Interpret results with him/her?

_____ Review transcript to assure completion of NCAA requirements?

_____ Help student-athlete develop a list of schools?

IN-SEASON

Did I:

_____ See if athlete has initiated college application process?

_____ Periodically check grades to assure completion of NCAA requirements?

_____ Notify parents if athlete is performing poorly in classroom?

_____ Meet with highly recruited athletes to assess schools?

_____ Maintain contact with coach and parents to provide recruiters with academic information as appropriate?

POST-SEASON

Did I:

_____ Discuss with coach athletes who are candidates for athletic scholarships?

_____ Change athlete's registration for second semester as needed to assure completion of NCAA requirements?

_____ Seek exceptions to admissions requirements at selective schools for athletes expected to sign Letter of Intent?

_____ Meet with coalition to determine processes?

FIGURE 1-3

Use the following checklist to remind yourself of your coalition tasks.

PRE-SEASON

Did I:

_____ Organize statistics of college-bound student-athletes?

_____ Notify colleges of student-athletes who are likely to compete at that level?

_____ Tell student-athletes to apply to college as if they had no interest in playing football?

IN-SEASON

Did I:

_____ Maintain statistics of student-athletes?

_____ Motivate students to perform well in the classroom as well as on the field?

_____ Assure appropriate press coverage for deserving athletes?

POST-SEASON

Did I:

_____ Consolidate statistics and forward to appropriate colleges?

_____ Meet with athlete and parents to identify schools that are consistent with athletic abilities?

_____ Seek post-season honors and recognition for deserving athletes?

_____ Review NCAA bylaws regarding recruiting and financial aid?

_____ Determine from recruiters and other university personnel graduation rates of student-athletes?

_____ Maintain contact with the coalition?

FIGURE 1—4

COALITION CHECKLIST—ATHLETIC DIRECTOR

Use the following checklist to remind yourself of your coalition tasks.

PRE-SEASON

Did I:

_____ Distribute to coalition updated NCAA legislation?

_____ Provide in-service experiences for coaches?

_____ Discuss with junior athletes and their parents in the spring of the year the realities of athletic scholarships to college?

_____ Supervise coaches to assure their involvement in the coalition?

IN-SEASON

Did I:

_____ Continue to inform coalition of changing NCAA legislation?

_____ Maintain helping relationship with coaches to sustain their involvement in the coalition?

_____ Continue to secure needed PR for team and player accomplishments?

POST-SEASON

Did I:

_____ Meet with coach prior to the initial meeting of the coalition?

_____ Continue supervisory relationship with coach?

_____ Share all relevant information with the coalition?

_____ Coordinate schedules of members of coalition and arrange for initial meeting?

FIGURE 1–5

TOWNSHIP HIGH SCHOOL DISTRICT
Athletic Code—PHILOSOPHY

High School District _____ officials and coaches of athletic teams believe that those students who are selected for the privilege of membership on teams should conduct themselves as responsible representatives of their schools. In order to insure this conduct, athletic directors and coaches will enforce this Athletic Code. Members of teams who fail to abide by this Athletic Code are subject to disciplinary action as prescribed by the Code. As recognized representatives of their schools, members of District _____ teams must demonstrate the character and behavior outlined in this Code. Behavior of team members is to be monitored by coaches and school officials in or out of season, in or out of uniform, whether on campus or off.

The close contact in District _____ activities of advisors and coaches provides them with a unique opportunity to observe, confront and assist young people. District _____ therefore supports education and awareness training in adolescent chemical use problems, including the symptomatology of chemical dependency and special issues affecting District activities for administrators, athletic directors, coaches, advisors, participants and their families.

SECTION I

A. An athlete at District _____ will be subject to disciplinary action if he or she commits any of the following violations:
1. Falsification of a signature on the athletic permit card or physical form. (If falsification is by a parent or another student, the athlete will be held responsible.)
2. Theft or vandalism of any school property.
3. Acts of unsportsmanlike conduct during the sport season in which the athlete is involved, such as cheating, fighting, or verbal abuse of officials, contestants, coaches or spectators.
4. Use of or possession of tobacco (all forms), alcohol, marijuana or any illegal drugs or related paraphernalia, look-alikes, or abuse of prescription/nonprescription drugs.

Each coach has the prerogative to establish additional rules pertaining to the activity supervised. These rules may include attendance at practice, detentions, curfew, dress and general conduct of participants during practices, contests and trips, and will be handled by the coach. These rules are also to be clearly communicated to the student/athlete.

SECTION II

Any violation of the stated policy while the athlete is enrolled in District _____ will result in the following action:

A. FIRST OFFENSE:
1. Suspension from all athletic contests for two (2) consecutive interscholastic events, or two weeks of the season, whichever is greater, with the student expected to participate in all practice sessions during that time. No exception is permitted for a student who becomes a participant in a treatment program.
2. If drugs or alcohol are involved, a mandatory conference with the Substance Abuse Coordinator and/or the Athletic Director, the parent(s) or guardian(s) and the student athlete is required for reinstatement. The athlete may not practice until his or her coach has received notification from the Coordinator or Athletic Director that a preliminary contact has occurred.
3. Voluntary admission of an infraction of a training rule regarding substance abuse will not result in a two-week suspension, but will count as a first offense. In such cases, a mandatory conference with the Substance Abuse Coordinator and/or the Athletic Director is still required. (The purpose of this provision is to allow an athlete to seek help.) This voluntary admission may *not* be used by a student if the school is already aware of the rules infraction. This provision may be used only one time by any athlete.

B. SECOND OFFENSE:
1. After confirmation of a second violation, the student shall lose eligibility for the next six (6) weeks in which the student is participating, but will be expected to practice. If necessary, this suspension may be carried over from one sports season into another, or from one year into the next year. The athlete must complete the season during which the penalty is being served. (In addition to the above penalty, if the second offense occurs during the same sport season in the same school year, the student shall lose eligibility for all practices and contests for the remainder of that season.) No exception is permitted for a student who becomes a participant in a treatment program.
2. If drugs or alcohol are involved, a mandatory conference with the Substance Abuse Coordinator and/or the Athletic Director, the parent(s) or guardian(s) and the student athlete is required for reinstatement. The athlete may not practice until his or her coach has received notification from the Coordinator or Athletic Director that a preliminary contact has occurred.

C. THIRD OFFENSE:
1. After confirmation of a third or subsequent violation, the student shall lose interscholastic eligibility for one full calendar year.
2. If drugs or alcohol are involved, a mandatory conference with the Substance Abuse Coordinator and/or the Athletic Director, the parent(s) or guardian(s) and the student athlete is required for reinstatement. The athlete may not practice until his or her coach has received notification from the Coordinator or Athletic Director that a preliminary contact has occurred.

These sanctions apply to all athletes whether or not they are actively engaged in their sport(s) at the time of violation. The penalties shall be cumulative beginning with the student athlete's signing of this code and continuing throughout the athlete's high school career. This policy is in effect throughout the calendar year and does not supersede District _____ school disciplinary policies.

_____
Athlete's Name (please print)

Year of Graduation _____

I understand and agree to abide by all the provisions of the Athletic Code.

_____   _____
Date   Athlete's Signature

I understand and agree to support all the provisions of the Athletic Code.

_____   _____
Date   Parent's Signature

FIGURE 1–6

10

COLORING OUTSIDE THE LINES

A few school districts across the country realize the value of engaging the high school coach in academic planning to the point of having him work with elementary and junior high school students to encourage their improved performance in the classroom. All too often he is called upon to quell spontaneous uprisings in the cafeteria or to introduce discipline to the "great undisciplined." Less often is his special reputation used to provoke academic uprisings or to inspire the "great unmotivated."

Let's admit it. To most aspiring young athletes, the high school football coach is a God-figure, a highly visible link between the boundaries of the home and community and the limitless possibilities that are football. High school coaches in all sports must tap into this resource of academic potential, and school administrators must provide the time and financial and professional support coaches need to do the job.

Years ago, Bob Mager indicated that education operates on the organizational principle that people "reallyoughttowanna," in essence that the storied commitment of teachers to education should result in their willingness to take on any task that helps kids. Well, experience indicates that many teachers do just that; others don't. Even those teachers who do take on added responsibilities require some kind of administrative recognition—beyond a pat on the back or a quick thank you.

Some coaches educate the "whole student," on the field and off. They extend their responsibilities beyond blocking drills and play-action passes; they take time off the field to work with a different set of fundamentals—the human needs of the students they coach. Other coaches see their jobs as a succession of Xs and Os, film analyses, and game-day strategies—de-personalized tasks that seek team victories, sometimes at the expense of the individual development of their athletes. Great coaches do both. They meet the personal and athletic needs of their players.

WE ALL NEED SUPPORT

Fortunately, coaches who care only about Xs and Os are a minority. The point, however, is that both kinds of coaches need administrative support, in the first instance to continue working with and for students; in the second instance to start to work with them. If coaches are to devote time to the activities of the coalition and, in some instances, to spend time in elementary schools and junior highs to inspire kids to work harder academically, they need administrative support: money and time.

In effect, if the educational and personal as well as the athletic needs of students are to matter to coaches, they must matter to the school's administration.

And they matter to the school's administration when the school puts its money where its proverbial mouth is. Coaches should be paid for their extra responsibilities and/or given extra free time to plan, to learn more about the curriculum, and to meet with students and their parents. A sense of school commitment is required if the coach is to feel the importance of his responsibilities.

WE'RE ALL IN THIS TOGETHER

Such a total commitment also requires the understanding of others in the school who might "get their noses out of joint" when coaches start getting into the academic act. Because their charisma generally extends well beyond athletics, many coaches will be working with a variety of students, not just student-athletes. Schools, therefore, are well-advised to explain at an early faculty meeting the coach's involvement in the program and to emphasize the fact that he is not replacing but complementing the involvement of others in the school.

If introduced thoughtfully to the rest of the school, the coach as academic advisor will be seen not as an intrusion but as a positive influence on the academic development of prospective high school students. Obviously, the concept is most appropriate within culturally deprived communities, but it has some value in all school districts. Of most value, however, is the coach's involvement in the school's coalition to help student-athletes and their parents find appropriate college experiences. That is the primary thrust of the remainder of this chapter.

THE COALITION: WHO DOES WHAT

To consolidate power within the coalition, each person within it has several specific tasks to perform. The accumulation of these tasks and the information they provide will result in the ultimate selection of the right college for each student-athlete. Incidentally, it also should result in the denial of certain university programs that fail to graduate a reasonable number of their student-athletes or otherwise abuse standards of academic and athletic integrity.

Following, then, is a list of the responsibilities of each member of the coalition. The responsibilities have been divided into three categories: Pre-season (which includes the spring preceding the senior year), In-season, and Post-season. The classification highlights the processes that must be followed and the information that must be shared if the student-athlete and his parents are to find a school that satisfies his academic as well as his athletic needs.

Notice that the specifics of athletic scholarships and the circumstances affecting the highly recruited athlete are discussed in later chapters. The purpose of this information is not to highlight ways to get scholarships but to plan intelligently for high school and college. As such, many of the tasks are relevant for all students, not just student-athletes. The student—in this case, the student-athlete—must assume much of the responsibility and perform many of the following tasks. The tasks are listed under the categories of parent or counselor only to emphasize the fact that they must be done, usually with the student-athlete to encourage relevant dialogue.

PRE-SEASON TASKS

Counselor

1. Meet with student-athlete to administer and/or to interpret career inventories.

    The primary purpose of college is to pursue a specialized field of study leading to a career. Encouraging the student-athlete to identify his interests as they relate to potential careers underscores the real reason for college.

2. Use the results of career inventories to identify and discuss with student-athlete the important variables that affect college selection: program of study, graduation rates, job placement possibilities, relative competitiveness of program, geographical location, size of school, and so forth.

    The identification and discussion of such variables is important for all students but particularly for the student-athlete. Most athletes, especially in high school, live in a world so crowded with the visions and sensations of football that little room is left for anything else. Big games overshadow big tests, and blocking assignments often obscure homework assignments. That student-athletes focus on the educational and social aspects of college, therefore, is critical.

3. Evaluate student-athlete's transcript to assure completion of NCAA requirements. Generally, it's wise to do this in the company of the athlete and his parents.

4. Develop with student-athlete a list of schools that satisfy his career and educational needs.

Parent

1. Meet with counselor in spring of athlete's junior year to discuss college selection process, including questions of financial aid.

    Athletes are allowed to supplement athletic scholarships with additional financial aid such as Pell Grants, if a documented need exists. Parents and athletes are well-advised, therefore, to meet with high school counselors and others who can explain the several options available to them.

2. Establish calendar with student-athlete to assure completion of career inventories and preliminary college selection process. Teenagers are people who have reached the age of dissent. When it comes to completing career inventories, they may need a gentle nudge, as the saying goes, to do what they "reallyoughttowanna."

3. Meet with counselor during registration for senior year classes to assure completion of NCAA academic requirements.

4. Discuss with student-athlete the list of colleges identified in consultation with counselor.

5. Visit selected college campuses to reaffirm such factors as size of school, geographical location, relative competitiveness of program, and so on. To many high school students, college is an exciting but distant and sometimes disturbing experience that happens to someone else. One or more visits bring home the reality that it is just around the corner and that the selection process, although at times stressful, requires immediate attention.

    All too often, football players who are interested in playing in college are content to wait for the end of the football season before they consider college selection. They and their parents are well-advised to find the right school, apply early in the senior year, secure one or more acceptances, then handle football as opportunities materialize at the end of the season.

Coach

1. Maintain personal statistics, including academic information, of prospective college-bound student-athletes. Such statistics should include size, speed, positions on offense and defense, nature of academic program, grade point average, ACT and/or SAT scores, game statistics (yards per carry, unassisted tackles, receptions, passes completed, etc.), uniform number, even educational goals in college. The information that eventually is shared with college and university coaches must not relate exclusively to athletic performance. It must include references to educational considerations to impress upon college coaches the high school's intentions to work with student-athletes.

2. Notify college and university coaches of student-athletes who are likely to compete on the college level. College coaches appreciate these kinds of contacts. They really don't do much with them until the end of the season, but if notified early enough, usually in the winter or spring of the athlete's junior year, they can maintain contact with letters and questionnaires throughout the season. These questionnaires will be more thoroughly discussed in a later section.

3. Meet with student-athletes in the spring of their junior year and again early in their senior year to encourage them to apply to college as if they had no plans to play football. The meeting provokes them to consider the educational and career variables that are most important in the college selection process. When football remains the only variable for high school athletes, it sometimes results in selections for the wrong reasons.

Administrator/Athletic Director

1. Secure and distribute to coaches, counselors and others, updated information regarding NCAA legislation. NCAA conventions are held yearly and often result in significant changes in rules and regulations. Coaches and counselors should be aware of such changes, especially as they affect the college selection process.

2. Encourage coaches and provide opportunities for them to learn more about high school and college athletics by watching tapes, reading books and articles, and attending relevant workshops and conventions.

3. Meet with junior athletes and their parents in the spring of the year to discuss the realities of athletic scholarships, to renew the requirements of bylaw 14.3, and to outline the college selection process. The athletes and their parents should be encouraged to apply to one or more schools early in the fall of the senior year—irrespective of football. Then, once the season has concluded, they can consider additional applications to schools that express interest in them as athletes.

4. Supervise coaches to assure their involvement in the informational sessions and the eventual coalition. Many coaches are inclined to think only of getting good players and using them strategically in practice and games. Who can blame them? Winning is the obvious goal of any football game. Getting them to think beyond win/loss records is critical, however, if coaches are to contribute their influence to the ultimate strength of the coalition. Administrators must let them know that such involvement is expected, and then recognize that involvement, assisting them with appropriate supervisory practices to see that they refine the skills necessary to make the coalition effective.

=========================== **IN-SEASON TASKS** ===========================

Counselor

1. Check to see that student-athletes have initiated the college application procedure. Certainly counselors will do this for all students, particularly in schools that send a significant majority of kids to college. It is especially

important for student-athletes, however, because of their disinclination to think about anything but football and homework during the season and, let's admit it, even homework takes a back seat, hence the counselor's second responsibility.

2. Check grades of student-athletes periodically to assure completion of NCAA requirements. Obviously, this isn't necessary for every athlete in school, just for those few who are marginal achievers and who require periodic "inspiration." Normally it isn't a good idea to wait until the quarter grades come out. It's generally wise to get a weekly update from teachers.

3. Notify parents of student-athletes who are performing poorly in the classroom. Such contacts provide the assistance from school personnel that parents of marginally achieving students sometimes need. They also help develop the foundation for future coalition activities.

4. Meet with recruited student-athletes to see if they are interested in applying to one or more of the colleges that have expressed an interest in them as players. If they are interested, their counselors may have to write recommendations for them and contact the recruiters to determine the advisability of sending the applications to the respective football offices for subsequent processing through the office of admissions.

5. Work with coach and parents to provide recruiters with academic information as appropriate. Giving recruiters transcripts and test scores early in the recruiting process can save everyone involved a lot of time. High school and college coaches don't want to waste their time seeking admission for students who will never meet a particular school's entrance requirements. That's why it's best to be up front with each player's athletic and academic credentials well before any actual recruiting begins.

Parent

1. Assure that student-athlete gains admission to at least one school that satisfies his academic and career interests. Scholarship offers to the right schools are icing on the cake. All high school football players, regardless of their pre-season press, should select schools as if football for them may end in a month or two—because it might. Injury and an overassessment of ability deny more scholarships to student-athletes than the most stringent NCAA regulations. Athletes must plan accordingly.

2. Maintain contact with high school counselor/advisor to assure the student-athlete's completion of NCAA requirements. Usually a phone call between grading periods and sometimes before the second semester (if course changes are necessary) is sufficient.

3. Maintain periodic communication with teachers to assure the student-athlete's satisfactory academic programs. Again, this is good practice for all students; it is critical, however, for the student-athlete who is a marginal achiever.

4. Meet with coach as necessary to determine procedure for dealing with persistent recruiters. "Blue Chippers" have a way of drawing crowds! High school coaches have the satisfaction of knowing that they *make* Blue Chippers; college coaches do their best to *recruit* them. Barry Switzer once told me that great players make great plays. He realized that great athletes transform good strategy into great strategy, so college coaches devote countless hours to getting the best high school players available each year.

   As much as parents might sympathize with coaches' needs, persistent recruiters, particularly when there are several of them, can throw any normal household routine into a top spin. Parents of highly recruited athletes, therefore, are well-advised to contact the high school coach to determine a process for dealing with recruiters. The specifics of this process are discussed in a later section.

Coach

1. Maintain and update athletic and academic statistics of student-athletes. Whether you do it or you get someone else to do it, the maintenance of player statistics is critical if athletes are to receive the recognition they deserve from the media as well as from college coaches.

2. Throughout the season, inspire student-athletes to perform to the best of their ability in the classroom as well as on the field. Good coaches create the circumstances and conditions within which such motivation occurs, and they provide the periodic inspiration needed by athletes to sustain such motivation. I inspired my backs one year to get on the stick academically by providing an early-bird study hall for non-performers in the classroom. It worked. Occasionally, kids need that kind of inspiration.

   Some teams identify their outstanding student-athletes at the end-of-the-year banquet. Such players are recognized along with "Most Improved" and "Most Valuable." That works, too. More will be said of such recognition later in this section.

3. Assure appropriate press coverage and honors recognition for deserving student-athletes. Some football coaches, normally bulldogs, turn into pussy cats when it comes to the local media. For some reason, they fail to hound the right people in recognizing the accomplishments of some of their athletes. Such recognition, academic as well as athletic, always influences the extent to which such athletes will be recruited at the end of the season.

Coaches are well-advised to realize that good publicity is a four-step process: one—identify something worthy of recognition; two—tell people; three—tell people; and four—tell people.

Administrator/Athletic Director

1. Continue to distribute relevant eligibility information to coaches and parents as needed/available. The NCAA holds a national convention each year to address relevant issues and to effect the legislation necessary to influence college athletics. Changes in NCAA bylaws must be shared regularly with parents and school personnel to assure compliance and to avoid the legal and PR problems that can result when athletes don't receive the right information.

2. Supervise coaches and sustain their involvement in coalition activities.

3. Continue to seek broad media coverage for the accomplishments of players and teams. The extent to which players receive the recognition and, ultimately, the scholarship offers they deserve is in large part a function of how hard we work for them. It's important for all school personnel to realize that, contrary to the self-perceptions of some sportswriters, they don't have Divine Knowledge. What they know is what we tell them. Regular phone calls and press releases, therefore, are excellent pipelines to the community and to college coaches.

=========================== POST-SEASON TASKS ===========================

Counselor

1. Initiate contact with the coach to discuss athletes who are candidates for athletic scholarships. Some athletes have received questionnaires, letters, and phone calls almost from the start of the season. Others have earned their way, on a game-by-game basis, into the college spotlight. Regardless of when they received the recognition, all such athletes need help narrowing their choices and coordinating them with their educational and career goals.

2. Make registration changes as necessary for second semester to assure completion of NCAA requirements. Normally, such changes are unnecessary. In the case of a few marginally achieving students, however, one or two courses may have to be added during the second semester to assure completion of the 13 core units.

3. Contact selective schools to determine admissions exceptions for students expected to sign the National Letter of Intent before such schools provide notification of acceptance. Many highly selective schools don't notify students of admissions decisions until early spring. Because the National Letter of Intent signing day is usually in early February, the offices of admissions of such schools have to make concessions for student-athletes being recruited by their coaches. Athletes who are interested in these schools must be informed of their admissibility earlier than normal if they are to sign the Letter of Intent.

   Admissions offices in highly selective schools, therefore, have a process appropriately dubbed a "squeeze play" that provides early admissions decisions to athletes being recruited by their schools. Without such a process, athletes are often compelled to sign with other schools. The particulars of the process usually require the input of both the high school coach and counselor. A quick phone call to the college coach and admissions office is advisable, and often a letter is required.

4. Meet with high school coalition (athlete, coach, AD, counselor, and parents) to organize the "who" and "what" of the college selection process. Important questions have to be answered about each school, including:

   - graduation rates of student-athletes (such information is now available to counselors and coaches by NCAA mandate.)
   - availability of program of study (if schools offering scholarships don't have the program of study, then what?)
   - housing accommodations (athletic or regular dorms?)
   - off-season time commitment (conditioning, weight training, etc.)
   - the placement possibilities in field of study
   - for a more extensive list, see Section 13, "The Highly Recruited Athlete."

Parent

1. Prepare with student-athlete a list of schools that meet his academic, career, and athletic interests. Unlike the pre-season selection of schools, this list reflects football as well as academic interests.

2. Meet with coaches to discuss the appropriateness of the list. Students and parents, particularly after a successful football season, sometimes find their expectations out of line with the real world of intercollegiate athletics. A meeting with the coach should affirm or modify the list of schools so that it ultimately provides a satisfying and potentially successful college experience for the student-athlete.

3. If the student-athlete is highly recruited, use the meeting with the coach to determine a process to have the coach coordinate activities with the recruiters. Recruiters should be instructed to call the coach and to check with him before visiting the student-athlete at home or at school. Ultimately, the coalition should assist with the identification of three to five schools that are realistic and appropriate choices for the student-athlete. Other colleges should be notified by the coach that their interest is appreciated but that the athlete is interested in other schools. (See Section 13 for additional information on this process.)

4. Accompany student-athlete on all college visitations to assure that the right questions are being asked and that the answers are consistent with the student-athlete's expectations and needs.

5. Sustain contact with the coalition to assure the different perspectives and the support needed to select the right school. Often all it takes is a phone call or a short visit with the right person to get needed information or assistance. Coaches and counselors must remind parents that the door is always open for such contacts.

Coach

1. Organize all personal statistics, including academic information, of student-athlete and forward to the appropriate colleges. Some players may already be on the mailing lists of certain colleges; other players—because of their senior year successes—warrant letters and phone calls as soon as the season ends, sometimes before. A cumulative sheet of personal statistics is the best way to attract the attention of college scouts/recruiters.

2. Meet with student-athlete and parents, as appropriate, to identify schools which are consistent with intended area of study and football abilities. Obviously, such a meeting should be held prior to any mailings or phone calls. Such assessments should be shared with other members of the coalition to assure that everyone is operating from the same base of information.

3. Aggressively seek post-season honors and recognition for deserving student-athletes. Having maintained lists of relevant statistics for selected athletes, coaches need only forward them to newspapers and other organizations to stimulate the kind of recognition such players deserve. Great players are not in it for the recognition they receive; usually their love of the game is at the top of the list. But great coaches guarantee recognition for deserving players.

4. Review NCAA bylaws regarding recruiting, student eligibility, and financial aid before recruiters start visiting. High school coaches must be familiar with all NCAA legislation, including recent changes, in order

to avoid jeopardizing an athlete's college career and to advise parents and other school personnel of proper procedures. In fact, it's often advisable to share materials with other members of the coalition. See Section 10 for additional information and reproducibles.

5. Determine from recruiters and other university personnel the graduation rates of football players in five years. Recent information released by the *Louisville Courier-Journal* reveals that graduation rates of football players in just the Big Ten universities ranges from a low of 18% to a high of 74%. The Southeast Conference is similar with a range from 16% to 65%. The average graduation rate for the SEC was 33%; for the Big Ten, 48%. High school athletes and their parents deserve to know such information.

6. Finally, maintain contact with the other members of the coalition to reaffirm the student-athlete's career and education plans and to guarantee that college coaches seeking visits with highly recruited athletes check in first with the high school coach.

Administrator/Athletic Director

1. Meet with the coach prior to the initial meeting of the coalition to reaffirm its purposes and processes. Members of the coalition have significant responsibilities prior to the end of the football season, but the real "coalescing" doesn't start until this initial meeting. That everyone understands his or her role, therefore, is essential. The student-athlete may be the main character, but the coach probably is foremost among the supporting cast.

2. Continue supervisory relationship with the coach to enhance his involvement in the process. The supervisory relationship is not evaluative or controlling but facilitating and helping. In essence, the athletic director's job is to continue to ask the essential question, "Is there anything I can do to help out?" The coach may be bumping into constraints involving time, secretarial help, scheduling complications, even comfort level with the process. The AD can help considerably by meeting periodically with the coach to identify these problems and help resolve them. In the process, he or she can review with the coach the NCAA regulations regarding eligibility and financial aid.

3. Share all relevant information with the other members of the coalition. If the athletic department has been sponsoring routine meetings to provide information regarding academic expectations and scholarship availability, student-athletes and their parents will be generally familiar with what the NCAA is all about. Some additional specifics might be helpful, particularly if they involve changes in NCAA bylaws.

4. Coordinate schedules of members of coalition and arrange for the initial meeting. Considering the telephone tag we all play at times, this may be the most difficult part of the whole process, but it's consistent with the AD's responsibility to facilitate the kind of dialogue that leads to good decisions.

════════ A FINAL WORD ABOUT THE COALITION ════════

As you can tell, the coalition provides primarily a coordinating function. It is not decisional. The final decision regarding the selection of a school rests exclusively with the student-athlete and his parent(s). The coalition does, however, influence the scope and direction of the decision by securing, sharing, and discussing relevant information about potential schools and their football programs. (See the Coalition Checklists—figures 1–2 through 1–5—for reproductions to be given to coalition members during informational meetings). As indicated already, characteristics deserving investigation are: program of study, graduation rates, size of school, location, relative competitiveness of academic and athletic programs, and many others. See Section 13 for a complete list of characteristics.

It is this influence on the final decision made by the athlete and his parents that consolidates the power of the high school coalition. The knowledge of specifics such as graduation rates of student-athletes and job placement possibilities after graduation is power—power which ultimately is granted only to those college coaches who can be expecting to use it in the best interests of their programs and of their student-athletes.

To extend the point for a moment more, consider the ultimate power of a national coalition of high school coaches. The thought of putting such a coalition together is staggering, but imagine such a group securing information about the graduation rates of all colleges and joining forces to isolate those colleges/coaches who fail to graduate an optimal number of their student-athletes. Further imagine the national coalition imposing sanctions (refusal to allow recruiting in high school, parental refusal to allow athletes to attend such schools, and so on) on colleges which consistently abuse players and programs. The NCAA has the authority to spank such abusers; a national coalition of high school personnel and parents would have the muscle to make it hurt. Such a national coalition, however, is the subject of another book.

Get Into the Feeder Schools

Dr. Rick Turner at the University of Virginia developed a pilot program several years ago that engaged high school football coaches in the academic planning and monitoring of junior high school students. He organized it on the assumption that high school coaches are "God figures" who command the attention of all students, particularly athletes. He further assumed that coaches would be able to convince students to take the appropriate academic programs and to work hard in order to satisfy high school expectations.

He was right. Dr. Turner's studies validated his assumptions. The junior high students in his control group did work closer to their ability levels, and they were more inclined to accept the challenges of an improved academic program. Common sense is often substantiated by research. In this instance, it also resulted in the improved learning experiences of a significant number of students, most of whom probably won't have to worry about the possible future implications of bylaw 14.3 (Proposition 48).

Could more schools engage in similar programs? Probably. Will they? Probably not. Convincing most schools to change is like convincing Vince Lombardi that winning is only incidental to a football game. They simply don't think in such terms. New ideas in education invariably experience the same fate. They don't last long. Why, for example, are ideas surrounded with so much enthusiasm at birth, neglected so obviously during infancy, abandoned so indifferently in their youth, mourned so little after death, and resurrected so blindly 20 years later? The answer is found in the systems within which we work. By definition, systems are resistant to change. To introduce the concept of getting high school coaches into the feeder schools, therefore, concerned persons will have to plan, hope, and then follow three important steps:

- Prove that a problem exists. Gather some statistics to underscore the reality of relatively poor academic achievement of selected students, athletes in particular. This is easier in some schools than in others, but it is relatively easy in any school. In every school, there are some students easily identifiable, who will respond positively to the advice of the local high school coach.

- Show that your solution will work. Dr. Turner has a convincing collection of statistics that prove the validity of his ideas. Supplement them with your own position if you agree that such an idea has merit.

- Show how the constraints of time and money can be overcome without overburdening any segment of the school staff. Periodic relief from one or more teaching and/or supervisory assignments is generally sufficient for the head coach. Providing substitute time or a small stipend is additional incentive for him to attribute the necessary importance to the task.

It's also important to meet with the counseling and even the special education departments to assure them that no one is stepping on their toes. The purpose of the head coach is to complement, not to replace, the work of the pupil personnel staff. Without this brief meeting, the concept could be undermined by the possible resistance of important persons within the school. As indicated already in this chapter, counselors and coaches must collaborate much more closely than they have in the past.

THE COLLEGE CONSULTANT

If your school has a college consultant, he or she should also be involved in some of the planning activities of the coalition. Counselors certainly have knowledge of college admissions requirements and programs of study, but the added expertise of a college consultant can make the information that much more valuable for the athlete and his parents. The consultant should be invited to the initial meeting of the coalition and should volunteer to assist parents whenever they require specific information. The college consultant can also represent the guidance department in the informative meetings that are presented for freshman and junior athletes and their parents.

BE TRUE TO YOUR VALUES

Saying that coursework is important to us as coaches is one thing; showing it in our behavior is another. We have all learned through our association with football that the ready hand wins more games than the ready tongue. It also emphasizes the student in student-athlete by providing incentives that help players see the value in hitting the books every bit as hard as they hit opposing players.

POST-SEASON AWARDS

On the reward side of such incentives, teams can recognize student-athletes at post-season banquets. When such recognition is provided to excellent students— and, surprisingly, it's done rarely—teams usually recognize the player with the highest grade point average with one award and the player with the most improved grade point average with another. This second award gives underachievers something to shoot at. They are often the ones most in need of incentives; the ones likely to be hit the hardest by bylaw 14.3

FOOTBALL STUDY HALLS

On the natural consequences side of the incentives are Early Bird Study Halls. Players who are close to falling short of in-season eligibility requirements established by the school, conference, or state, often see the light when coaches inform them that they have been assigned to an Early Bird Study Hall. The study hall may be just for the football team or it may be for all fall sports, but usually it starts about 45 minutes before the first period class, is overseen by one of the coaches, and can involve student tutors who have volunteered their time to help out. It is also advisable to provide the study hall for all athletes, in essence to make it preventative as well as remedial.

The National Honor Society and other service organizations in the school often seek opportunities to donate their time to school projects. You and I have learned that every once in a while a real "project" comes along, a player who would rather pull his own teeth than open a book. Well, Early Bird Study Halls for the team—*in-season*—may not be as painful as pulling teeth, but they are attention-getters. More important, they let athletes know that help is available, and they let everyone know, the community included, that we as coaches, contrary to popular perceptions, aren't all talk!.

=================== **LET'S WRAP IT UP** ===================

Any college coach worth his salt realizes that high school coaches wield a lot of power. Dr. Rick Turner realized much the same thing when he referred to high school coaches as "God figures." Such coaches can influence the academic experiences of athletes before they enter high school or college. Their personal charisma and their association with a sport rich in tradition make them very powerful people in the lives of students.

Most often we channel this power almost exclusively into winning football games. Less often do we use it to influence the academic experiences of our athletes. In this regard we may be as guilty as some of our intercollegiate counterparts by seeing our players primarily as so many means to an end. High school football needs coaches who recognize the power we have, use it to develop athletes as well as win games, and share it only with college coaches who share the responsibility to seek the total development of our players.

No one, not the finest coach in the most upstanding university program, is good enough or wise enough to be trusted with unlimited power. High school coaches must give it to them wisely. The high school coalition can help; so can the additional ideas outlined in this section.

SECTION 2

Motivation

Motivation Defined

Let's be careful to avoid any confusion between inspiration and motivation. G.K. Chesterton once said, "At its best, inspiration means breath, and only too frequently it means wind." Some of us know exactly what he meant. We have either played for or worked with at least one coach who could breathe fire into his players, and we have also experienced the coach who somehow managed to talk in someone else's sleep.

This section deals only marginally with our ability to inspire others. It deals primarily with a concept that each of us can master, the ability to manipulate the football environment in order to promote player motivation. For our purposes, let's define motivation as any internal stimulus to action which is affected by external circumstances and conditions. That's where you and I come in. First, we must be aware of the needs and interests that players already have; second, we must devise ways to promote the needs and interests they *don't* have.

Call one internal motivation, the other external motivation. The terms are unimportant. What is important is our awareness of the needs that every player brings to practice and games; the satisfaction he seeks from playing football. It's important for each of us to understand these needs and to promote ways to satisfy them.

What are the Needs?

A quick look at the basic ego and social needs of every young adult reveals that motivation for the football coach is a simple process. The mere fact that we are involved with *football*—and all that the word suggests—gives us an advantage that most classroom teachers pray for. At the risk of sounding professorial, I'd like to list the six ego needs identified by Henry A. Murray several decades ago. They are relatively unchanged today:

• Achievement

—To accomplish something difficult

- Counteraction
- Order
- Understanding
- Play
- Sensuous Experience

—To overcome weakness in one-self

—To put everything in its place

—To master a body of knowledge

—To participate in sports

—To be involved in events

Obviously, each of these needs relates to our desire to see ourselves as worthwhile, to develop and preserve positive self concepts. Like most sports, football offers players continuing opportunities to satisfy each of these needs. I need not explain how. The answers are too obvious.

The relationship of football to the satisfaction of a player's *social* needs is equally obvious. The social needs of all young adults involve:

- Deference
- Affiliation
- Succorance

- Abasement
- Exhibition
- Autonomy
- Dominance
- Nurturance
- Aggression
- Rejection

—To support a superior

—To work with someone

—To receive help (as from a team-mate)

—To accept blame

—To impress others

—To be free to follow impulses

—To control others

—To console others

—To oppose forcefully

—To dispose of an inferior

Just a cursory glance at the ego and social needs of young adults tells us that coaches live in the best of all possible worlds. Not only do these needs provide for the long-term involvement of athletes, but they sustain their interest and enthusiasm on a short-term basis. Whether in a game or at a practice session, players seek to satisfy their needs for affiliation, exhibition, aggression, and all the others. All we as coaches have to do is provide the right opportunities for them. That, too, warrants some brief discussion.

Motivation and Maslow

Most of us are familiar with Maslow's Hierarchy of Needs. It's a familiar cornerstone of many of the education courses we took in college. For the moment, let's strip away some of the ivy from his model and look at Maslow's ideas from a football coach's perspective. The time is well spent.

Figure 2–1 provides a look at Maslow's pyramid. Two of its characteristics are particularly important. One, movement up the pyramid is possible only when a lower-level need is satisfied. In other words, security needs don't come into play until physiological needs have been met. Two, unmet needs are motivators. The security needs become motivators as soon as the physiological needs have been satisfied.

What all this means to you and me is that the athlete's need to realize his full potential as a football player is dependent upon the satisfaction of several basic needs that coaches must recognize and acknowledge. Let's look at our players through Maslow's eyes. I'm not sure that he had football in mind when he developed his theory, but he'd certainly agree with how we're using it.

Physiological needs. Those of us working in the inner city already realize the problems of working with poorly fed kids. If they have the courage to even come out for football, they rarely perform well because of their physical and emotional limitations. Consider another example, one that is more obvious to all of us—the continuing question of water on the practice field.

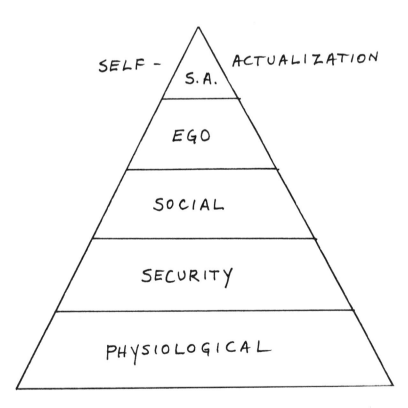

FIGURE 2–1 MASLOW'S HIERARCHY

Research has indicated that the loss of even 5% of our body fluids can drain us of as much as 25% of our mental capacity. A few of our "shining lights" can't afford any kind of a drain on their mental capacity. So when a player is thirsty, don't try to teach him anything. All he can think about is water. So give it to him. Maslow's Hierarchy may sound pretty academic, but, really, that's all it boils down to. When the team is thirsty, give them water, all they can drink— or you're wasting the rest of your practice session.

The rest of Maslow's hierarchy involves the same kind of common sense.

Security Needs. All of us want to feel safe—unless we're so hungry that we're willing to risk anything for food. Once we have food and drink, however, our need for safety becomes a motivator. Until football players feel safe, that is, until they feel confident of being treated fairly, they will not take risks, the kinds of risks that result in what we sometimes call "flashes of brilliance." Only a secure athlete is capable of such performances.

Such athletes don't require handling with kid gloves. They can take their share of verbal abuse, if they have it coming. All they expect and all they require is to be treated fairly, to feel confident that no one is "out to get them." This is as true for the third and fourth teamer as it is for the star performers, perhaps more so for them because they constitute the team.

Social Needs. Once athletes feel secure, they are ready to seek a sense of belonging, of acceptance, of giving and receiving help; in essence, of team membership. This characteristic of Maslow's Hierarchy warrants repeating. Once the lower levels have been satisfied, the higher levels become motivators. Athletes desire a sense of team membership. Molding a team is not the difficult task that some coaches make it.

So if you have a problem developing a sense of team unity, look at your behavior and the sense of safety that prevails among your players. Without the security that comes from being treated fairly, either by you or the other players, athletes spend most of their time worrying about themselves and are unable to develop the spontaneous bonds that result in a team. Once such bonds have been developed and strengthened, the team will form and ultimately become a family. More of the family concept will be discussed later in this section.

Ego Needs. Nurturing families provide the atmosphere for individual growth. Consider some classrooms in some schools and universities. The levels of competition for grades and the relative absence of cooperation among students usually thwarts a real sense of belonging—of the feeling that "we're in this together." Only the brightest and most capable, therefore, are able to develop a sense of competence or independence. In such a climate, one that fails to satisfy the student's social needs, it is virtually impossible for all but a few to satisfy their ego needs.

Contrast this with a successful football team, not one with just a good win/ loss record, but one that values the contributions of everyone, from the smallest prep teamer to the biggest star. Such a team convinces every player that he is vital to the team's success, that the team wouldn't be the same without him. They convince players of this fact because they mean it. Prep teamers may not score many touchdowns on game day, but the job they do during the rest of the week makes all those touchdowns possible. So if your prep teamers bear the traditional title "hamburgers," get a "Hamburger Helper" out there to praise their contributions. Everyone will grow as a result.

The worst athlete on the field, once he gains a sense of team membership, will start to work on his ego needs—the needs for achievement, competence, recognition, and appreciation. He may realize that his athletic skills are weak, but the confidence he builds being a contributing member of the team will carry over into his classroom and personal behavior. Players who persist in acting like winners soon become winners. That's how you and I motivate.

Self-Actualization Needs. All of us spend the better part of each day trying to realize our potential. Some of us are better than others at actualizing it. Usually, the ones who are most successful have satisfied their social and ego needs to the point where they are able to become creative in the broadest sense of the term. Coaches are among the most privileged persons in schools when it comes to providing opportunities for young adults to realize such potential.

We've already seen how fair play and recognition of each player's contributions enable the entire team to move up Maslow's Hierarchy. Few other professions provide such willing "workers," young men capable of such significant growth. Our job simply is to provide the conditions and the circumstances that foster such growth, but the building blocks must be laid thoughtfully if we hope to foster self-actualization among our players.

Consider, for example, the advice we often give to young athletes: "Trust your body." We've learned that without that ability a tackle will never master an area block, a quarterback will never develop the "feel" he needs to consistently complete passes, and a running back will never capitalize on the kinesthetic sense that gives him "eyes in the back of his head." It is a critical insight, important for every player but mastered by only a few. Why?

Well, one reason may involve the inability of most players to satisfy the safety, social, and ego needs as identified by Maslow. Remember, until they are satisfied, players cannot move up the hierarchy. If a talented running back is constantly intimidated, therefore, or is ostracized for whatever reason by his teammates, don't expect him to trust his body. Trusting your body is a weaker need than trusting your teammates or your coach.

Another Perspective

We've all worked with players who did just enough to get the job done, to make the team or to keep their starting positions. And if we've been fortunate, we've also worked with one or more "115 percenters" who always seem able to give just a little more whenever it's needed. The difference between these two types of players is generally the difference between the kinds of rewards they receive.

Countless studies support the idea that fair treatment, good human relations, and security are sufficient to get an athlete to do enough to get the job done. This same research also indicates that more of the same is *not* enough to get players to go beyond bare expectations. More is needed.

To exceed expectations and to give what Frederick Herzberg calls the "performance investment," players require a sense of autonomy, esteem, recognition, and continuing opportunities for self-fulfillment. Having established this position as a framework, let's focus on some specifics within it.

Putting Maslow to Work

A good theory is nothing but a road map that leads the way through and around the obstacles and opportunities that face us daily. Maslow's theory is better than most, especially as it gives coaches a way to understand and predict the individual and collective behaviors of football players. Let's look at a few.

The Unmotivated Player

First of all, no player is unmotivated. He may be motivated in directions different from yours, but he *is* motivated. Your job—"if you should choose to accept it"—in essence, if the player is worth the trouble, is to determine why his motivations are inconsistent with yours. Once you make that determination, get him to change directions.

Simple inquiry may uncover personal problems, an unmentioned injury, or identification with a group outside the team: another sport, a gang, a clique, or so forth. He may also be identifying with a sub-group on the team, one that may be violating training rules and/or disregarding the authority of you and the coaching staff. This sometimes happens in very insidious ways but becomes apparent after close scrutiny.

Injury, even minor but recurring injury, sometimes won't allow a player to progress beyond his physiological needs—hence his apparent unmotivation. Personal problems may not allow him to progress beyond his safety needs. And affiliation with an outside group or an oppositional sub-group on the team will satisfy his social needs but in a way inconsistent with yours.

Whatever the cause, you're going to want to know what it is. Personal problems and injuries are dealt with in one way, oppositional sub-groups in another. Maslow would remind us that if a player's social needs are being satisfied, neither they nor his security needs are motivators. Make them motivators again! John Wooden indicated once that one of his best weapons in the battle of wills was "the bench" or, in the case of training rules violations, expulsion from the team.

These are not drastic measures. Once a player's security becomes a motivator, he is more inclined to listen to you. If he genuinely enjoys football, he will suddenly become more motivated. Then you can work with him again regarding the ways he chooses to satisfy his social needs. Recognize and accept that if he's a standout player, you may lose a game or two in the process, but in the long run your program will be better off—much better off.

The Highly Motivated Player

Don Coryell, when he was coaching the San Diego Chargers, once said, "The country is full of good coaches. What it takes to win is a bunch of interested players." Let there be no doubt about it, interested players make a coach's job a whole lot easier. And just think, all it takes to keep them interested is a positive stroke or two. Such players also provide a different perspective on the whole question of motivation.

Contrary to popular opinion, the highly motivated athlete is not really a rarity. My experience has been that most football teams are loaded with them. They just don't tend to dominate the ranks of standout athletes. Gifted athletes, especially in high school, sometimes take their gifts for granted and require from their coaches an occasional boost to use them consistently.

Less talented athletes, by the mere fact of their being on the field, are often highly motivated. Just try to convince me that the prep teamer who takes a beating day after day and keeps coming back for more is not highly motivated. If his love of the game is not pure and unencumbered with such things as recognition issues, then I've missed the boat for most of my career.

The key for the successful coach is to build his program around such kids, irrespective of their talents as football players. Recognize them by establishing awards for them or, more appropriately, by talking with them to reinforce their values and, by so doing, letting other players know that what they represent as athletes and as young men is what you are looking for in your team. The gutsy prep teamer, if appropriately acknowledged by his coaches and teammates, can be an inspiration to even your most talented starters. Capitalize on his strengths, too.

The Highly Talented Player

A coach once asked me how I motivated one of my All-State running backs, a kid with enough kinesthetic sense to put cats to shame. I replied that the knowledge came only with years of experience and involved my saying to him: "Way to run, Billy!" I learned long ago that open admiration is often the best motivator. I also learned not to compromise raw talent with too much coaching.

Remember, motivation is nothing more than creating the conditions and the circumstances within which an athlete does his own thing. The best circumstance for some highly talented athletes is simply to let them do their own thing. Getting out of the way is difficult for some coaches, but for the highly talented player, particularly if he's highly motivated, there really isn't much for us to do, except recognize him and appreciate him.

It's also important to keep in mind, however, that the recognition and appreciation should always occur within the context of team values. No player, no matter how talented, is responsible for a team's success—just as no player is ever responsible for a team's lack of success. One of our most significant accomplishments as coaches, therefore, may be to keep the highly talented athlete's feet on the ground, where they will do him, you, and your team the most good.

The Untalented Player

Talent is relative. Scholarshipped athletes in college are, by definition, talented players, but some of them routinely get pounded every game day. Consider Coach Rick Venturi's comment when he was taking his lumps at Northwestern: "The only difference between me and General Custer is that I have to watch the films the next day." Let's admit it, we have all identified with Coach Venturi and with General Custer on more than one occasion.

A part of the reason may involve a lack of talent as well as our inability to use what talent we had. Maslow also wrote very extensively about the term "synergy," a force created when the combined sum of the parts is greater than their individual sums. It's a fascinating concept and underscores the importance of cooperative effort.

Sometimes the synergistic combinations of untalented and quasi-talented athletes can result in surprisingly successful seasons. The key is the cooperative effort the team displays on game days. One part of that effort can result from the offensive and defensive strategies established by the coaching staff. This element will be discussed in a future chapter. Another part involves the scouting format and how it affects game day strategies. This, too, is a subject of future discussion.

This section involves motivation and the effects it can have on a team with no standout performers. If we provide the circumstances within which players learn to believe in themselves, we can stand back and watch them grow—taller and heavier. They even start to look faster. Within Maslow's framework, belief in oneself leads to generous doses of self-actualization. Within the coaching rubric, belief in oneself is little different from what English poet John Dryden said about it: "For they conquer who *believe* they can."

We took the practice field in mid-August one year with a team of almost no seniors. Our starting eleven promised to be so young that our biggest fear on hot practice days was diaper rash. Because they learned early, however, that only a concerted effort would get the job done, they soon established a collective identity, and then they believed in themselves. The rest was hard work and satisfaction— for all of us.

The Coach as Model

Hard work and satisfaction are the hallmarks of the successful football coach. Coaches who model these characteristics in their own behavior soon see them reflected in a team's performance. In fact, successful coaches model all the behaviors they expect in their players. They don't just talk motivation; they are motivated—in all the right directions.

- *Hard work*—Coaches should be the first ones on the practice field, and they should have on hand a knowledge of fundamentals and a complete breakdown of everything the upcoming opponent is likely to do. Midway through the week, every player on the team should have the same knowledge of the opponent's tendencies, and the only way he'll have it is if your scouting report is complete and in his hands the first day of practice.

  Coaches have to work hard to provide such information. The specific tasks they have to perform are discussed in a future chapter, but the commitment they make to the report will be reflected in their hard work and ultimately will spill over onto the team. Laziness is collectively restricting. It begins like a cobweb but soon binds like a chain. So does hard work.

- *Values*—Be what you believe—or you really don't believe it. The proverbial commitment to excellence is a universal value, and it goes well beyond the world of athletics. It is found in the behavior of all great coaches. It transcends their win-loss records, even the innovations they may have introduced to their sports. Their commitment is found in what they *represent*. Let's put it this way. Coaches are people who can explain what they represent; good coaches are people who can teach what they represent; great coaches are people who are what they represent.

  Their greatness in relationship to their values is found not only in their ability to inspire others but also in their ability to be inspirations. They inspire humility in victory and resolution in defeat. They realize, for example, that there may be a million reasons for defeat—but not one excuse. They make none and they allow their players to make none.

  Some segments of our society call coaching values old-fashioned: fair play, self-sacrifice, team commitment, and hard work. Well, they may be, but they're still as relevant as love of family and basic honesty. They are values that are as desirable today as they were centuries ago, and no one said they are easily achieved. The old saying reminds us that living up to such values is easier than dying for them. But if we don't live up to them, how can we expect our players to?

- *Adult behavior*—Coach Ray Malavasi once said, "They say losing builds character. I have all the character I need." His comment may be funny, but it ain't no joke! Not only does losing build character—sometimes—but it becomes habitual. If unchecked, losing breeds losing, and it breeds losers. That's its worst effect. Coaches, however, can do something about it.

  Childish responses to a loss include making excuses, laughing it off, and quitting. It's unfortunate but true that many players and some coaches are inclined to respond in one of these ways. Sometimes they do it without realizing it. A "what's-the-use" attitude often results in less work, and excuses always obscure any possibility of learning from failure.

  To an adult, an occasional failure is an opportunity in disguise, a chance to learn, to be better in the next attempt. Coaches must reflect this attitude. Failure provides them the opportunity to work harder, to show their players what it takes to stand up to adversity. It represents the chance to show young adults that they may fail—many times—but *be* failures only when they start making excuses or blaming someone else.

  Success provides similar opportunities. It represents the chance to accept victory graciously, without arrogance, and to affirm the importance of a team effort. Vince Lombardi once said, "Coaches who can outline on a blackboard are a dime a dozen. The ones who win get inside their players and motivate." One of the best ways to get inside them, as Lombardi knew so well, is to *be* what you expect from them.

- *Caring*—John Wooden once indicated that he always assured his players of his availability to them when they faced personal problems. His players can attest to the many hours he spent with some of them off the court to help them resolve personal issues. They also will attest to his expectations that these same problems were never allowed to interfere with their on-court performance.

  Wooden, first of all, realized the importance of caring for the entire player, not just his athletic ability; he also realized, however, that young men don't become strong until they can face personal problems and continue to accept their responsibilities. All effective coaches reflect a similar attitude. Caring for our players rejects any attempts to make excuses for them.

  It also rejects the idea that we somehow have to become "buddies" to them. The 17- or 20-year-old isn't alive who needs a 40-year-old pal. What he needs is a friend, a respected adult who values his contributions no matter how small, and who seeks only what is in the player's and team's best interests—no matter how difficult.

Inspiration and Motivation

This section already has emphasized the distinction between inspiration and motivation. Now it's time to emphasize the importance of both, as long as we continue to realize that motivation operates inside the player—inspiration outside. And the inspiration on the outside won't have its effect unless the motivation on the inside is willing to accept the message. This is a critical point. The coach who relies on his personal charisma or his speaking ability to inspire but fails to incorporate at least some of what we've discussed in this chapter is in for a lot of frustration and disappointment.

Pep talks work on motivated kids. They intensify the fires in players who already want to do the job; they momentarily warm everyone else. The athlete must be the source of the fire. Inspiration (literally, it means breath) simply gives motivation intensity. Inspiration, therefore, is essential, but it is lost on the unmotivated athlete.

It can be lost on the motivated player as well if it is inadequately prepared or delivered. How about the coach who when he returned home from the big game was asked by his wife: "How did your pep talk go?" His answer: "Which one? The one I prepared? The one I delivered? Or the one I gave in the car on the way home?"

Sometimes a good pep talk is spontaneous; most often it is planned, even rehearsed. The inspirational moment in the big game can't be left to chance. The speaker is rare who can inspire dozens of young men, no matter how badly they want to be inspired, without at least identifying a focus for his speech and giving it some organization.

He must be prepared for at least two possible contingencies. If the team is emotionally sky high already, any attempts to get players up may be counterproductive. The purpose of a good pep talk is not to work players into a "feeding frenzy," but to heighten their desires to perform to the best of their ability. There are times when some teams have to be brought down if they are to execute their assignments intelligently. The good coach must be prepared for both possibilities.

Slogans

Good slogans are abstractions of the coach's philosophy, the commitments he expects from his players and the reflections of his own behavior. If placed conspicuously throughout the lockerroom and surrounding area, they constantly remind players and coaches of their reasons for being on the team. Like pep talks, they are moments of inspiration and serve as motivators only to the degree that they remind players of the needs they bring to the sport.

In that regard, the best slogans contain catchwords that are traditionally important to the team. I spent many years at a school which emphasized the family concept, for example, so just above the doorway exiting the lockerroom was the slogan "One family, one destiny." I had never seen the slogan anywhere else; neither had the players. So it became theirs—and hopefully still is.

This school also had the following slogan in the hallway leading to the practice field: "Pain is temporary; pride is forever." It reminded each athlete, every day, not only of the commitments expected of him but of the esteem needs he was seeking to satisfy. Obviously, the school's coaches never mentioned esteem needs to the players! They were very conscious of them, however, when thinking about motivation.

Effective slogans, then, probably should have at least two characteristics. One, they should suggest ways to satisfy the motivational needs that players bring to their sports. Two, they should contain catchwords that embody the themes that are traditionally important to the team and school. It is best, then, to avoid hackneyed phrases like "It's not the size of the dog in the fight but the size of the fight in the dog" and to create a few of your own slogans. They will be more personally relevant to the players and that much more inspirational.

Speaking of inspirational, a team I know developed the tradition of touching the slogan above the door every time players left the lockerroom on the way to the game field. The slogan was simple—"Unity – Pride – Total Effort"—but it embodied everything the coaches emphasized each year. Of special importance to me during a recent visit was the fact that it also reflected—in order—Maslow's higher order needs: social, ego, and self-actualization.

The Social Context

Sports really are unique in our country. In a society where a love of things is reflected on TV and brightens the eyes of every kid who helps populate the local shopping mall, sports emphasize denial and self-sacrifice. In communities sometimes characterized by their excesses and their "Me-first" values, sports emphasize self-control. And in a world grown increasingly tolerant of mediocrity, sports represent a continuing commitment to personal excellence.

Coaches, therefore, constantly bump into competition from a wide range of social groups: the media, schools, peer groups, parents, and others. Many of the temptations offered by these competing groups are powerful inducements away from the practice field. Compared to the attraction of football, however, they are fighting a losing battle. No "high" or material possession compares to the sustained thrill of athletic competition or to the sense of self-satisfaction that derives from a game well-played. So we can continue to take heart; motivation is still on our side.

The Family Concept

A football "family" has value not in the sense that adults develop children but that children become adults. Such a focus is very important because it determines the nature of the interrelationships among everyone on the team. For one thing, it places the responsibility for growth squarely on the shoulders of the players. It is not so much what coaches do as what players do that influences player growth.

Like good parents, coaches realize that love, not control or authority, is at the core of every happy and productive family. Certainly control is important but only as it assures the ordered relationships that nurture everyone in the family. Family members genuinely care for each other, and the act of caring ultimately produces a synergy that can transform good teams into great teams.

Kids overcome injuries faster when they know they are needed. Players who are inclined to stand on the edge of total commitment dive in enthusiastically when they realize that others are diving in, too, and that no one is pushing them. Practices become opportunities to improve rather than drudgery to overcome. Games become visible commitments that players make to each other. Family members learn quickly that such commitments are not a way of talking, but a way of walking.

The actions of the head coach, the father of the family, are equally important. To him falls the task of emphasizing and modeling important family values. It is a well-known fact that most juvenile delinquents have little knowledge of their family values, let alone a sense of commitment to them. This is perhaps the most easily identified variable that distinguishes between the causes of delinquent and non-delinquent behavior.

Similarly, the identification with family/team values is one of the clearest influences on player behavior and performance. A child on the verge of misbehavior, for example, may well visualize a respected member of the family to assess how he or she would behave in a similar situation. The same is true of teammates and coaches. They, too, serve as models of appropriate and successful behavior.

It's perhaps safe to say that if values are visible in the behavior of respected coaches and players, they exert continuing influence on teammates. The degree of their visibility determines the degree of their influence. The family, then, if caring and nurturing, brings important values to life—every day, on the field and off.

Values do not allow fighting and bickering among family members. They provide a sense of constant support to every member of the family. We had a team manager one year who, before he joined the team, was constantly picked on in the halls by a couple of the school's "losers." Nothing physical transpired between the bullies and the football players; we would not allow that. But the manager was soon able to walk through the halls without fear or intimidation. Families are like that.

The effective family also establishes appropriately high expectations of its members. The football family simply doesn't permit mediocrity, on the field or in the classroom. The search for individual excellence, the goal of every family member, does not end on the way home from practice. The values that are important to the family are important all the time and can never be emphasized enough.

We have all known the player who improved his grades during the football season but started falling apart a month after it ended. His associations with family values ended, and their daily visibility no longer influenced his behavior. Perhaps that's why classroom teachers use the coach as a resource so often and why more and more schools (See Section one) are getting coaches to advise younger students in feeder schools regarding their study habits and selection of courses.

The family concept, therefore, provides the most effective way to establish the conditions and circumstances within which motivation occurs. It's a unit that is both familiar and desirable within our culture. It may be taking a beating in some of the media, but the family remains the strongest foundation for individual growth and the best model available to me and you for team unity.

Motivation and Assistant Coaches

It is no startling revelation to say that coaches, especially in high school, are not in it for the money. After all, we realize what the Good Lord thinks of money. Look who He gives it to! Our priorities are a whole lot different; we're in it for the intangibles: commitment, self-sacrifice, self-fulfillment, satisfaction. There's a whole lot of "self" in those needs, too, but they also allow us the chance to touch a whole lot of lives in the process.

Assistant coaches, therefore, bring to their jobs the same kinds of internal needs that motivate the players: recognition, achievement, affiliation. Head coaches capitalize on these drives in several ways. First of all, they acknowledge contributions in the media and thank assistants publicly whenever possible. They also thank them privately. Admit it, there is as much greatness in the recognition of a job well done as in the act of doing one.

Similarly, head coaches recognize the value of distributing responsibilities. Responsibilities shared with others not only reduce our work loads but engage those who receive them. Obviously, the responsibilities must be commensurate with the assistant's ability to perform them, but once assigned, they become reasons for the coach's growth and for his sense of belonging.

Trust is a two-way street. The head coach expects it from his assistants, and the assistants expect it from the head coach. The easiest way to show it is to share it. Give coaches responsibilities; value their input by seeking it regularly; recognize their efforts. The synergy that results from this kind of team cooperation will provide a heightened sense of direction for you and your team. Values are most effective when they are shared values, when they are made visible by a common sense of purpose.

Let's Wrap It Up

I went out on a limb in the beginning of this section. I dared to dip into the world of academe to find a foundation for our discussion of motivation. The concepts were so important, however, and so clearly related to what we do as coaches that such a foundation had to be laid. The interests and the needs of athletes provide their motivations, and you and I must understand them if we are to create the conditions within which they are realized. That's how we motivate.

To make this point further, we discussed the distinctions between motivation and inspiration that exists between them. And we agreed with Maslow that self-actualization—the search for personal excellence—is the ultimate need of all of us. In that regard, let's borrow a quote from Harry Broady once more: "Excellence is a state the human psyche craves and just as regularly does without."

Perhaps one of the reasons we love our jobs so much is that we can do something about that.

SECTION 3

Team Discipline

Coach John Wooden tells the story of a former athlete, one of UCLA's finest, who was unable to abandon his "free spirit" personality. As we all know, free spirits are not atypical on the UCLA campus nor, for that matter, in most corners of California. They were not, however, favored sons on a John Wooden basketball team, which typically allowed about as much deviation from the norm as a grizzly gives her cubs. And like Mrs. Bruin, Coach Wooden, the head Bruin at UCLA, made his position very clear well before his players had the first inclination to try their legs.

Early each season he announced that they were expected to be clean-shaven and well-groomed, from the tops of their heads to the tips of their Converses™. And he allowed no deviations, even in the case of his All-American free spirit who announced to friends a few days before the NCAA championship game that he was going to grow a beard. Needless to say, word of his intentions got to Coach Wooden just about the time the player's face was bristling with potential problems.

Coach Wooden called the player into his office and said, "_____, it's apparent to me that growing a beard is very important to you." The player responded that, yes, a beard would enable him to reflect his independence and that, yes, it was very important to him.

Coach Wooden responded: "Well, I certainly would never come between a young man and his values. They are far too important to him. You obviously have strong feelings regarding the beard, so I guess I'll have to respect your decision. It's too bad. We'll miss you in the championship game, but . . . ."

Nothing more need be said. The player shaved his beard, made his usual outstanding contribution in the championship game, and joined his coaches and teammates in the celebration of another national championship. As important, discipline in the John Wooden basketball program was reaffirmed in the simplest, least disruptive way possible. And the whole process reflected not only Wooden's strength of conviction but his courage and his commitment to the UCLA program.

Ernest Hemingway once described courage as "grace under pressure." John Wooden, particularly in anecdotes such as this one, is the embodiment of grace under pressure. The prospect of losing one of basketball history's great players

43

just before the national championship game is like fighting Mike Tyson with one
arm. You'd probably be a whole lot better off to stay home.

For Wooden, however, the decision probably was easier to make than most
of us realize. Like all good coaches, Wooden realized the value of maintaining
"the program" over the occasional player who challenges it. This is not to say
that coaches like him don't consider the extenuating circumstances of a player's
departure from expected behavior.

We all make such allowances, but we also realize that "the program" is not
a depersonalized abstraction that systematically disregards the human needs of
our players. To the contrary, "the program" *is* our players, and the enormous
good it provides can't be compromised by the occasional player who wants to do
things his way. Nor are we interested in squelching independence or personal
expression. Athletic activity provides ample opportunity for personal expression—in all its forms. It also acknowledges the necessary limitations that inhere
in the word "independence." Our job as coaches is to foster a sense of independence
in our players, but within an environment of shared responsibilities and mutual
consideration.

Maintaining the program, therefore, is not seeking refuge behind a bureau-
cratic shield. Rather, it is stepping out in the open to risk occasional censure to
defend what the program represents to so many athletes. And you know as well
as I do that every time we take that step into the open, we risk losing a game
or two—maybe several—and feeling the wrath of the inevitable critics who take
pot shots at us.

But that's all right. If folks weren't taking pot shots at us, we'd have to start
questioning our own motives. My favorite definition of critics is that they are
people who knock—without entering. We enter; that's what we're all about. So
the next time you stand up for "the program" over the self-indulgent behavior
of an athlete who needs your censure, take heart. It's just a whole lot easier to
be critical than to be correct.

════════ A GOOD GUIDING PRINCIPLE ════════

One more quote from John Wooden. I asked him once how he abstracted his ideas
about discipline: "Simple," he said. "Make the rules clear and the penalties
severe." It worked for him, and it has worked for me over the years. In the first
place, most players want to do the right thing. And it's much easier for them
when they realize that you mean business.

A case in point. Bob Devaney, one of college football's great names, shared
a similar philosophy. Coach Devaney was my coach at Nebraska back in those
thrilling days of yesteryear when my knees could still make it up a flight of
stairs. I recall him standing before us indicating the exact amount of time al-
located for each day's drills. He never deviated from his schedule, even when we

didn't perform up to par in a particular drill. If he scheduled 15 minutes for a pass blocking drill, we spent exactly 15 minutes running into our fellow man.

If we didn't do it well, however, we knew that during the next day's practice we'd work on pass blocking for half an hour—with a very predictable increase in intensity. We learned soon that our time was better used and Coach Devaney's expectations were better served when we worked as hard as we could during the original drill. It made his practices more predictable, and it saved a lot of wear and tear on our bodies.

"Clear rules and severe penalties," therefore, don't always relate to issues as serious as training rules violations or academic ineligibility, nor are they always severe. They are immediate and forceful enough, however, to develop the sense of discipline that football players require to make a continuing contribution to the team and to become upstanding young men. Discipline, then, involves a great deal more than punishment.

Punishment is the external response when self-discipline breaks down. The focus for coaches, then, is to inform players of consequences for misbehavior but, more important, to avoid the misbehavior by encouraging in them a sense of self-discipline. In essence, punishment is a last resort. Believe me, after sticking my face mask in the numbers of countless teammates during blocking drills, I knew what was expected of me, and I didn't need a coach in my face screaming consequences if I missed a block.

I need not mention even one of the many studies conducted over the years that have concluded that punishment has little effect on learning. Yet many coaches, particularly new coaches, perceive punishment as a motivator. Well, it can influence the security needs of an athlete, but if used recurringly, it doesn't teach, nor does it allow athletes to satisfy their social and ego needs. It's important, then, to look at discipline in the broadest sense and to understand the basic principles that can put it to work for you and your players.

CLARITY

The expected behaviors of players must be communicated clearly to everyone. The principles of substantive and procedural due process demand it legally; so does common sense. Players can't be expected to perform in ways that are unfamiliar to them or beyond their capabilities. Athletic Codes (see Section 1) and Athletic Permit Cards such as the one in Figure 3–1 are necessary, therefore, to establish a record of expected behaviors.

Even the fundamental skills to be performed in practice must be communicated clearly and practiced repeatedly so that athletes become disciplined in their execution. The team, for example, that conducts its first scrimmage without drilling players on the fundamentals of blocking and tackling risks injury to players and possible legal action against the school if someone is seriously hurt.

PLEASE PRINT IN INK

DISTRICT _____ —ATHLETIC PERMIT CARD

ID# _____

Fall: Sport _____ Season # _____
Winter: Sport _____ Season # _____
Spring: Sport _____ Season # _____

Name _____ Date _____
        (last)   (first)   (middle)

Address _____ City _____ Zip _____

Phone _____ Counselor _____ Present year in school _____

Father's Name _____ Work # _____ Mother's Name _____ Work # _____

Date of birth _____ Place of birth _____
      (mo/day/year)   (city)   (county)   (state)

Physician _____ Dr. phone number _____

In case of emergency call _____
           (name-relationship)   (phone number)

ATHLETIC AGREEMENT

District _____ believes that it is the function of the athletic department to provide sports which are interesting, wholesome, stimulating and enjoyable for all students. Their overall objectives are to develop physical fitness, sports habits and skills, sports understanding, sportsmanship, and a spirit of competitiveness in each boy and girl. All parents and athletes are asked to read and discuss the implications of participation in the high school athletic program before signing this form. THIS FORM MUST BE *ANNUALLY* FILED IN THE ATHLETIC OFFICE BY THE FIRST DAY OF PRACTICE OF THE ATHLETE'S SPECIFIC SPORT SEASON.

An athlete in District _____ will be subject to disciplinary action if he or she commits any of the following violations:

1. Falsification of information on this form.
2. Theft or vandalism of any school property.
3. Repeated acts of unsportsmanshiplike conduct.
4. Use of or possession of tobacco (all forms), alcohol, marijuana, look-alikes, any other illegal drugs or related paraphernalia, or the abuse of prescription/non-prescription drugs.

ALL ATHLETES AND THEIR PARENTS MUST ATTEND AN ATHLETIC CODE MEETING TO RECEIVE AND SIGN THE ATHLETIC CODE AT LEAST ONCE DURING AN ATHLETE'S HIGH SCHOOL CAREER. I and my parent(s)/guardian have attended an Athletic Code Meeting. (Please circle)   yes   no

We advise all athletes to be adequately covered by hospitalization insurance. Your signature indicates that you will accept financial responsibility in case of injury to your child sustained in connection with these activities. Please indicate your insurance preference:

_____ We plan on insuring our child in the school insurance program.
_____ We do not wish to purchase the school insurance. We believe that our present accident insurance provides adequate coverage.

Our son/daughter has our permission to practice and compete in the interscholastic athletic program. We realize that such activity involves the potential for injury which is inherent in all sports, and on rare occasions a severe injury, including permanent paralysis or death may occur.

Each athlete is responsible for any uniform and/or equipment issued to him/her. Any article lost or damaged, other than ordinary wear and tear, must be paid for by the athlete. Should a lost item be found after it is paid for, it must be returned to the athletic office, and no refund will be made.

Date _____ PARENT PERMISSION _____
                                     (signature)

I agree to conduct myself in accordance with the athletic agreement. Failure to do so may result in disciplinary action.

Date _____ ATHLETE'S SIGNATURE _____

DOCTOR'S PERMIT (freshman use school physical form only)

I have examined this student on this date and find him/her to be physically fit for athletic participation.

_____ MD _____
      (doctor's stamp required)   (date of examination)

FIGURE 3–1

If players are to become disciplined athletes, therefore, they must understand how they are to behave and perform and must have opportunities to practice these expected behaviors. The coach who expects his athletes, for example, to avoid fighting during a game sends an inconsistent message to his players if he argues with the opposing coach or baits the officials during a game. As mentioned in Section 2, the coach who models the behaviors expected of his athletes communicates them most clearly to everyone on the team.

REPETITION

Having communicated team values clearly, the coach must provide the time to practice them. Like the fundamental physical skills expected of good football players, self-discipline requires practice. One of the best ways to assure successful practice is to praise the efforts of the player who performs or behaves as expected. Praise is the best way to assure conforming behaviors. Players should constantly be praised, therefore, when they curb their anger, when they help younger players, when they reflect a solid work ethic by running ten yards farther than everyone else in an offensive timing drill, when they help the equipment manager pick up towels in the lockerroom, or when they take control of a noisy huddle.

Being self-disciplined often runs contrary to the basic urges of young men. Not only do they battle their own impulses, but they usually risk the censure of at least some of their teammates when they act self-disciplined. In that regard, they require the support of their coaches and teammates who share their values. You see, without such players, the constant modeling of the values important to winning is left only to the coach—a mighty big order for anyone.

Winning is a habit. As indicated in the previous section, players who act like winners soon become winners. And players who act like winners are self-disciplined players who know what is expected of them and try most of the time to perform accordingly. The coach who sustains a focus on the task at hand, therefore, whether during a blocking drill, a halftime speech, or an informal conversation in the cafeteria, provides the modeling and the repetition necessary for athletes to develop a sense of self-discipline.

The repetition doesn't have to be overt, and the reminding doesn't have to be punitive. Sometimes a knowing glance, even if acknowledged only by the player, communicates volumes, including the fact that you noticed and that you respect the player enough to withhold a remark. Saying something isn't always important; noticing everything *is* important. All coaches are well-advised to heed the words of Pope John XXIII: "See everything; overlook a great deal; correct a little." Let self-discipline do its thing.

Let's look at self-discipline another way. If expectations have been spelled out and players have had the opportunity to practice them, deviations from them can be handled in two fundamental ways. One, the coach can draw attention to the problem, and as appropriate, decide whether or not to apply a reasonable consequence. In this instance, the coach has assessed the situation and is personally invested in the outcome.

The second way to handle deviations from expected behavior or performance—and remember, we're not talking about training rules violations exclusively—is to oversee a process whereby the athlete acknowledges the problem and determines corrective action. In this instance, the player has assessed the situation and is personally invested in the outcome.

I don't like to ask rhetorical questions, so I won't. But I will answer the obvious one that comes to mind. I much prefer the situation that requires the athlete to self-evaluate and to identify and invest himself in solutions. When I identify the solution, I'm invested in the outcome. When the player identifies the solution, he's invested in the outcome. I like it when he's invested. I know *I* am. How this is to be accomplished will be discussed later in this section.

IMPORTANCE

One of the best ways to underscore the importance of any responsibility is to sustain a focus on it. Whether seeking to maintain control during a meeting or a practice session or to develop a sense of self-discipline in each team member, coaches are well-advised to maintain a task-oriented approach. Kids with a focus tend to remain focused; kids without a focus tend to reflect a lack of self-discipline. The more evident the task at hand, the more athletes will pay attention and reflect our expectations of them.

Consider, for example, the behaviors of athletes the closer we get to game day. Early in the week, when the pressure of the previous game has disappeared and the next game is several days away, the focus may not be as intense. The behaviors of the athletes at that time may be loose enough to interfere with any real learning. This is not all bad. Players need the time early in the week, particularly if they performed as expected, to loosen up a little.

These are the times, however, when control can become a problem. Focus, then, enables learning, and it provides the relative levels of intensity required for the development of team and self-discipline. For a further example, look at focus in relation to motivation. When players are highly motivated, in a game for example, an admonition directed at one player will be acceptable to the entire team. When player motivation is low, however, as in certain practice sessions, the same admonition directed to one player may cause some members of the team to think of the coach as unfair or unreasonable.

This makes for a very interesting and revealing observation. Admonition (external discipline) is least effective with the least motivated athlete—or child—

or employee. The very person who seems most in need of punishment or external discipline is the person least influenced by it. The person who needs it least, the highly motivated athlete, is most affected by it. Maybe that's why the good get better; they're inclined in that direction.

Countless studies support the previous observation. They also support the related observation that if we expect self-discipline in our athletes, we must provide the conditions and the circumstances that stimulate their motivation. We might go so far as to say that the degree of their self-discipline is directly proportional to the degree of their motivation to complete the task—whatever it is. Motivation and discipline, then, go hand in hand. Consider the obvious example of the hungry student. Rarely will self-discipline interfere with his determination to eat. Similarly, self-discipline rarely influences the behavior of the intimidated player or the isolated player. The key for coaches, therefore, is to acknowledge the motivational needs of athletes when seeking to develop self-discipline in them.

BALANCE

When balance is lost, someone invariably gets hurt. Whether it involves a running back hitting the turf, a quarterback throwing off the wrong leg, or a guard punching an opponent, the loss of balance is the surest sign that something has gone wrong. It is also conclusive: the back is tackled; the pass is incomplete; and the guard is out of the game. Balance, therefore, must be taught to, and expected of, players. Just as drills in running fundamentals emphasize high knees for balance, coaches must emphasize high standards of behavior to secure the balance players need to perform as expected on the field, in the classroom, and at home. And coaches must model similar balance when teaching such fundamentals. Passion is fine at halftime when players' emotions need stimulation. It is to be avoided when player learning is the focus.

OBJECTIVITY

A key, therefore, to effective team discipline is the objectivity of the coaching staff. Psychologists have advised parents for years not to take the misbehavior of their children personally. We must acknowledge misbehavior and respond to it, but we must not take it as a personal assault. I have three children, all of whom blessedly are now adults, so I understand the difficulty at times of accepting and following such advice. And, frankly, the coach in me is often disinclined to moderate my voice and behavior. Maybe that's why we named our dog "Coach;" all he does is sit around and bark all day.

But I learned. I discovered the more objective I became in dealing with occasional misbehavior, the more inclined my children were to listen to me. I also discovered that I was a whole lot more effective—as a parent and a coach. I learned, for example, to show how deviations from practice interfered with the team's need to learn—not how much it bothered me. I certainly acknowledge distractions and subtle misbehavior; they are persistent interferences to learning. But I try not to react to them as insults to my coaching.

Admonitions from effective disciplinarians, therefore, tend to be simple and casual—non-confrontational. So are the consequences they give for misbehavior. The really effective consequence on the football field is the one that provides something good while it gets the player's attention. Examples of such consequences will be discussed in the next section.

THE WHAT AND THE HOW

Disagreement often means we're moving in the right direction. We can't expect our players to agree with everything we say or expect of them. They would be rather disappointing as young men if they did. The same would be true of our assistant coaches. If you have one assistant coach and you both agree on everything, one of you is unnecessary. Occasional disagreement is healthy. It is the form that disagreement takes that can be unhealthy. That's why effective team discipline always provides a forum for the discussion of grievances and/or input into decisions. Such a forum obviously is not available to complain about laps or wind sprints, but it is open informally whenever a coach gives players the leeway to block a point of attack in a way that's best for them, and formally when team meetings are held without coaches to discuss such things as sagging motivation.

Such meetings are not frequent. A team may have only one every five or six years. What is important to players, however, is the awareness that coaches acknowledge their ability to make such decisions and to influence the direction the team is taking. As they experience such opportunities, particularly on an informal basis, they become more willing to accept standards of performance and to develop the self-discipline that is so important for them as players and young men.

Effective discipline, then, involves two basic considerations. One, if internalized by players (self-discipline), it introduces long-term advantages to the development of the team and the individual players. Two, if considered in relationship to motivation, it assumes a different perspective and can be handled more effectively than if motivation were not considered. To illustrate each of these points, let's consider a few typical examples.

Poor Performance During A Game

We discussed player self-evaluation earlier in this chapter. Hopefully, we agreed that when people have opportunities to self-evaluate and to have input into corrective action, they tend to be more invested in the success of that action.

OF OFFENSE

Directions: Watch yourself on last week's game film/tape and use the following form to analyze and evaluate your offensive performance. Complete the evaluation by placing one mark next to the word under each category that best describes your performance during each play.

Line or Backfield Blocking (Includes at the point of attack *and* downfield)

Good _____

Fair _____

Poor _____

Running

Good _____

Fair _____

Poor _____

Passing

Good _____

Fair _____

Poor _____

Pass Receiving

Good _____

Fair _____

Poor _____

Ball Handling

Good _____

Fair _____

Poor _____

Faking

Good _____

Fair _____

Poor _____

Reactions

Offensively, I need work on: _____

_____

_____

FIGURE 3–2

OF DEFENSE

Directions: Watch yourself on last week's game film/tape and use the following form to analyze and evaluate your defensive performance. Complete the evaluation by placing one mark next to the word under each category that best describes your performance during each play.

Tackling

Good _____

Fair _____

Poor _____

Pass Defending

Good _____

Fair _____

Poor _____

Executing Stunts

Good _____

Fair _____

Poor _____

Meeting and Breaking Down Blockers

Good _____

Fair _____

Poor _____

Reading Keys and Keeping Proper Pursuit Paths

Good _____

Fair _____

Poor _____

Reactions

Defensively, I need work on: _____

_____

_____

FIGURE 3–3

Football players, therefore, who analyze, evaluate, and suggest ways to improve their own performance have a greater investment in that performance than players who do not have such opportunities.

The key is to provide them such an opportunity. It can be done in one of several ways. Exactly which way is dependent upon your individual situation. The focus, however, is on the forms illustrated in Figures 3-2 and 3-3 and the time provided for players to use them. Players, individually or collectively, should review game films and use the forms to analyze and evaluate their own performance. Having conducted such a review, players should give the forms to coaches to have their suggestions incorporated into the week's practice schedule.

They might review the game tape at home with teammates, at school during free periods or study halls, or in a team meeting before Monday's practice. Whenever and however they meet, their completed forms are to be given to a coach sometime before they go home after Monday's practice. Coaches then review them to incorporate their suggestions into the remaining practice sessions for the week.

The process has several advantages. First, evaluations generally are consistent with the coaches' evaluations, so they are mutually reinforcing. Two, the players benefit almost immediately from an observed poor performance, one which probably has been observed as well by one or more teammates. Three, a movement from first to second string by the coaches is reinforced by the player's perception of his own performance. (If players don't see anything wrong, that fact is a good subject of conversation with them.) Four, the weekly repetition of using the form provides ongoing reinforcement of what is expected of each player. Finally, players are inclined to work harder during drills *they* suggest.

Obviously, coaches still make the major decisions regarding practice, but even in this regard, any punishments for poor performance should not be arbitrary but must seek positive results. The running back who persistently fails to lower his shoulder, for example, should run through the blaster or a gauntlet of standup dummies 20 times. The punter who shanks a punt should punt the ball 50 or more times the following week. The team that runs out of gas in the fourth quarter should double up on the wind sprints. These may seem like punishments, and to some extent maybe they are, but they also are directed toward the improvement of individual and team performance and are that much easier to defend.

THE PLAYER WHO MISSES PRACTICE

Missing practice involves a similar situation. More importantly, it has a direct bearing upon the survival of "the program." Nothing is as destructive to a sense of team discipline as players cutting practice. When players are misbehaving at practice, at least the coach has the opportunity to correct their behavior. When they simply cut practice, the coach's hands are effectively tied. It cannot be tolerated by the team.

    That's why the team has to be informed sometime in the pre-season of the consequences of cutting practice. Because some parents rely on the family lawyer the way others read Dr. Spock, it's always wise to inform the team in writing. Substantive due process requires that people look at something rather than listen to it. See Figure 3-4. And it's much more acceptable to everyone when consequences are applied objectively, in essence when coaches emphasize the value of the program and sell the idea that cutting is destructive to it.

    One cut generally is acceptable to most coaches, but the second cut, if there are no extenuating circumstances, subjects the players to automatic dismissal from the team. Questions of reinstatement can involve petitioning the coach, or the coach can require dismissed players to petition the team for their approval to be reinstated. Generally, this latter way to petition is best because it gives the team additional credibility and reinforces the social aspects of motivation.

    This process for handling the cutting of practice meets all the requirements for effective team discipline. The expectations are clear; they are repeated often enough; their importance is emphasized reasonably; the process underscores the necessary balance between practice and performance; and it involves the objectivity needed to assure that any consequences are not just punitive but learning experiences for the athletes involved.

PENALTIES AND FUMBLES

An occasional penalty or fumble is like a pothole in the road. It might be damaging; it's always bothersome; but it's easily overlooked. A road full of potholes, however, stops progress, so when the team starts losing its cool and the ball with careless abandon, something needs to be done. Each of these situations is handled easily, primarily because football players know immediately how badly they've goofed when they've dropped the ball—literally and figuratively. They *expect* some kind of consequence. Our job is to apply the right one. Generally, removing the athlete from the game to punish him is not a good idea. Believe me, his guilt is far more effective than anything we can do. In fact, it may be so extreme that the best alternative is to keep him in the game to reaffirm our faith in him.

    Several years ago, I worked with a young running back who, in his first varsity game, fumbled the ball four times. He had great potential, but inexperience and exertion were causing him to lose control of the ball. At that point in a young athlete's career, it's difficult for the coach to determine who's at fault for the fumbling, player or coach. I chose to accept at least some of the blame and communicated that to him. Fortunately, we won the game in spite of his fumbles, but more importantly he went on to become a standout player in high school and a scholarshipped athlete in college.

    As important, he and I enjoyed a productive and rewarding relationship, the kind that sparked his training, performance, and level of commitment to the team. I'll never forget a comment following the awards banquet during his senior

ATTENDANCE AT FOOTBALL PRACTICE AND GAMES

Introduction

Regular attendance at football practice and games is essential if players are to learn the skills and the strategies that make them and the team successful. The cutting of practice jeopardizes this success. Such cutting lets the team down and reflects a clear lack of commitment to its goals. For these reasons, it cannot be tolerated.

Cutting Policy

Football players are allowed one unexplained, unauthorized absence from practice. They are allowed none from games. Players who miss one such practice will not be questioned or penalized in any way, and they will resolve the absence only if they volunteer an explanation. If the explanation is acceptable, the missed practice will not be considered a cut, and the one-cut policy will again be in effect. A second cut from practice or a first cut from a game will subject the player to automatic dismissal from the team.

Possible Reinstatement

Football players dropped from the team for unauthorized absences may petition for reinstatement. The petition will be made to the head coach, who will refer it to the team for disposition. Coaches enjoy their associations with players; the team *depends* upon them. Because players who cut practice harm the team more than the coaches, the team will determine reinstatement.

A Final Word

A player's commitment to the game of football is reflected in everything he does: how he applies himself academically, how he behaves on and off the field, and how he commits himself to team goals. Practice involves one such commitment. Players or parents who require additional information regarding this policy are encouraged to contact the head coach.

FIGURE 3–4

year; "You know Doc, I still remember the faith you had in me during that first
game a couple years ago. It really helped."

It does help. When we expect the best from players, they almost always
deliver. Consider all the educational and psychological research out there that
confirms the fact that children from non-punitive homes appear to be better
adjusted than children from homes where external discipline is frequent and
sometimes arbitrary. Internal discipline—reasonably expected of athletes—is
far more effective than punishment.

At those times, however, when punishment is necessary, it should be applied
reasonably. Coaches, therefore, should fight the prototype of the bull-necked
cyclops grinding his clipboard to pulp every time a player drops the ball on the
field. If the family concept is what we seek in player relations, coaches should
behave more like Ward Cleaver than Freddy Krueger.

That's not to say that consequences are inappropriate, but they should be
delivered casually, even humorously. Just as my running back recalled my early
faith in him, he also never forgot—nor did his teammates—the 100 up downs
we did after Monday's practice. Our team has a policy: ten up downs for every
fumble or pass interception and one up down for every yard penalized. Four
fumbles and 60 yards in penalties resulted in 100 up downs that week.

We did them all after practice and after our usual wind sprints. The players
expected them; they knew they were coming. And believe me, my young athletes
paid close attention the next day during a fumble drill, and the entire team
applied more than a little peer pressure each time someone went offside—even
in practice. The right consequences, appropriately applied, can save us a lot of
time.

=============================== **SWEARING** ===============================

Swearing on the game or practice field is one of the most obvious breakdowns
in individual or team discipline. Young men and even coaches may discover in
a moment of anger that the wrong word has slipped out. If it happens infrequently,
no real response, other than a knowing glance in the player's direction, is required
from the coach. If the problem is recurring, it must be acknowledged because it
reflects a lack of self-discipline which is likely to repeat itself in other ways.

That's how to present it to the team. Most football coaches would be hard-
pressed to claim that swearing was personally offensive. The "vernacular" is as
common at coaching clinics as defensive strategies for stopping "the bone." Swearing does, however, represent a relative absence of self-discipline, a commodity
that winning football teams—classy football teams—require in large doses. If
explained to players in such terms, they are usually willing to live up to expectations.

========================= **QUITTING THE TEAM** =========================

I am one of those old-fashioned derelicts who clings to the idea that quitting is destructive to a positive self-image. A quitter shouts to the world and to himself that he can't do it. And maybe that's not all bad. A realistic assessment of one's strengths and weaknesses is critical to our self-knowledge. But quitting isn't the appropriate response to the sudden awareness that we have weaknesses. Personal growth is always a function not only of strengths exploited but of weaknesses overcome, and sometimes the weakness extends beyond physical limitations to an unwillingness to extend oneself. See Figure 3-5.

To say that all athletes can't be first teamers is no startling revelation, but they can provide something for the team within the framework of their physical limitations. We had a tackle one year who was so overweight that we had a tough time finding game pants for him. Although we never found out for sure, we suspected that his parents pushed him into football to lose weight—which is all right with us. We never cut players. Any kid who wants to play football, for whatever reason, should have the chance—but more about that in a future section.

This young man must have considered quitting the team at least ten times a day. If he hadn't considered it, I would have questioned his sanity. But he stayed with us, knowing that his playing time would be limited and that on occasion he might even embarrass himself during certain drills. His courage, however, and his willingness to do everything everyone else did endeared him to his teammates. They would cheer him during wind sprints as he invariably brought up the rear, and they would use him as an example in the huddle when a game started to get tough.

As I write these words, I hesitate to think what might have become of him had he quit the team, for that matter had he become a quitter. Heaven knows, it would have been easy for him, and few people would have blamed him because of his physical limitations. But he recognized, as many of us do, that football isn't all Xs and Os; it's one of life's opportunities to become more than we are— in our own way to elevate ourselves above the ordinary. And such elevation doesn't require scoring touchdowns. Often it means simply sticking it out.

When players quit, therefore, they affect many people. Most obviously, they deprive the team of any help, no matter how insignificant, they might otherwise provide. They deny their teammates the chance to help them, an act which is as beneficial to the person who gives help as well as to the one who receives it. They reaffirm the popular misconception that football is little more than bumping into each other. And they deny themselves the personal growth that results from a good fight with adversity. The young man who scores touchdowns receives our recognition; the young man who overcomes adversity receives our respect and admiration.

With few exceptions, therefore, I always try to discourage a young man from quitting. But if he does, we part ways amicably and I tell him that if he decides

QUITTING THE FOOTBALL TEAM

Introduction

Quitting often avoids a very healthy battle with some kind of adversity. For that reason, the _____ football program is opposed to quitting, regardless of each player's physical abilities. We are committed to the idea that every player in our football program makes an important contribution to the team's success and that when a player quits, he deprives the team of that contribution.

Policy

If a player determines to quit, however, we ask that he meets first with the head coach to discuss his decision. After the meeting, appropriate action will be taken.

Reinstatement

Players who quit the football team will be allowed to petition for reinstatement, such reinstatement to be determined by the team. Players seeking reinstatement are encouraged to see the head coach, who will turn the disposition of the case over to the football team. *They* are the ones affected by players who decide to quit.

A Final Word

Every player on the _____ football team is very important to us. We believe that our job involves much more than developing a winning program. It involves the development of upstanding young men who are willing to face their limitations and commit themselves to a *team* effort. We encourage every player, therefore, to remain a contributing member of the team and to talk to coaches before making a decision to quit.

FIGURE 3–5

© 1992 by Michael D. Koehler

to rejoin the team at some time in the future, I will be pleased to have him back but that the final decision involving his reinstatement will be with the team. The reasons are simple. He really hasn't hurt me at all by quitting. I may be disappointed in him and I might miss him, but I am largely unaffected by his decision. He has hurt himself and his teammates. The decision, therefore, is theirs to make.

THE CRITICAL PLAYER

Some football players, like some adults, think criticism is motivation. I hope our discussion in Chapter Two blows a hole or two in that idea. Criticism is usually threatening, often demeaning, and only occasionally constructive. That's perhaps only one reason why my coach at Nebraska, Bob Devaney, never allowed players to criticize each other's performance. NEVER. I don't either.

One more dip into the world of academe reminds us of Abraham Maslow's ideas about synergy, a combined output that results in a more powerful effect than the sum of the individual parts. High synergy results when those parts are mutually cooperative; low or no synergy results when those parts are mutually antagonistic. When players criticize each other, they create a competitive, mutually antagonistic situation.

Mutual antagonism destroys the team and family concepts and often results in the "individual parts" doing their own thing. Teams may win occasionally if those individual parts are highly talented, but they will never develop a football machine that generates the habit of winning. Criticism among players, therefore, must always give way to encouragement and praise, and coaches must model such expectations. If we believe in the positive approach, the team will, too.

LET'S WRAP IT UP

System theorists tell us that, by definition, systems are resistant to change. My body tries to maintain a certain temperature; my car seeks just the right air and fuel mixture; and my football team strives to maintain the level of accomplishment with which it has grown comfortable. Some teams are comfortable losing. They have grown accustomed to it and in many instances have developed behaviors associated with it: missed practices, training rules violations, dissension among teammates, swearing, laughing after losses, and so forth.

This can be changed. And it doesn't require a time-consuming psychological overhaul of attitudes and values. Contrary to popular opinion, attitudes don't have to change before behaviors change. Contemporary research has proven that changed behavior ultimately can result in changed attitudes. To repeat a recurring idea in this section: if football players act like winners, they ultimately will become winners.

The key, then, is to influence their behaviors; their attitudes will follow. Over the years, I have worked with several football players with lousy attitudes. Our program hasn't changed all of them, but we've turned around most of them— through expectations, not punishment. We reminded a lot, applied natural consequences occasionally, modeled continuously, bit our lower lips more than once, and finally found ourselves with the kinds of players we wanted.

The focus, then, is self-discipline—first ours, then the athletes! I learned a long time ago that the best time to keep quiet is the time when I'm absolutely certain that something has to be said. As the old saying goes: never pass up the opportunity to keep your mouth shut. Once a football team develops the self-discipline that comes with learning such a lesson, they reflect it in almost everything they do, and they become winners, for you, for their parents, for their teachers, and, most importantly, for themselves.

SECTION 4

Offensive and Defensive Football: Guiding Principles

Motivation and discipline may be the heart and soul of a football team, but offense and defense are the arms and legs. They provide the action that attracts spectators and showcases the talents and teamwork of the players. In another sense, motivation and discipline provide the interpersonal principles that help coaches transform children into young men. Offense and defense provide the strategic nuts and bolts that help coaches transform students into football players.

Barry Switzer, the former head coach at Oklahoma, once told me that "great players make great plays." We had been discussing the merits of misdirection and how it increases the unpredictability of a team's offense. His position was that great players can transform even the most unimaginative offense into a thrill-a-minute spectacle for coaches and fans alike. His argument was interesting but unconvincing.

I have seen too many gifted players stifled by their own teammates when the offense discovered only a few minutes into the first quarter that they had a lousy game plan. Pardon me, Coach Switzer, but great plays *do* make great players. Better yet, properly organized great plays make great players. The finest, best-conceived offense in the world isn't worth the paper it's diagrammed on if it's used in the wrong situation.

Any game plan is a solution to a problem. And a problem is the discrepancy between "what is" and "what should be." Coaches, therefore, have to answer both questions before decisions are made regarding offensive and defensive strategies. The "what should be" as it relates to the scouting format and game preparation is discussed in the next section. For now, we will focus on "what is," in essence the offensive and defensive weapons we have in our football arsenal to effectively defeat any opponent.

Any military commander will tell you that the more a weapon can do the better its strategic value. What we want in our offensive and defensive arsenals, therefore, is a sophisticated combination of weapons that will enable us to adjust to any new or unexpected situation. That makes the "what should be" aspect of planning that much easier. Without the consideration of both—"what is" and "what should be"—we never really identify the dimensions of our problem and might be guilty of applying a great solution to the wrong problem.

61

If the game plan is the essential solution to the problem, the offense and the defense are the essential elements of the game plan. And the more sophisticated and comprehensive the offense and defense, the more successful the game plan, if the players carry out their assignments effectively. The development of any offense or defense, therefore, must take into account several basic characteristics that give the scope needed to provide the strategic edge for a variety of game situations.

=============================== THE THREE ESSENTIALS ===============================

Continuity

Let's talk first about offense. Any good offense is like a well-coordinated academic curriculum. Sounds funny, but it's true. And, like the school curriculum, a great offense provides the substance for a level of higher-order thought process that rivals the toughest challenge of any advance placement course. Higher-order thought process may be receiving recent emphasis in all those classrooms out there, but it has been a reality on the football field almost since Walter Camp helped introduce the game as you and I know it.

When we line up our offensive team early in the week, show them three or four of the defensive fronts they're likely to see in the next game, and ask them to point to the player they'll be expected to block, we are engaging our players in the highest levels of evaluative thought. As a matter of fact, I often find myself wanting to drag a few of the academicians out of the school building to let them see higher-order thought process in action.

When we ask football players to analyze a defense, evaluate its potential stunts, and identify the most appropriate blocking scheme for a number of different plays, we're expecting the best of higher-order thought. And we're using our "curriculum" as the framework to provide it. Benjamin Bloom and his taxonomy would be proud of us.

An important component of that offensive curriculum is continuity, the repetition of major elements from freshman through varsity levels of competition. Obviously, the major elements involve the fundamental series emphasized by the program and the basic plays within each series. Coaches who favor the triple option, for example, are advised to teach the basics of that offense at every level of student participation.

Too many schools allow lower level coaches to use their favorite offenses and, in effect, disregard the offense used by the varsity. Although such a practice may keep lower level coaches happy and acknowledge their autonomy within the program, it fails to provide the continuity that football players require if they are expected to master their assignments. One offense, repeated and refined every year, gives players the experiences they require to understand the offensive "Big Picture," and coaches the consistency they require to teach and refine their favorite plays.

Our program has consisted primarily of Wing T plays, but we have traditionally emphasized two basic series, the Crossfire and the Inside Belly. They will be used as examples throughout the remainder of this section. The basic plays are illustrated in Figures 4–1 and 4–2. These basic plays within each series are introduced at the freshman level and are complemented by more sophisticated plays at each successive level of competition. The more sophisticated plays will be illustrated in the next section of this chapter.

Different blocking schemes also are introduced at a later time. Obviously, the easiest block to master at the lower levels of the program is the straight block. As illustrated in Figure 4–3, however, football teams have a variety of formations and blocking schemes to employ against different defensive sets and possible stunts. The smart coach develops a chart that illustrates all of what he likes to do with each series. The chart has replaced the playbook in our program. It provides an excellent teaching tool and a ready reference for sideline communication on game days. Figure 4–4 provides a reproducible copy.

The point to emphasize, however, is that the entire offense, everything from favorite formations and motion to backfield execution and blocking schemes, involves a continuity that is interwoven throughout every level of the school's football program. It is this continuity that provides the foundation for the additional plays that ultimately transform a basic offense into a diversified and unpredictable game plan. Such a game plan, then, requires appropriate sequencing, the *second* essential element in an effective offense.

SEQUENCE

Misdirection as a concept isn't particularly new. The term has received recent favor, but the principles are as old as Pop Warner's hidden ball trick and Stagg's Statue of Liberty, both introduced at the turn of the century. Misdirection's recent emphasis, however, has encouraged some coaches to complement their philosophies of "three yards and a cloud of dust" with "12 yards and a trail of confusion." And the only way to cause such confusion in an opponent is to maintain a properly sequenced offense. Having established the necessary continuity in the offense, coaches must sequence it—i.e. assume that successive experiences for players provide plays of increased complexity and sophistication. In other words, the basic plays and the fundamental offensive philosophy are repeated every year at every level within the program; the more complex plays within the offense are introduced as players are able to understand and execute them, usually at the varsity level.

Figures 4–5 and 4–6 illustrate examples of the sequencing that we provide in the crossfire and inside belly series to complement the basic plays diagrammed

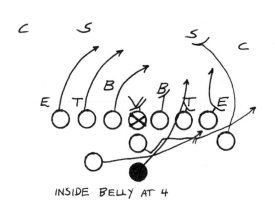

INSIDE BELLY AT 4

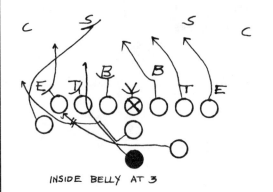

INSIDE BELLY AT 3

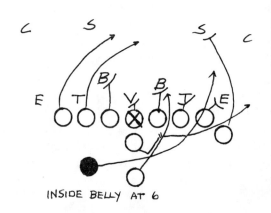

INSIDE BELLY AT 6

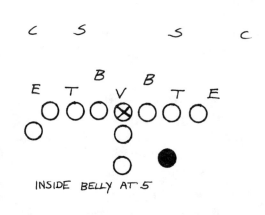

INSIDE BELLY AT 5

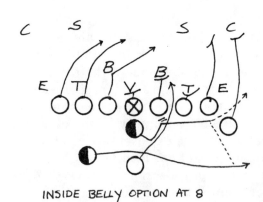

INSIDE BELLY OPTION AT 8

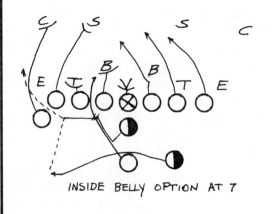

INSIDE BELLY OPTION AT 7

FIGURE 4–1

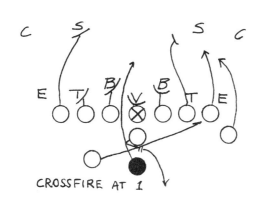

CROSSFIRE AT 1

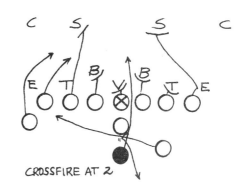

CROSSFIRE AT 2

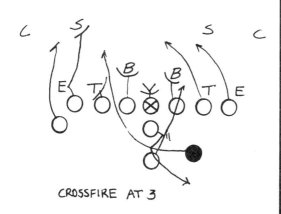

CROSSFIRE AT 3

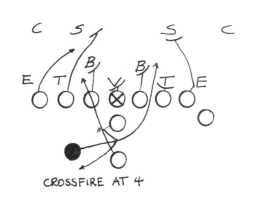

CROSSFIRE AT 4

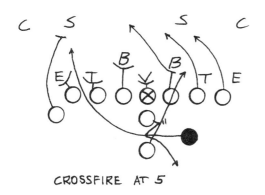

CROSSFIRE AT 5

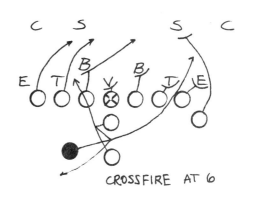

CROSSFIRE AT 6

FIGURE 4—2

RUNNING OFFENSE

	Formations					Blocking Schemes										
SERIES / Plays	FULL HOUSE	T	WING	PRO	I	STRAIGHT	TRAP	ISO	CROSS	EXIT	LEAD	HAMMER	WHEEL	D EXIT	T TRAP	SWITCH
CROSSFIRE	✔	✔	✔		✔											
XF 10, 20	✔	✔	✔		✔	✔			✔	✔	✔			✔		
XF 1, 2	✔	✔	✔		✔	✔			✔	✔	✔			✔		
XF 12, 21	✔	✔	✔		✔		✔							✔		
XF 3, 4	✔	✔	✔		✔	✔	✔	✔	✔	✔	✔			✔		
XF 5, 6	✔	✔	✔		✔	✔	✔	✔	✔	✔		✔	✔	✔		
XF 7, 8	✔	✔	✔		✔	✔						✔	✔		✔	✔
XF ctr. 5, 6	✔	✔	✔		✔		✔								✔	✔
INSIDE BELLY																
IB 12, 21	✔	✔	✔		✔	✔	✔									
IB 3, 4	✔	✔	✔		✔	✔		✔	✔	✔	✔					
IB 5, 6	✔	✔	✔		✔	✔	✔	✔	✔	✔		✔	✔			
IB option 7, 8	✔	✔	✔		✔	✔										
IB ctr. 5, 6	✔	✔	✔				✔								✔	
QUICK																
Q 1, 2	✔	✔	✔	✔		✔			✔				✔			
Q 3, 4	✔	✔	✔	✔		✔			✔							
Q slt. T 1, 2	✔	✔	✔				✔								✔	
Q option 7, 8	✔		✔			✔										
Q 5, 6	✔	✔	✔			✔			✔					✔		
Q QB kp. 7, 8	✔	✔	✔	✔		✔									✔	
Q ctr. 5, 6	✔	✔	✔				✔						✔			
Q power 5, 6	✔					✔			✔							
POWER																
P slt. T 3, 4			✔				✔								✔	
P 3, 4	✔	✔	✔	✔			✔				✔					
P right & left	✔	✔	✔	✔		✔							✔		✔	
P ctr. 5, 6	✔	✔	✔	✔			✔								✔	
P reverse 7, 8	✔	✔	✔	✔		✔									✔	
P toss r & l				✔			✔					✔	✔		✔	

FIGURE 4–3

RUNNING OFFENSE

	Formations	Blocking Schemes
SERIES		
Plays		

FIGURE 4–4

67

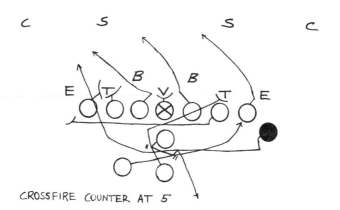

CROSSFIRE COUNTER AT 5

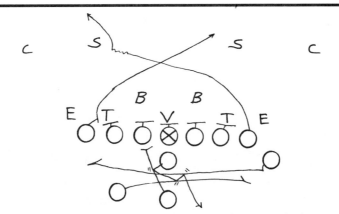

CROSSFIRE COUNTER ACTION PASS

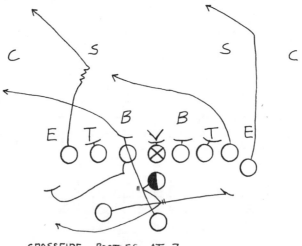

CROSSFIRE BOOTLEG AT 7

FIGURE 4—5

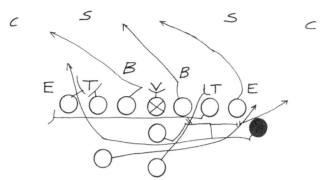

INSIDE BELLY COUNTER AT 5

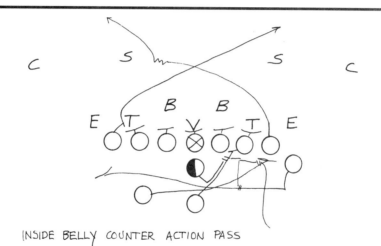

INSIDE BELLY COUNTER ACTION PASS

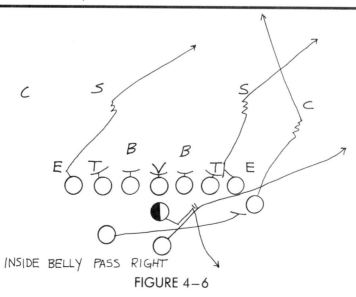

INSIDE BELLY PASS RIGHT

FIGURE 4-6

must be done during each play to counteract defensive maneuvers. That's not to say that they represent the staple of our offense. They don't. Often the more fundamental plays are more effective when circumstances require that we "take the game to the opponent." Well-sequenced plays, however, do provide the necessary complements to assure unpredictability in the game plan. Once we begin to experience limited success with the crossfire at 4, for example, we find that the crossfire counter at 5 is likely to pick up yardage. And once a hard-nosed safety stuffs the counter play at the line of scrimmage, the crossfire counter action pass is a potential touchdown. Sequencing is the key.

And successful sequencing is dependent not just on the inclusion of complementary plays in the offense but on the offensive team's ability to call them at the right time. Appropriate sequencing is dependent upon the strategic knowledge of the coaching staff. Sometimes a play action pass is the best call, sometimes the fullback up the middle. Such calls should be made, however, based on the knowledge of what the defense is giving you. So successful sequencing is a function of both a well-conceived and a well-executed offense.

Figure 4–7 provides a model for charting defensive reads. The chart should be part of every game plan, particularly if the team uses phones to communicate to the sidelines. Many teams assume that all coaches are familiar enough with the offensive ready list to be able to provide systematic feedback to the sidelines without following a prescribed form. Don't believe it.

Some coaches can provide such feedback. Even they, however, find themselves getting so wrapped up in occasional plays that they forget to make their defensive reads. A chart may not keep them from forgetting all the time, but it will help sustain their focus most of the time. And the feedback will be more comprehensive.

Figure 4–7 illustrates the chart before the game. It consists simply of the ready list (the plays which have been emphasized for this particular game) and the "reads" that are needed in order to sequence follow-up play calls. Notice that the chart emphasized the XF 12, 21, T, the XF 3, 4 lead, the XF 5, 6 hammer, and the XF counter at 5, 6. All of these plays are complementary. Each hits a different hole, but the backfield action is fundamentally the same in all of them. See Figure 4–8. Notice that the plays are all run from the full house formation; it causes the defense the additional problem of being unable to determine tendencies by formation.

The chart, then instructs spotters, usually assistant coaches, to watch certain players on defense in order to identify the complementary plays that will capitalize on the weaknesses in the defense. Figure 4–9 reveals what the chart might look like during the game, when the assistants are making their notations. Notice the remark that the offside safety is keying and reacting quickly to our left halfback. The counter play became the perfect call to capitalize on the area he vacated. Later in the game the crossfire counter action *pass* became even better!

Obviously, the chart includes more than one page. There must be room for all observations, including defenses and observed weaknesses in them. In addi-

READY LIST	PRIMARY AND (SECONDARY) DEFENSIVE READS	WHAT IS THE DEFENSE?	WHAT ELSE DID YOU SEE?
XF 12, 21 T	Linebacker keys and reactions (line slants)		
XF 3, 4 lead	Same as 12, 21 Trap Outside man — Can we hammer?		
XH 5, 6 hammer	Outside man on defensive line. Is he slashing, boxing, keying end?		
XF ctr. 5, 6	Offside safety (linebacker adjustments)		
IB 3, 4 lead	Outside man — can we hammer? (D back reactions what does pass look like?)		

FIGURE 4—7

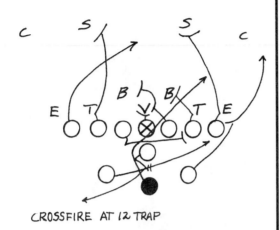

CROSSFIRE AT 12 TRAP

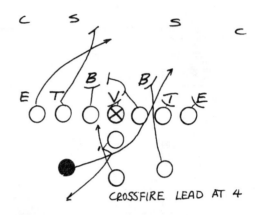

CROSSFIRE LEAD AT 4

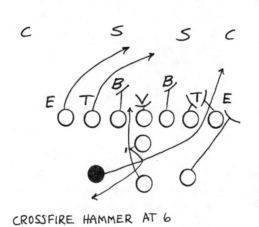

CROSSFIRE HAMMER AT 6

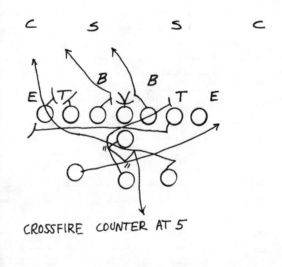

CROSSFIRE COUNTER AT 5

FIGURE 4–8

tion, observers must jot down anything else they see. The observation that the offside safety was reacting hard to play side was information that was requested in the form. The observation that the noseman was slanting consistently to the wide side of the field was *not* requested. It was picked up by the observers during the course of the game but was every bit as helpful as the information requested.

Sequencing, then, is dependent upon how well a coach conceives his offense and, later, how well he uses it. It's important to recognize, therefore, that sequencing may introduce plays of greater sophistication as players reach the varsity level but that is also reaffirms the importance of the basic plays. Our Running Offense chart, for example, reveals a Quick at 3 and 4. It is nothing but the old-fashioned dive play, as old as the split T and every bit as effective.

In certain game situations, our coaching staff may become officers on a submarine by shouting "Dive! Dive!" The dive play suddenly may be our best strategy against the defensive stunts we're facing. Sequencing, therefore, doesn't necessarily go from basic to sophisticated; it may go in the opposite direction. A sophisticated defensive read may tell us a basic play is required. Figure 4–10 provides a reproducible chart to allow for such reads.

INTEGRATION

Integration refers to the horizontal relationship of player experiences, in essence the elements that are emphasized and repeated in all the series and throughout the entire offense. A good example of one element integrated within the entire offense is line blocking. Good football teams can attack any hole along the line of scrimmage in a variety of ways. Usually, they can vary their blocking schemes for any single play. The blocking scheme called is the one that is most likely to be successful against a particular defensive set or combination of stunts.

Consider the Crossfire at 4. It can be blocked several different ways, depending upon the relative predictability of defensive stunts. If the opponent is slanting his line with some predictability into the wingside of our formation, we are likely to call a Crossfire trap at 4 in order to double-team the noseman, angle block the linebacker and trap the left defensive tackle, who is angling away from the point of attack anyway. See Figure 4–11.

If the offside linebacker is reacting with our pulling guard and jamming the play at the line of scrimmage, we can call a crossfire tackle trap at 4. See Figure 4–12. Or if we are unable to contain the noseman and want to eliminate the guessing game at the point of attack, we can double team him with the Crossfire at 4 lead. See Figure 4–13. The same blocking variety is true of other plays within the Crossfire series. See Figure 4–14 for the Crossfire at 6.

Who calls these blocking schemes and when they are called is a matter of team preference. We usually call the traps in the huddle but encourage the

DEFENSIVE READS

READY LIST	PRIMARY AND (SECONDARY) DEFENSIVE READS	WHAT IS THE DEFENSE?	WHAT ELSE DID YOU SEE?
XF 12, 21T	Linebacker keys and reactions (line slants)	S2/S2/S3!	LB's getting caught in
		S2/S3/61-?	wash — good play
			Noseman stunting
			consistently to wide side!
XF 3, 4 lead	Same as 12, 21 Trap (Offside safety — what's he doing?)	S2/S2/S3	Hammer better vs - S3!
		S2/S2/S2	Offside safety reacting
			hard to play side!!
XH 5, 6 hammer	Outside man on defensive line. Is he slashing, boxing, keying end?	S3/S2/S3/S2	Good vs. S3! They're giving
		S3/S3	us the S3 on 1–10!
			Stay with it —
			They can't stop it — at least
			5 yds. each time we run it!
XF ctr. 5, 6	Offside safety (linebacker adjustments)	S3!	TD!!
			Counteraction pass
			looks good, too —
			Second half?
IB 3, 4 lead	Outside man — can we hammer? (D Back reactions what does pass look like?)	S2/S3/S2	Outside man boxed —
			Hammer looks good
			Still boxing —
			Call hammer —

FIGURE 4—9

DEFENSIVE READS

READY LIST	PRIMARY AND (SECONDARY) DEFENSIVE READS	WHAT IS THE DEFENSE?	WHAT ELSE DID YOU SEE?

FIGURE 4–10

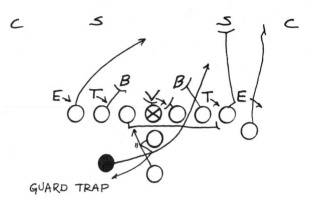

GUARD TRAP

FIGURE 4-11

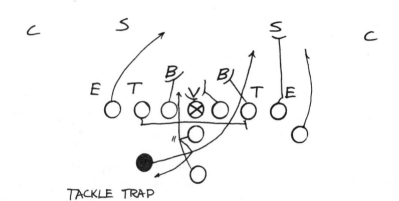

TACKLE TRAP

FIGURE 4-12

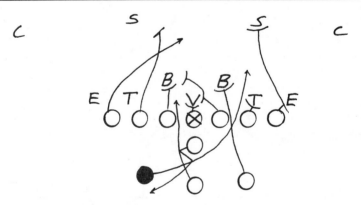

LEAD BLOCK

FIGURE 4-13

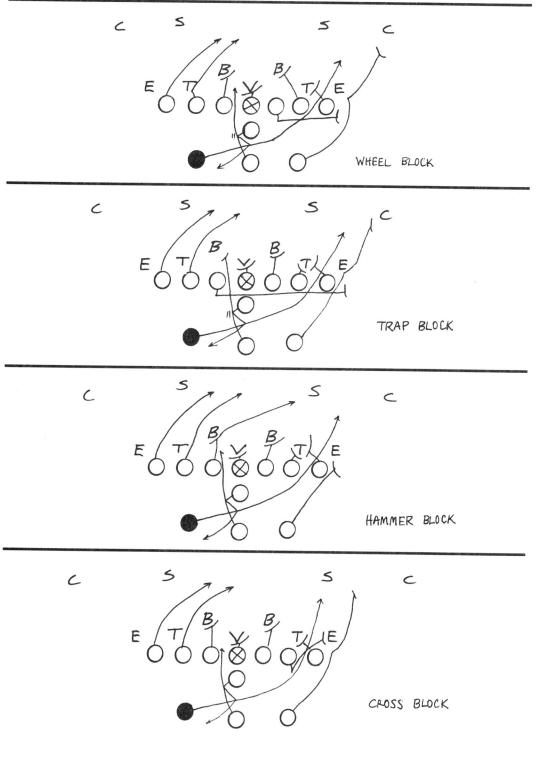

FIGURE 4—14

linemen to call the others on the line of scrimmage. Once they develop that higher-order thought process we discussed earlier, they are the best ones to determine appropriate blocking schemes, particularly if the defense is showing a variety of different looks.

The point is that variable blocking strategies are integrated throughout the offense and are repeated and emphasized within each series. Such repetition makes them easier to learn and makes the offense that much more effective. Similar principles apply to the need to integrate play-action passing as a complement to the running game.

The Play-Action Component. Rarely is a complement of play-action passes introduced at the freshman level in high school. Most freshmen are too busy trying to stay with the snap count on each play. It's a rare freshman end who can simulate a block at the line of scrimmage, sneak into the seams in the secondary, and catch the ball for a 15-yard gain. So we coaches spend more time on the basics with them and keep the principles of sequencing and integration in mind as they work through the program.

Play-action-passing becomes an element that introduces increased sophistication. When it is carefully integrated within the offense, it provides two important advantages to the offense. One, it is remembered easily by the players. If play-action pass plays are well-conceived, the pass routes should simulate the blocking responsibilities on the running play they complement. See Figure 4–15. The play call is "Inside belly pass right." You can see by comparing the pass play to the running play diagrammed underneath it that the pass patterns effectively complement the blocking responsibilities.

This suggests the second advantage of a well-integrated play-action passing attack. It is very confusing to the defense. If the selection committee for the Academy Awards genuinely tried to reward all creative acting performances, they would have to award an Oscar to the "Best Pass Receiver in a Supporting Role." Pass receivers executing play-action passes must first be pass deceivers. They must sell RUN to the defense before they break into their pass routes.

If integration is to be realized, coaches have to guarantee that players understand and execute their play-action passing assignments correctly. Most young pass receivers, particularly early in the season, pump so much adrenalin that they can barely contain themselves on the line of scrimmage. At the snap of the ball they race through their pass routes like greyhounds chasing well-oiled rabbits, and the quarterbacks execute fakes as if they were nuisances that get in the way of a quick drop back.

Effective integration, then, is as much a function of the execution of the offense as its development. This same characteristic is true of "sequence." Both reaffirm the fact that the truly successful coach is the one who can create a well-conceived offense on paper and then bring it to life on the field. Neither is really successful without the other. Keeping that thought in mind, let's look momentarily at passing offense.

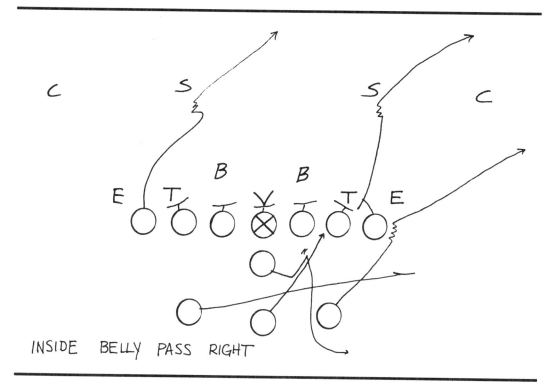

INSIDE BELLY PASS RIGHT

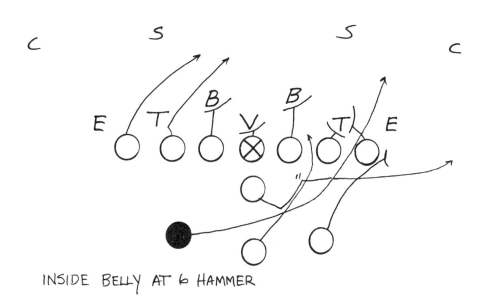

INSIDE BELLY AT 6 HAMMER

FIGURE 4–15

=============================== **PASSING OFFENSE** ===============================

This chapter already has suggested the distinction between a play-action passing attack and a conventional dropback attack. The distinction is important if each is to be successful. Play-action passes complement run action—and vice versa. Dropback passes complement both by adding another dimension to the offensive attack. They force the defensive line into a pass rush and provoke the secondary into different coverages.

=============================== **CONTINUITY** ===============================

Play-action. The major elements of a solid play-action passing attack must be repeated each year as young football players work their way toward and through varsity competition. They must learn:

- the modified fire-out block in order to simulate run action.
- how to "stalk" pass defenders before breaking into pass routes.
- how to fake run action in the backfield before blocking the pass rush.
- how to simulate blocking responsibilities and execute the appropriate pass route.
- to accept the fact that "he who hesitates is boss!" Good receivers in a well-conceived play-action passing attack often delay at the line of scrimmage and then *feel* their way into the secondary. Such smart receivers surrender speed for intelligence—and they make a lot of receptions.
- to execute play-action passes that are basic within the offense and that are likely to be repeated each year.

Dropback. As with play-action passes, the major elements of a dropback attack must be repeated each year. Players must learn:

- how to execute the basics of protection—linemen and backs.
- the primary pass routes that are used by every level of participation in the program.
- the quarterback drop: three, five, and seven-step depending on the pass routes called and the yardage needed.
- how to read the secondary in order to make necessary adjustment in the pass routes. Some players learn to run pass routes as if they're following the yellow brick road. Every time they run such a pass route, their behavior screams to us that they don't understand what we're trying to accomplish. This kind of improper execution should be corrected every day in order to assure that players have a basic understanding of the passing attack.

- to key a certain player on the defense in order to determine the primary receiver for any given play. Sometimes quarterbacks are told who their primary receivers are when the play is called. The demands of a game situation often require such calls. At other times, however, quarterbacks must throw the ball where "the defense ain't." Such execution requires the ability to watch defenders early in the play instead of their primary receivers. Quarterbacks must understand this principle early in their careers.

SEQUENCE

As with the running offense, the passing offense must introduce responsibilities of increasing complexity as football players move each year through the program. Sophisticated plays should build upon basic plays in order to establish within the total offense the kind of diversity required to confuse any defense the team may encounter during the season.

Play-action. Players must learn:

- to execute play-action passes that complement more complex running plays.
- to complement the modified "fire-out" block with a knowledge of area blocking techniques, particularly against attack defenses.
- to execute pass plays of increasing sophistication: bootlegs, counter action passes, and play-action screens.
- how to simulate blocking responsibilities and read the openings/seams in the secondary coverage.

Dropback. Players must learn:

- to complement basic pass protection blocking with a knowledge of area blocking techniques.
- to complement the three to seven-step dropback with the ability to throw from a roll-out or sprint-out action.
- to read defensive coverages of increased sophistication.
- to execute run or pass options out of roll-out, sprint-out, or bootleg action.
- to coordinate pass plays that attack the secondary with variable speed and variable death of penetration. See Figure 4–19 for an example of this principle.

INTEGRATION

Play-action passes and dropback passes have several characteristics in common. These common characteristics provide the kinds of repetitive experiences that refine the fundamental skills of football players. In essence, the integrated characteristics of the passing offense are the skills that receive constant drilling, because these are the skills and techniques that bring effective strategy to life.

Both kinds of passing attacks requiring players to know how to:

- execute the fundamentals of an effective pass protection block.
- "spot pass" the football, i.e. throw the football to a spot near the receiver where only he can catch it. Such passes may look bad to spectators, but the quarterbacks who can throw them are gifts from heaven to coaches.
- find the seams in the secondary. Receivers and quarterbacks are always looking for "holes" in the secondary. Quarterbacks are throwing the ball into them, and receivers are always trying to find ways to exploit them.
- run a pass route that complements the pass routes run by teammates. Again, refer to Figure 4–19 for an illustration and explanation of this principle.
- maintain a level of unspoken communication that results in a receiver breaking a pattern or "coming back" to the football when the coverage demands it. Sometimes excellent defensive coverage of a fly or streak pattern (deep move downfield) results in the quarterback's purposely underthrowing the receiver. Good receivers anticipate such decisions from the quarterback and break their deep patterns in order to come back to the ball. Such unspoken communication results only from the experience of working together.
- finally, the receivers in both kinds of passing attacks must always maintain a reserve of speed and the body control necessary to make adjustments in their pass routes. A receiver running "with the pedal to the metal" can't put on a burst of speed to run under an overthrown ball, nor can he adjust his forward momentum fast enough to come back to an underthrown ball. Smart receivers rarely use all their speed on any given pass play until it is required.

AN EXAMPLE OR TWO

Let's avoid a thousand words by looking at the picture. The principle of continuity tells us to introduce a basic play-action pass at a lower level and use it repeatedly at each successive level of player participation. The play must be easy to communicate, learn, and participate in. The "power action pass," which is illustrated in Figure 4–16, provides a perfect example.

The play is run from the "Full House" formation and complements the blocking responsibilities of the "Power Right," one of football's most basic plays. Because of this complementary relationship, it is taught easily to the freshman team, yet provides enough sophistication to be run with success at the varsity level.

The "Power bootleg pass at 7," however, involves more sophisticated backfield action as well as line blocking and requires different skills from the players. As diagrammed in figure 4–17, the right guard acting as personal protector must be familiar with pulling techniques and must have developed the skills needed to block a very mobile defensive end. Similarly, the quarterback must know how to make a good bootleg fake, then have the know-how to decide whether to run or pass the ball to the left.

Additional examples of continuity and sequence, this time from dropback action, are illustrated in figures 4–18 and 4–19. Figure 4–18 illustrates the "Dropback/Right In" pattern, a relatively easy pattern that can be taught to even the youngest football players. Quarterback and receiver are looking at each other throughout the entire play, and neither is required to find seams or holes in the defense.

Figure 4–19, however, illustrates a relatively sophisticated crossing pattern that requires the receivers to vary their speed and depth of penetration into the secondary. It requires additionally that they complement each other's patterns as well as react to the coverage of the secondary. A description of how it's taught provides the best example of its sophistication.

Because in most "combo" secondary coverages, the left cornerback is responsible for the first deep move in his area, the play almost forces him into "man" coverage. It also forces the onside safety into a deeper drop because he is responsible for any deep or "in" move in his area. This particular play, therefore, instructs the offensive right end to run his pattern at 12 to 14 yards at 85% speed in order to encourage both defenders into a deeper drop.

It then instructs the slotback to run his pattern at seven to eight yards and at 60% speed before he breaks to the flag. We have found that the slotback is often open underneath the coverage because of this variable speed and depth of penetration into the secondary. On occasion, the right end is wide open if the safety begins to anticipate the slotback's out move and vacates his area.

You have plays in your passing attack that probably are superior to this one. The point, however, is that basic plays are introduced at lower levels (continuity) and repeated throughout successive levels of competition. Then as players mature, they are introduced to complementary, more sophisticated plays (sequence) that capitalize on their growing skills and talents as athletes. And throughout all this, they continue to work on the refinement of skills and strategies that are common to all levels of sophistication (integration).

These three principles provide the framework within which any offense can be developed. They represent concepts to guide our thinking. And they work just as well for the development of an effective defense.

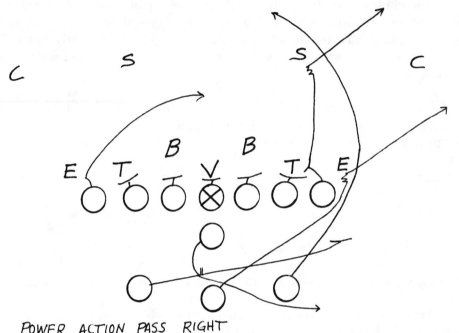

POWER ACTION PASS RIGHT

FIGURE 4-16

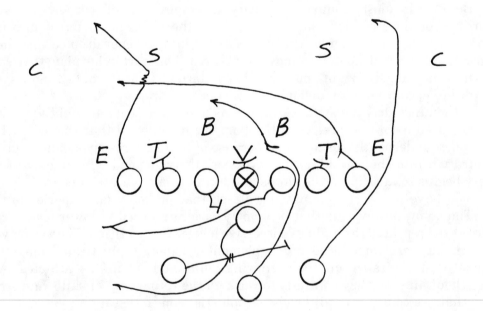

POWER BOOTLEG PASS AT 7

FIGURE 4-17

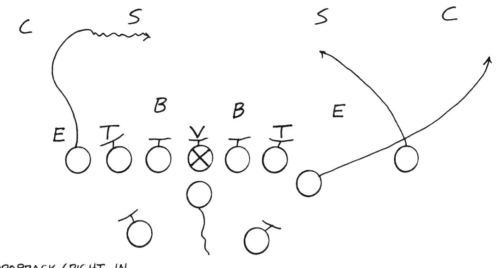

DROPBACK/RIGHT IN

FIGURE 4-18

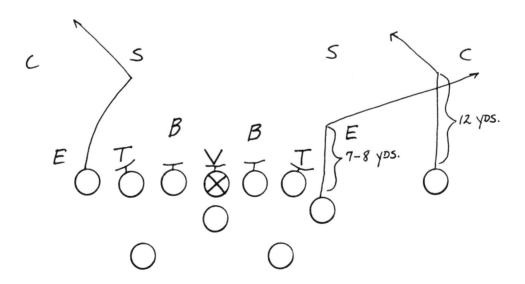

FIGURE 4-19

=========================== **DEFENSE** ===========================

The late General R.R. Neyland, when coaching at Tennessee, had a sign in the lockerroom which read: "There are more ways to score on defense than there are on offense." And none of his players disagreed. How could they? It's tough enough having to fall in line for the head football coach, let alone an Army General. Players learned to agree with everything he said.

Besides, he was most always right. His Tennessee teams did score by returning fumbles, intercepting passes, blocking kicks, returning punts, and scoring safeties. They did capitalize on his West Point military training by benefitting from philosophies like General Sheridan's Civil War mandate to "Get there first with the most." It was an exhortation that inspired the Union troops in the Shenandooah Valley Campaigns and, in essence, has become the battle cry of the contemporary attack defenses that cause sleepless nights for so many offensive coaches.

The evolution of defensive football, as reflected in the relatively recent growth of attack defenses, has underscored the importance of continuity, sequence, and integration in the development of the defense as well as the offense. Years ago, football teams aligned their defenses in a single set, dug in, and slugged it out with the offense. Players moved around a little but generally preferred to protect their pieces of turf. They forced offensive players to root them out of their bunkers in order to gain yardage.

As such, the battle plans of earlier defensive players focused more on trench warfare than strategic mobility, which is the primary characteristic of today's defenses—and which requires more sophisticated skills of the players. The continuity, sequence, and integration of the total defensive program, therefore, are critically important if defensive personnel are to be strategically mobile by the time they reach the varsity.

=========================== **CONTINUITY** ===========================

The sophomore team, therefore, should not be learning to slug it out in a traditional 52 set when the varsity uses an attack 43. Continuity of player skills suffers considerably when varsity players have to relearn fundamental skills and become acquainted with substantively different responsibilities. Inside linebackers in the 52 must read different offensive keys and play their positions differently from middle linebackers in the 61 or 43 defenses.

As illustrated in figures 4–20 and 4–21, the keys and range of responsibilities are different for 52 and 61 inside/middle linebackers. The inside backers in a 52 set are expected to help each other versus both run and pass action. Middle linebackers have more expected of them and require more experience to learn their positions. Even the keys tend to be more complicated for middle

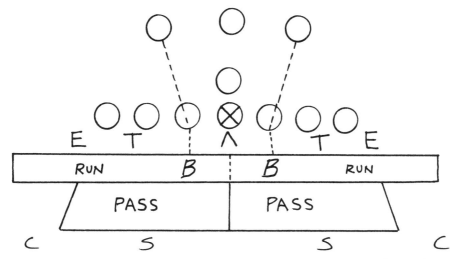

AREAS OF RUN AND PASS RESPONSIBILITY FOR 52 BACKERS

FIGURE 4-20

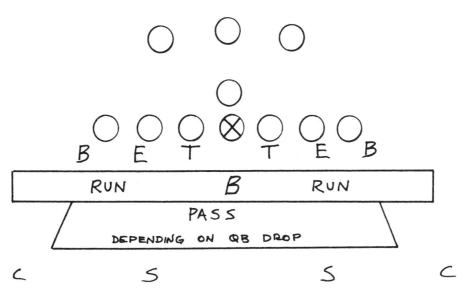

AREAS OF RUN AND PASS RESPONSIBILITY FOR MIDDLE BACKER

FIGURE 4-21

backers. Backers in the 52 normally key through the guard to the near halfback, whereas middle backers in a even front usually key the "triangle."

A similar situation is true of the down tackles in an even defense versus the noseman in an odd. Their responsibilities are substantively different, depending upon the team's preferred strategies. Nosemen must have the quickness to penetrate either gap between center and guard and still have the strength to muscle the center on certain plays. Some high schools use a small, quick noseman and slant him one way or the other on every play. While this may be solid strategy for a patterned 52 stunting defense, it is devastating to the school's total program if it is done at a lower level and something else is done on the varsity.

The principle of continuity, therefore, dictates that one defensive scheme prevail throughout the entire program. This is not to say that teams should not use multiple defensive sets and stunts to confuse offensive blocking schemes, particularly if they are blessed with talented personnel. But they should not surrender the principle of continuity to an attempt at diversity that could result in players becoming "Jacks of all trades, masters of none."

SEQUENCE

In addition, without a solid and continuing base of defensive strategies and fundamentals, football players have nothing to build upon. Again, consider the middle linebacker as an example. During his first year in that position, he learns the proper stance, how to meet and defeat the center's block, how to key the fullback, and how and where to drop in pass coverage. During his second year he may learn a few defensive stunts and begin to read "the triangle," the pattern of movements of the fullback, the center, and the two guards.

As he gains more experience with the varsity, the middle backer learns to read the triangle (See Figure 4–22), drop to pass coverage while locating all possible receivers, execute a variety of stunts, call the defensive signals, and provide the kind of leadership the defense needs to develop as a unit. It's important to remember that all these skills are acquired incidentally; they are refined with each passing year. As such, they must start with a solid foundation.

Certainly, there are blocking schemes in addition to those diagrammed in figure 4–22. Offensive teams have a variety of inside blocking schemes based upon the sophistication of their total attack. The point is, middle backers must learn to read such schemes in order to make quick decisions about the offense's point of attack. If their early experiences in football are with 52 or 44 defenses, they are denied the kinds of sequential experiences they need to develop into outstanding players.

Even if the team emphasizes a primary defensive scheme within every level of competition, players must still develop refined skills. As indicated already, middle linebackers don't learn to read the triangle overnight. Such knowledge comes with sequential steps. The same is true of the ability of linemen to "swim" past blockers and of defensive backs to execute multiple coverages.

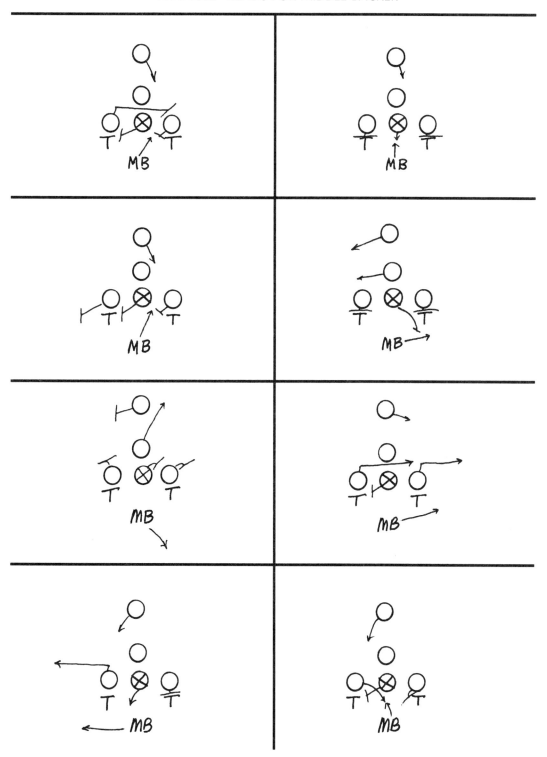

FIGURE 4–22

Some programs emphasize the sequential nature of fundamental football skills by using checklists that do two things. First, as illustrated in figure 4–23, they list the skills that players must have to play a certain position. In essence, they describe for lower-level coaches the fundamental skills that players must have before reaching the varsity and then, for the varsity, the skills that players must have to play that particular position successfully. Expectations, therefore, are clarified for players as well as coaches.

The second advantage of such lists is that they enable coaches to talk to players at the end of the season or during the off-season and point out the skills they need to work on. Successful coaches learned a long time ago that exhortations of "Get out there and play football" may be moderately inspirational, but they don't communicate to players exactly what is expected of them.

A careful review of the appropriate list with each player—perhaps even giving him a personal copy—lets him know exactly what he has to do by next year if he wants to be an accomplished player in that position. During the off-season, he might be encouraged to read books, watch video tapes, attend camps, or set up his own individual practice plan. Whatever he does, it will involve purposeful activity which responds to the information on the skills form.

Coaches are advised to reproduce several copies of the form provided in figure 4–24, give them to their assistants to make preliminary input, then meet with the entire staff to develop skill lists for every position, offensively and defensively. The process of developing such lists results in two things: one, a focus on an essential sequence of player development and, two, the investment of the coaches in the realization of that development. "Ownership" is an important word in any organization.

If coaches identify the skills players must have, they will work that much harder to assure that players develop them. Conversely, once players understand the specifics of what is expected of them, they will be more inclined to work on them. Such an investment on the part of players and coaches helps as well to realize the third necessary characteristic of the organization of a good defense, integration.

INTEGRATION

No matter what defensive alignment or pattern of stunts is preferred by the team, all defensive players must execute several basic skills, which are repeated and emphasized every year. They must:

- Learn to anticipate certain plays from certain offensive formations. Obviously, the scouting report is very important in this regard, but even more fundamentally, players on defense must realize that certain formations hit certain points along the line of scrimmage or in the secondary

KEEP IN MIND: To become good football players, athletes must play with their head, their hearts, and their bodies. They must have both the desire *and* the necessary skills to compete successfully. Following are the skills required of a good   Middle Backer . Some of them are basic, some advanced. Players must work to develop all of them. The coaching staff will help in any way possible.

BASIC SKILLS: *Before* competing at the varsity level, the
Middle Backer   must be able to:

_____ Establish a solid hit position/stance

_____ Deliver an effective forearm blow and react

_____ Drop correctly to appropriate hook zone

_____ Learn basic defensive calls

_____ Pursue correctly and "face up" to ball carrier before tackling

_____ Execute basic scrape maneuver

_____ Demonstrate "inside-out" pursuit path

_____ Key the fullback

_____ Execute fundamentally sound tackle

ADVANCED SKILLS: To be successful on the varsity level, the
Middle Backer   must be able to:

_____ Execute hand shiver and other avoidance techniques

_____ Execute all of the foregoing basics

_____ Drop to hook zone, find all eligible receivers, and read the quarterback's eyes

_____ Learn all defensive calls

_____ Recognize and call out all offensive formations

_____ Call out likely plays from formations based on scouting report

_____ Execute appropriate blitzing techniques

_____ Key the "triangle"

_____ Execute "gather and dip" technique before tackling

FIGURE 4-23

more effectively than others. Much of this comes from experience but is in no small part a reflection of coaching effectiveness.

- Consistent with identifying the strengths of certain offensive formations, most defensive players must learn to read and to trust their offensive keys. Even in the most active attack defense, certain players have to read their keys in order to anticipate the point of attack. For the young middle linebacker, his key may just be the fullback; for the veteran linebacker, it may be the triangle. Whatever it is, he has to learn to read and react to it.

- Demonstrate the ability to defeat an offensive block. Whether the player is a lineman, a linebacker, or a defensive back, he must possess the skills to destroy or avoid an offensive block. To resurrect a quote from Coach Neyland: "Your value to the team varies inversely with your distance from the ball." The key, then, for every defensive player on every level is to destroy or avoid a block and work hard to get to the ball. Nothing is more demoralizing to ball carriers than to be tackled on every play by almost every player on the defense.

- Execute solid tackling fundamentals, whether they have to hit a big fullback low to stop him or a quarterback high to prevent a pitch, tacklers must know how to stop a ball carrier. They must have mastered the fundamentals well enough to stop the opposition and prevent injury to themselves.

- Know how to react to passing situations. Linemen must execute at every level a determined pass rush; linebackers must drop to their zones; and defensive backs must cover all receivers. Again, the skills involved may vary in complexity from level to level, but the basics are performed every time at every level.

Integration, because it requires the horizontal repetition of basic skills within any defense, is an important principle for coaches to keep in mind. In fact, no one principle is more important than the others. All three must be kept in mind if coaches are to develop the kinds of offensive and defensive strategies that win football games and establish winning programs.

Other principles are important, too. In addition to the organizing concepts of continuity, sequence, and integration, coaches are advised to keep four other concepts in mind. These four are dependent upon the first three but provide added dimension to the organization and delivery of a good offense and defense.

═══════════════════ TEACHABILITY ═══════════════════

I guess it's not too surprising that it was Vince Lombardi who reminded football coaches everywhere that it's not how much you know but how much you teach that makes you a good coach. What we do as strategists is completely dependent

KEEP IN MIND: To become good football players, athletes must play with their head, their hearts, and their bodies. They must have both the desire *and* the necessary skills to compete successfully. Following are the skills required of a good _____. Some of them are basic, some advanced. Players must work to develop all of them. The coaching staff will help in any way possible.

BASIC SKILLS: *Before* competing at the varsity level, the _____ must be able to:

- _____
- _____
- _____
- _____
- _____
- _____
- _____
- _____
- _____

ADVANCED SKILLS: To be successful on the varsity level, the _____ must be able to:

- _____
- _____
- _____
- _____
- _____
- _____
- _____
- _____
- _____

FIGURE 4–24

upon when and how we do it. Our job is to handle the "what" and "when." Our players handle the "how," and as Shakespeare said—"There's the rub!"

During my first few years prowling the sidelines, I experienced more than a little frustration calling one play on the sidelines and then watching a different one run on the field. Being a young coach, I ranted and raved a lot at the athletes' failure to run the play I called, expecting, I guess, to make up in volume what I was losing in substance. Fortunately, like most of us, I learned eventually that when something goes wrong the first place to look for the problem is in the nearest mirror.

It was at this point that I realized I had better take a careful look at how our system was being taught to the players and how it was being communicated to and among them. I discovered that we were doing different things at different levels. We had failed to provide the continuity and the sequence that a well-organized program requires.

The freshman level was running a sweep and a quick opener series, primarily because each series was easy to teach to beginning football players. The sophomore level was running an inside belly series, which was consistent with what the varsity was doing, but was blocking it differently; and the varsity was running the crossfire and inside belly series, in essence having to teach many of the most important plays from scratch.

The sophomore team was also using the 52 as their primary defense, and the varsity was using the 43. Sequencing of appropriate skills and strategies, therefore, was a problem for us. The players were denied a process not only to develop and refine their football skills but to use a consistent terminology that was reinforced each year and that ultimately could become second nature to them.

Once we started heeding the principles of continuity, sequence, and integration, our program developed better plays and improved player skills. We even considered ways to improve communication regarding such things as our offensive formations. When we took the time to determine what we wanted from our formation-calling system, including a minimum of words to communicate it, we developed a very simple format. (See Section 5 for a detailed explanation.)

The point is, "teachability" is a crucial consideration if we want the offense and defense to do what each has been designed to do. This point is equally valid when it comes to decisions regarding players and the skills they bring to the task.

PERSONNEL CONSIDERATIONS

"Give me the right players and no matter what I run, I'll win most of my games." Right? Wrong! You might win some games you should have lost, but you'll lose just a whole lot more that you should have won. Teams with lesser talent are beating teams with gifted athletes every day. And they're doing it with just a whole lot more than inspirational pep talks.

These teams are providing a diverse enough offense and defense to capitalize on the skills of their lesser talented players, and they are providing enough continuity within the program to assure that all players have mastered their responsibilities. A solid program, therefore, doesn't depend upon superior personnel to sustain a winning team, particularly in high school, where significant talent isn't available every year. That's why "the program" is so important. It transcends the talent or the lack of talent of individual players in order to provide the coordination of combined effort that makes the most of whatever strengths the team possesses.

Certainly football has its share of universals. I have learned over the years, for example, that there is no substitute for speed. Excellent speed and quickness can make up for a multitude of mistakes. On the other hand, I also have learned that there is no substitute for brains. If the offensive line knows how to block every defensive alignment they face and can adjust to every stunt (a mighty tall order!), they will at least be in the right place at the right time.

They may not be able to execute the most devastating block I've ever seen, but at least they'll get in the way. In many instances that's good enough. Sometimes a good shield block is even preferred to a solid shoulder block. The player knowledge that results from constant exposure to an offensive or defensive program often results in the kind of program that wishes it has more blue chippers but that wins a whole lot of ball games—year after year.

It also consists of the kinds of players who are able to execute a variety of basic and sophisticated plays (sequence) that enhance the unpredictability of both the offense and the defense. If the coach calls the right play at the right time, and the players execute their assignments, the team doesn't need someone with a 4.2 forty to get into the end zone. Speed may be one of our universal desirables, but brains can give us just as much. And that's an element we can control.

ADAPTABILITY

Stand-up comics aren't the only opportunists who "steal" from each other. Good coaches seize opportunities; they don't wait for the knock on the door. A good idea belongs to everyone, and there's no reason why coaches can't learn—and borrow—from each other, as long as their programs are adaptable to good ideas.

That doesn't mean they imitate. Originality is essential within any program because it means that the coach is still looking at his world through fresh eyes. But when those eyes spot a good idea, there's nothing wrong with customizing it a little. Solid programs are built by coaches who sustain a focus on the evolution of their offensive and defensive attacks and the incorporation of new ideas.

Adaptability, therefore, is most dependent upon the coach's mind set. Static programs are sustained by coaches who adapt their behavior to outside influences. These are coaches who define team performance in terms of player skills and attitudes, budget, parental support, assistance from colleagues, park district programs, Booster Clubs, and so forth.

Dynamic and adaptable programs, on the other hand, are established by coaches who perceive themselves as the primary influence on team performance. They are the ones who seek out problems in team performance and look to themselves for answers. They are open to new ideas, irrespective of who has the idea, and they know how to secure the input of colleagues and players to help them. Adaptability, therefore, is much more a process than a product, and if it is to be realized in a particular program, it will be established by a coach who is himself adaptable.

LET'S WRAP IT UP

The purpose of this section was not to emphasize a particular offense or defense. It was to provide a set of principles to guide your thinking while you develop and/or refine your own. A process that meets our special needs and interests is often better than a product which may or may not. It might take more time, but it's always more effective.

Only a part of the time in overseeing the process is going to be spent in staff and team meetings. The substance for those meetings will come from the analysis and discussion of books and articles, information derived from workshops and conventions, discussions with other coaches, and the knowledge which is an essential by-product of watching other teams.

Most important, however, is the mind set that seeks out better ways to do things offensively and defensively. Such a mind set is not interested in change for its own sake. Just as all movement on the football field is not forward, all change in our programs is not progress. But if we take the time to look carefully at what we're doing each year, open ourselves up to new ideas, and sustain a process that accommodates these ideas in a relevant way, we're going to be mighty happy with the result.

Game Preparation

Remember Rick Venturi's quote? "The only difference between me and General Custer is that I have to watch the films the next day!" He probably had to watch them a whole lot more than once. Win or lose, coaches analyze films into the wee hours of the morning, and the coaches who do it systematically win much more often than they lose. If a well-designed offense and defense are serviceable tools, the process of game preparation determines how they will be used.

Good coaches use their tools like master craftsmen, not day laborers. Winning football games is a major construction project, requiring a well-conceived blueprint for action. The first element that must go into the blueprint is a thorough knowledge of the opponent.

KNOW YOUR OPPONENT

Good coaches live with game films, scouting reports, and practice schedules. They try to get inside the opponent's head. They study him, assess his strengths and weaknesses, identify what he likes to do, evaluate his personnel, and ultimately decide what they must do to win. Then they coordinate their practices to assure a maximum effort from their teams. They also seek commitment from all their assistant coaches.

Fortunately, such commitments are relatively easy to come by, if the purposes requiring them are reasonable. Former players become coaches because they love the game, and they are willing to sacrifice time, even quality time on weekends with their families, if it is spent profitably. The time is not spent profitably if the scouting format is poorly organized and the subsequent analysis and organization of data are frustrating.

Simplicity is the essence of creative scouting. It is what communicates to players, and it keeps coaches looking for the strategic keys that open doors to improved player performance and winning records. It was this search for simplicity that led us ultimately to our scouting format, a process that can be handled completely by one coach and that results in a thorough knowledge of what we must do to win each football game.

Gathering the Information

Obviously, we prefer to send more than one coach on each scouting assignment, but anticipated play-off competition sometimes sends all of us scurrying in different directions to scout possible opponents. At such times, we are particularly grateful for the simplicity of our format. We also come to rely heavily on tape recorders, which capitalize even further on the verbal format we have developed.

The fact that our format consists exclusively of words and numbers makes it compact, so that we deal generally with no more than five or six sheets of paper. Its greatest strength, however, is that it also enables us to communicate formations to our players in the fewest words possible. Sending formations and plays into the huddle is as easy as extracting other teams' tendencies from scouting reports. As a matter of fact, our scouting format evolved from our formation-calling system.

Its simplicity and flexibility are advantages in the huddle as well as in the stands when we scout an opponent. We run our offense from several basic formations, each of which is diagrammed in Figure 5–1. Each has been given an arbitrary name, and each is easily learned by our players. Figure 5–2 illustrates other formations, used infrequently by a few of our opponents. The point is, each has a name in order to keep the scouting format simple.

Names and Numbers. Once combined with numbers, the names enable us to identify in a very few words hundreds of different formations—certainly all of our formations and most that are used by our opponents. The number assignments are similar to those used by most teams. As indicated in Figure 5–3, the left end is designated a five, the left tackle a three, the left guard a one, and the center a zero. The right side receives the even numbers.

In addition, a spot approximately one yard to the outside of the offensive left end is designated the seven position; another spot anywhere from 10 to 15 yards outside the left end is designated the nine position. Conversely, the 8 and the 10 positions are located similarly to the outside of the right end.

A final point involves the positioning of the ends. If we want the left end split, we initiate the formation call with the term "Open." If we want to split the right end, we conclude the formation call with the term "Split." If neither of these terms is called when we designate the formation, both ends are tight. If we want to "flex" either end, i.e., position him approximately three to five yards outside his tackle, we initiate the call with the term "Flex" for the left end and conclude the call with the term "Flex" for the right end. We use the flex positions so infrequently that we see no reason to use distinct terms for each end. That's really all there is to it.

When combined with the names of the backfield sets, the numbers and the end designations enable us to identify quickly any formation we see while scouting, or for that matter, to call any of the over 300 formations that we might use

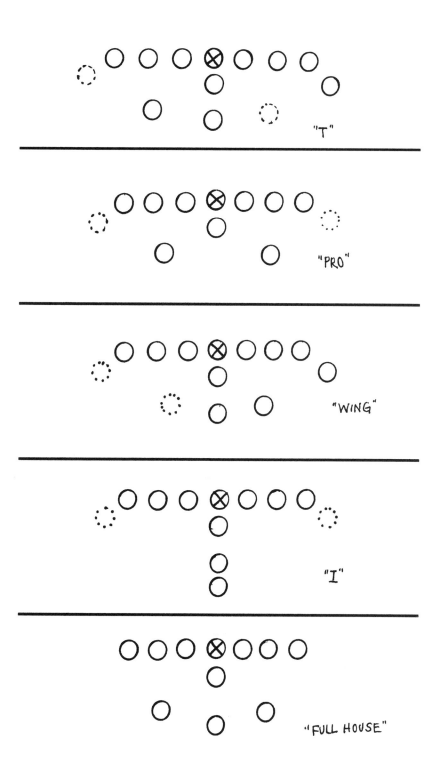

FIGURE 5-1

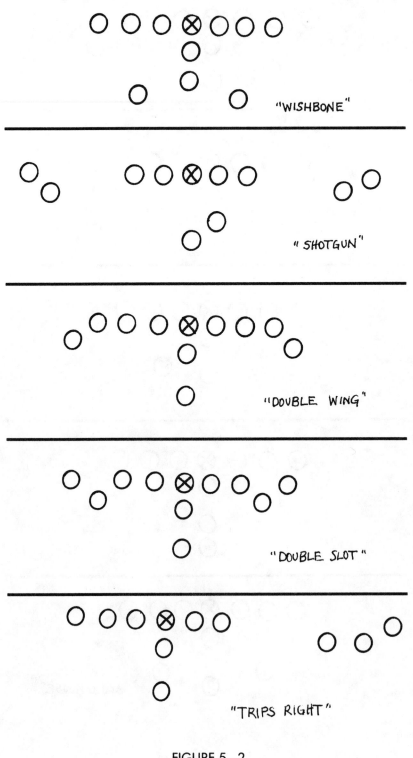

"WISHBONE"

"SHOTGUN"

"DOUBLE WING"

"DOUBLE SLOT"

"TRIPS RIGHT"

FIGURE 5—2

100

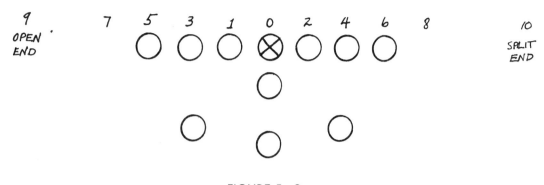

FIGURE 5–3

during a game. The players pick up the system with amazing ease. All they have to remember is what each backfield set looks like and that the odd numbers in the call instruct the left halfback where to position himself; the even numbers instruct the right halfback. Finally, if the call begins with either "Open" or "Flex," it refers to the left end; if it concludes with either "Split" or "Flex," it refers to the right end.

Figure 5–4 illustrates six different formations, all of which currently are very popular, either in college or in the pros. Look at all six and try to name each before you read the answers which follow. The terms are, starting from the top left hand corner, the "Open-Pro 10," a very popular pro formation; the "T 8," a formation that we use very often; the "I 9-Split," a popular formation used by many colleges; the "Open-Wishbone," one of the basic alignments for the triple option; the "Pro 9-Split," another popular pro formation; and the "Flex-Pro 5-Split," an interesting concoction that no one seems wild about but that someday may be fun to throw at someone. The possible combinations, especially as more backfield sets are introduced, are endless.

We feel that our crossfire, belly, power, and quick series also describe most of what we might see other teams run while we scout them. Certainly they use different designations, but the backfield action and the general play sequencing seem to be fundamentally the same. If they do run from series fundamentally different from our own, we'll give it a name on the spot, diagram one play to show the basic backfield action, and continue to simply write down the names of successive plays. Most of the plays that we see, however, are much like ours or are simple variations of our own, so we have never had much of a problem with this part of the scouting format.

As a matter of fact, we have never had much trouble with any part of the scouting format because it is so easy and quick. Our staff, while scouting a triple option team, for example, might observe a "Wishbone-Split/Inside Belly at 5." The scouting report would contain "W-S/IB5." Such a format certainly involves an economy of words and allows us enough time, even if only one or two coaches are scouting, to look for other things. While our colleagues from other schools

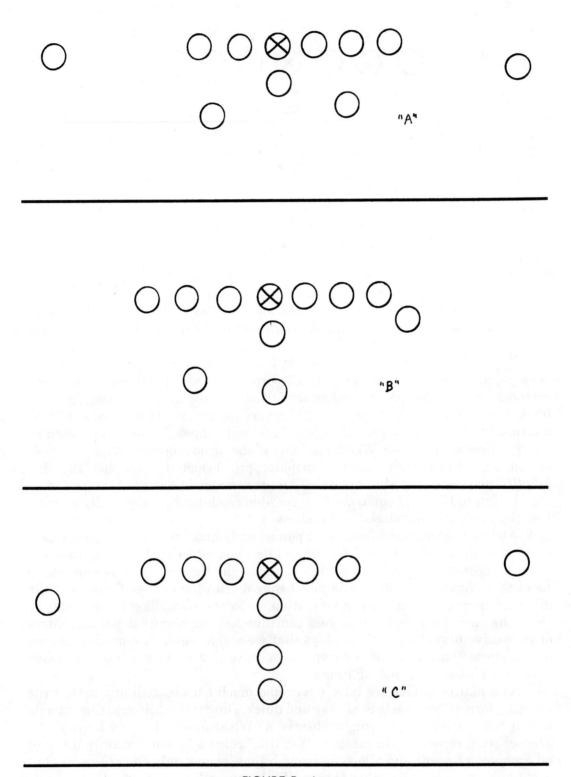

"A"

"B"

"C"

FIGURE 5-4

102

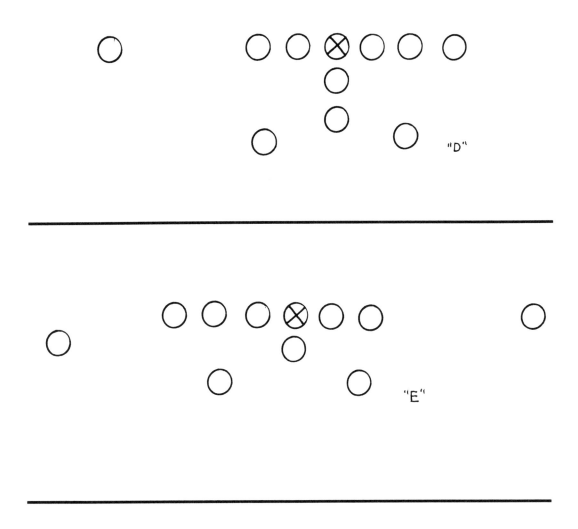

"D"

"E"

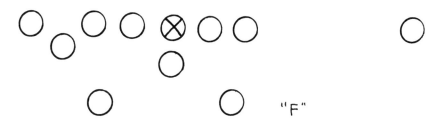

"F"

FIGURE 5–4 (*Continued*)

103

are drawing X's and O's and are diagramming backfield action, we are writing down "W-S/IB5" and are watching for traps, cross blocks, finesse blocks, or any of several insights into what makes the team tick.

An added advantage of this format is that with a few simple modifications, the scouting reports for an upcoming opponent can be computerized, and his tendencies can be identified and systematized in a matter of seconds. We have saved much valuable time in preparation for an opponent by letting the computer do most of the work. By not having to break down the scouting reports, we can devote more time to the analysis of our offense.

THE SCOUTING FORMAT

This scouting format handles time like money. We learned long ago that the less we have, the farther it has to go. Time is a precious commodity to coaches. One week doesn't provide much time to re-tool for a new opponent, so the smart coach spends every minute wisely. Following is a general outline of the actual scouting format and several reproducible copies of essential pages. Examples of each page will be presented later in the chapter when the game plan is discussed.

Opposing Personnel

Figure 5–5 is the first page of the scouting format. When scouting one of the opponent's games, coaches simply write down the numbers of the offensive players in the circles provided. They can get the names and other information later from the program they picked up at the gate before the game. They identify defensive personnel by writing the numbers of the players in their respective positions. The final copy to be given to the team will have even more information and will be illustrated later in this section.

Special Teams

Figure 5–6 illustrates the form used to gather information about the opponent's special teams. Ultimately, it identifies the particulars about the opponent's kickoff team, the kickoff return team, punt and punt return teams, extra-point teams, and related statistics. It provides valuable information about the average distance of kickoffs and punts, the personnel responsible for each position, and the opponent's return strategies.

An obvious reason for the value of such information involves the need to kick away from the opponent's best runner or, less obviously, to discover significant personnel changes: the second-string quarterback entering the game as a

OFFENSIVE TEAM

DEFENSIVE TEAM

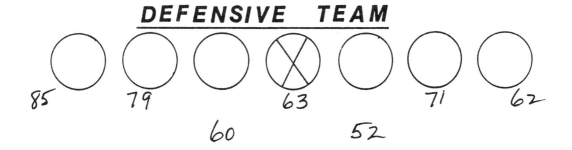

FIGURE 5–5 *(Continued on next page)*

OFFENSIVE TEAM

DEFENSIVE TEAM

FIGURE 5–5 (*Continued*)

106

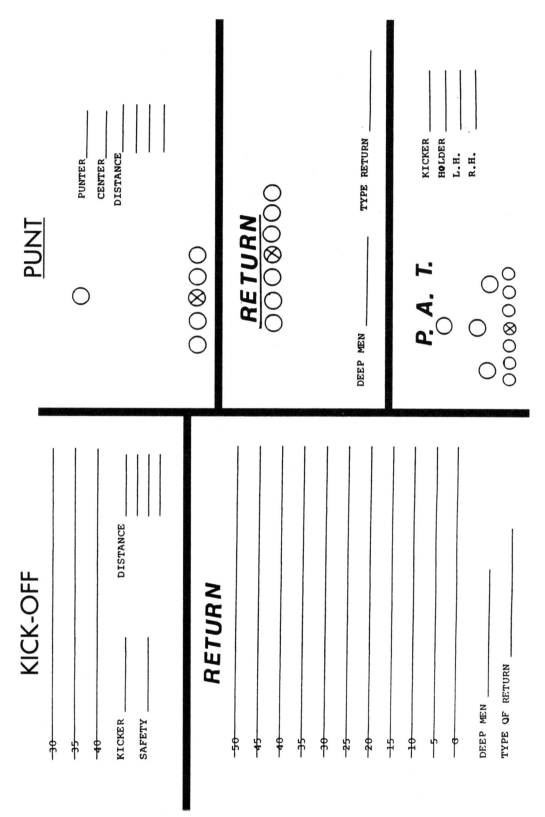

FIGURE 5-6

107

punter or any second or third stringer replacing an injured player, particularly in a skill position like center or PAT holder. A knowledge of such changes during the game causes coaches to rethink defensive alignments or strategies such as PAT or punt blocks.

As important, a knowledge of your opponent's special teams personnel and tendencies reaffirms in the minds of each of your players that you have done your homework. It provides further encouragement for them to do theirs, and it helps provide that intangible sense of confidence in a game plan that fosters superior performance on the game field.

Defense

Figure 5–7 illustrates the sheet on which scouts will identify the opponent's primary defenses along with favorite adjustments and stunts throughout the game. If they can record such information verbally, so much the better. We can always draw the defenses later for distribution to the team. Scouts might, for example, write "straight 52 with occasional inside and outside LB scrapes on first downs" or "straight 43 with line slants into home halfback."

Generally, however, they will draw the defense, showing with arrows the direction of LB stunts and line slants. Each defense will be drawn, including loosen and prevent defenses and goal line or short-yardage adjustments. This is not a time-consuming task because most teams, even those with attack defenses, prefer a basic defensive set and a limited number of stunts. They need be drawn by scouts, therefore, only two or three times during the game.

Passing

This is the toughest part of scouting. It is virtually impossible for one scout to identify all the pass routes during a given play, particularly if it involved play-action. Two coaches, however, can watch both sides of the offensive formation and identify the routes of two, even three players. And given the fact that several of the opponent's pass plays will be similar to yours or a few of their favorites will be repeated throughout the game, scouts can simply record them verbally.

This section of the format, however, is among the most critical. Teams often introduce new running plays in big games, but the difficulty of timing good pass plays usually requires them to stay with their favorites throughout the season. Those are the plays that can break a game wide open. A knowledge of how they're executed and when they're likely to occur is often the key to a winning effort.

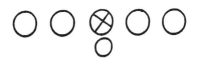

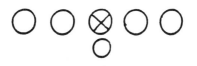

FIGURE 5–7

109

Running

The significant majority of our opponent's running plays will be recorded verbally. A few may be so unique, however, that they have to be drawn. See figure 5–8. This should be done immediately in order to look for the play's less obvious elements the next time it is run. Usually, a short trap or a cross block can be added after the formation and the basic backfield action are drawn.

After several scouting reports have been gathered, the incidence of such unique plays or formations can be determined. To know whether the play was used for a particular game or has become a staple of the opponent's offense will influence your preparation for the game. Such determinations are relatively easy once the scouting process is complete.

Play-by-Play Sheet

The primary focus of our scouting format is the play-by-play sheet as illustrated in figure 5–9. The accumulation of the information it provides constitutes the meat of our scouting format and subsequent game preparation. Ultimately, the play-by-play sheet identifies most of the opponent's offensive tendencies. Generally, tendencies by formation are the most useful, but field position tendencies, game-situation tendencies, and tendencies by down-and-distance provide the additional insights needed to get inside the opposing coach's head in order to get a picture of what he's trying to do with his team—or of understanding the limitations that are preventing him from doing what he'd like to do.

Experienced coaches realize the need to stay a play or two ahead of the opponent throughout the game. The art of anticipating his next move prevents him from sequencing his offense or from setting up his favorite plays. In essence, he becomes predictable. Then, he becomes frustrated, and frustrated coaches make mistakes—just before they lose.

How we determine tendencies and then share them with our team will be discussed later in this section. Let's first discuss the use of the play-by-play sheet and provide an example or two.

═══════════════════ **BRINGING THINGS INTO FOCUS** ═══════════════════

What can be an unclear picture early in the season comes into focus with the addition of each scouting report, particularly if the opposing team runs from a variety of formations. Just one scouting report, however, can provide a clear picture of certain tendencies if the opposing team has a well-sequenced but basically unimaginative offense. Many coaches ask their teams to do only a few things but to do them well. Predicting what they like to do, therefore, is relatively easy. Stopping them may be another issue.

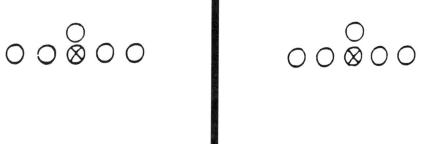

FIGURE 5-8

PLAY BY PLAY _____ vs _____ PAGE _____

PLAY #	YARD LINE	DOWN	FORMATION	PLAY	BALL CARRIER	GAIN	REMARKS
1							
2							
3							
4							
5							
6							
7							
8							
9							
10							
11							
12							
13							
14							
15							
16							
17							
18							
19							
20							
21							
22							
23							
24							
25							
26							
27							

FIGURE 5—9

Since prediction is the first step, however, let's look at a sample play-by-play sheet to see what it tells us. We're scouting DHS and, as evidenced by figure 5–10, we see that they started their first drive on the MS 23 yard line, ran from three different formations, used three different plays and three different runners, and finally had to punt the ball.

What may be unclear during the first drive comes into focus after the next three drives. It seems the DHS coach likes a deuce backfield with a wingback, sometimes with an open left end and a flanker, as his favorite alignment, and he wants to run the power play ("P right" and "P left"), pulling both guards ("Gds."). His left halfback may be his best runner, probably because his right halfback ("big kid") is a good blocker from the wing position.

At least as far as this scouting report is concerned, DHS likes the power play with play-action complements, and the team runs at least one misdirection play, a Power counter at 5 ("P ctr. @5") from its favorite formation. DHS also dropback passes from the pro formation and, one time at least, ran its fullback on a Crossfire at 12 trap ("XFT 12").

Obviously, the more scouting reports you accumulate on any given opponent the better your understanding of what he likes to do and where he seems to be heading offensively. Once his direction becomes apparent, you can cut him off at the pass with the defensive ambushes you develop in your pre-game staff meetings, which will be discussed later in this section.

Figure 5–11 illustrates a sample page from a sample follow-up scouting report. It reveals that DHS is still favoring the pro set backfield alignment with the power play and its variations as its favorite running offense. It also reveals the increasing tendency to use the T formation with the Crossfire (XF) and the Inside Belly (IB) series as complements. DHS seems to favor play-action passing as well as a conventional dropback passing attack, and it uses misdirection sparingly, often enough, however, to give the defense a problem.

This kind of added information helps round out the picture of the opponent's tendencies and provides substantive material for planning activities in staff meetings. In addition, because most of the staff in attendance have helped collect the information, each will be able to complement the objectivity of the information with a feel for the opponent and a reaction in terms of what has to be done to beat him. That fact brings up the question of who does the scouting—and when.

THE WHO AND WHEN OF SCOUTING

Now that we've answered much of the HOW of scouting, the WHO and WHEN should be discussed. An overriding principle governing who should scout upcoming opponents is that every member of the varsity staff should see every opponent as many times as possible. Watching an opponent on tape provides a systematic look at blocking schemes and backfield execution. It even provides a general idea

PLAY #	YARD LINE	DOWN	FORMATION	PLAY	BALL CARRIER	GAIN	REMARKS
1	MS 23	1–10	Pro 8	P right 9ds.	27	+3	Good speed
2		2–7	Pro 7	P left 9ds.	23	+4	Big kid
3		3–3	OT 10	XFT 12	36	+2	
4		4–1	Punt				
5	MS 16	1–10	Pro 8	P trap 4 Gd off	27	+2	
6		2–8	Pro 8	P action pass			Inc.
7		3–8	0 Pro 10	DB screen right	23	+5	
8		4–3	Punt				Almost blocked Up gut —
9	MS 19	1–10	0 Pro 10	P right 6ds.	27	+8	
10		2–2	0 Pro 10	P right action pass		+23	Flood right / ladder
11	mid-field	1–10	Pro 7	P left	23	+1	This kid's slow
12		2–9	Pro 8	P ctr. on S	23	—	Stuffed!
13		3–9	0 Pro 10	DB pass			Right 'A' Inc.
14		4–9	Punt				
15							
16							
17							
18							
19							
20							
21							
22							
23							
24							
25							
26							
27							

FIGURE 5–10

Play No.	Yard Line	Down	Formation	Play	Ball Carrier	Gain	R
51	WW 19	1–10	Pro 7	P trap 3	23	+4	
52		2–6	T 10	XF 1	36	+7	
53		1–10	O Pro 10	S 8	27	+3	
54		2–7	Pro 8	P right	27	+1	
55		3–6	Pro 9 S	DB pass		Inc.	
56			Punt				
57	WW 48	1–10	T 9 S	XF 2	36	+3	
58		2–7	T 9 S	XF action pass		+32	
59		1–10	T 8	IB 6	27	+4	
60		2–6	T 8	IB 4	36	+2	
61		3–4	T 9 S	XF 2	36	+5	
62		1–10	T 9	XF action p.		+18	TD
63	next possession	1–10	Pro 9	P left	23	+6	
64	DHS 36	2–4	Pro 8	P right	27	+1	
65		3–3	Pro 9	P trap 3	23	+2	
66		4–1	Punt				
67	DHS 40	1–10	T 8	IB ctr @ S	23	+11	
68		1–10	T 8	IB 4	36	+2	
69		2–8	T 9	XF action pass		Inc.	
70		3–8	O Pro 10	DB pass		Inc.	
71		4–8	Punt				
72							
73							
74							
75							

FIGURE 5–11

115

of defensive tendencies and personnel strengths. But tapes do not communicate that feel that tells a coach just how good an opposing team really is.

For that reason, we expect all varsity coaches to scout an opponent as often as possible. This may be a problem for coaches in rural areas. As circumstances permit, however, they should scout opponents as often as possible. When we play our game on Saturdays, we divide the staff on Friday nights to scout as many games as are played that night. Conversely, we all scout someone on Saturdays when we have a Friday night game. It makes for a full weekend, particularly when Sundays often involve meetings, but the information we receive and the feel we have for upcoming opponents makes the investment of time worthwhile.

Freshman and sophomore level coaches provide the final scouting dimension we need to plan for upcoming games. Usually, the freshmen play in the mornings, so the coaches are available on Saturday afternoon to scout opponents who play on the same day. Obviously, the additional information they collect is more important to us than the feel they get from an upcoming team. The varsity staff has to know every aspect of the opponent's game, so we scout as often as possible, and we encourage each varsity coach to watch available tapes of the opponent on Sunday before the meeting and during the week of the game.

ABOUT FILMS AND TAPES

Varsity coaches can watch tapes or films Sunday mornings, at home during the week, or during free periods during school. After watching a tape or film, they are asked to fill out the Film Evaluation Sheet and get it to the head coach sometime before the staff meeting. Each is asked to review the tape independently of his colleagues to guarantee an individual opinion. We have discovered that minority opinions in the beginning of the staff meeting eventually become majority opinions at the end once we've taken the time to analyze them.

The film evaluations provoke considerable discussion, some of which gets pretty heated. Without such discussion, however, a coaching staff is unable to transform a body of information into a comprehensive plan of action. The film evaluations provoke enough educated opinion to provide a range of different perspectives. When the opinions regarding elements of the opponent's offense and defense are unanimous, the staff can feel confident about the need for action and the directions it should take.

The Evaluation Form

The Film Evaluation Form, as illustrated in figure 5–12, asks each coach to make a routine assessment of the opponent's offensive and defensive packages. One evaluation form is expected for each film or tape that is available for review. Obviously, as the season wears on, particularly when playoff competition begins,

Directions: Find the time to do this by yourself. Jot down any of your reactions to the tape or film while you review it. Use the appropriate heading, and don't worry about rewriting the form when you're done. Just give it to me.

A. What do you see as their offensive strengths?

B. What do you see as their defensive weaknesses?

C. How can we capitalize on these weaknesses?

D. What defensive adjustments must we make to counter their offensive strengths?

E. What are their personnel strengths? Weaknesses?

F. <u>Summary</u>
   1. What do they like to do?

   2. What *must* we do to beat this team?

FIGURE 5–12

117

more and more of the opponent's films or tapes may be available. Reviewing all of them can be a chore, hence the beauty and the simplicity of the form.

If our expectations of varsity assistants become unreasonable, some or all of the coaches are going to start hedging on their responsibilities, usually unconsciously but almost always certainly. The form, therefore, is designed to provide just enough space for each coach's *abstracted* assessment of offense, defense, personnel, and necessary adjustments. The two or three observations and subsequent suggestions made by coaches in each category provide all the information the entire staff needs later to get a handle on the opponent's likes and dislikes.

The form's summary and the two questions it asks ultimately provide the focus the staff needs to prepare for the upcoming game. Specifically, the answers to "What must we do to beat this team" translate into a game plan and a series of practice schedules that reflect not only the objective awareness of documented tendencies, but the subjective feel for the opponent that keeps you one step ahead of him.

COACHES' MEETING

The staff meeting is the final process that takes all the bits and pieces of information and consolidates them into a game plan. The standardized agenda for our coaches' meetings (see figure 5–13) is to the game plan what our naming and numerical system is to our scouting format. It gives organization to the information we have gathered and a sense of direction to the varying opinions expressed by the coaches. The first part of the meeting requires each coach to roll up his sleeves and get to work. Each scouting report has to be broken down to reveal personnel strengths and weaknesses, special situations, and offensive and defensive tendencies.

Identifying the personnel strengths and weaknesses is relatively easy, given the recurring comments made by coaches on the scouting reports. The experienced coach has learned that personnel strengths are not as revealing as personnel weaknesses. Every offensive football team has at least one pretty good lineman, and if the team is right-handed, you'll find him at right tackle. Their good running back is the player who's carrying the ball all the time. By definition, it's hard to hide standout players.

What good scouts have to realize is that most football teams try to hide their weaker players, cover for them, give them help. These are the players we want to find. Although not as easily identifiable, once they are found, they provide a range of offensive and defensive exploitation possibilities, taking the form of defensive stunts, offensive adjustments, and personnel changes.

These are all subjects of conversation during the coaches' meeting. Similarly, it's important to identify from the scouting report any special situations: unique defensive adjustments and/or stunts, special substitutions of offensive or defensive personnel, unique two-point plays, particularly from kick formation, quart-

1. Break down scouting reports

2. Determine tendencies
   —by formation
   —by down and distance
   —by field position

3. Organize tendencies for scouting report

4. Discuss film/tape evaluations to identify common opinions

5. Discuss the question: "What must we do to beat this team?"

6. Identify defensive adjustments

7. Develop new plays as needed

8. Discuss personnel changes

9. Develop practice schedule(s)

10. Consolidate game plan for distribution to the team

FIGURE 5–13

erback audibilizing, trick formations and shifts, tactical motion, and other strategies that may be out of the ordinary.

If used often enough, an opposing coach's attempts at unpredictability become in themselves predictable. This fact is most evident in his selection of offensive plays. Even the best football coach slips occasionally into a predictable routine of play-calling. Most obviously, the coach may be left-handed or right-handed and may favor one side of the line of scrimmage over the other. In key situations, he may be inclined to run toward his own sidelines in order to see the execution of the play for purposes of play sequencing. Or, more usually, he will try as much as possible to run his best back behind his best lineman. In addition, some coaches have favorite plays against a 52 defense or a stacked 44, and they run them irrespective of the opponent's personnel and game-day adjustments.

The scouting report must be organized and analyzed so that it reveals the opponent's favorite formations and the plays he runs from them. The early part of the coaches' meeting is devoted, therefore, to a simple listing of all formations the opponent has used throughout the season and the plays he has favored. Figure 5–14 illustrates a sample format used to organize the information.

Favorite formations are listed horizontally across the inside of a manila folder, and plays run from each formation are noted, the hashmarks after each one identifying the number of times it was run. Formations that were used only a few times are disregarded. The folder can be used to store the remainder of the scouting report, then can be filed for reference in future years.

Once the tendencies by formation have been recorded, the staff can use the play-by-play sheets to determine tendencies by down-and-distance—if the upcoming game is important enough to justify the additional time. We determine these tendencies by recording the plays within five categories: first and ten, second and short, third and short, third and long, and fourth and short. These categories cover most game situations and serve as excellent complements to the

PRO 8	*PRO 7*	*T 9S*	*T 8*	*T 9*	*O Pro 10*	*OT 10*
P right III	P left II	XF2 II	IB 6	XF action p. II	DB pass III	XFT 12
P trap 4	P trap 3	XF action pass	IB 4 II		P right pass	
P action pass			IB ctr 5		Sweep right	
P ctr @ 5						

T 10	*Pro 95*	*Pro 9*
XF 1	DB pass	Power left
		P trap 3

FIGURE 5–14

opponent's formation tendencies. Normally, however, we take the additional time to determine down-and-distance tendencies only before important playoff or championship games. They require a lot of time, and the tendencies by formation often give us all the information we need anyway.

"What Must We Do to Beat This Team?"

The middle third of the coaches' meeting is devoted to a discussion of any Film Evaluation Forms that may have been completed prior to the meeting. Because our meetings usually are held on Sunday evenings, some of the coaches already have reviewed one or two tapes and have brought evaluation forms with them. The discussion solicits the opinions of each coach and results ultimately in consensus regarding necessary adjustments in our offense or defense.

The question "What must we do to beat this team" usually provokes general reactions such as "Get to the quarterback" or "Gang tackle Jones every time he touches the ball" or "Pick up their stunts in the 44 Gap Stack." Whatever the general consensus initially, it soon translates into specific adjustments in personnel and in the offensive and defensive game plan. This is the time to adjust the defense to accommodate their offensive tendencies and to add new offensive plays or blocking schemes to capitalize on their defensive weaknesses.

══════════ *PERFECT* PRACTICE MAKES PERFECT ══════════

Having made these decisions, the coaches are ready to discuss what must happen in practice to guarantee the success of the game plan. Players will need time to master offensive and defensive adjustments in addition to the time they usually spend on timing and execution. They will need time to work on fundamentals, particularly the skills required for new blocking schemes. They will need some early-week conditioning and some work, usually later in the week, on special teams: kicking, kick receiving, and two-point plays.

The practice schedule, as illustrated in figure 5–15, enables the coaches to coordinate needed activities and to have the appropriate equipment on hand. During the following week, each coach receives a copy of the day's practice schedule and one is given to the team manager, who sets up equipment before the drills and blows a whistle after each drill to signal movement to the next activity.

══════════ PRACTICING THE GAME PLAN ══════════

One of the last items in the meeting is devoted to the organization of the game plan for distribution to the team early in the week, usually in a meeting before Monday's practice. The packet is a compilation of everything we have discovered

DAILY PRACTICE PLAN   DATE _____

1. _____ to _____	ACTIVITY	EQUIPMENT	REMARKS
GUARDS			
TACKLES			
CENTERS			
BACKS			
ENDS			

2. _____ to _____			
GUARDS			
TACKLES			
CENTERS			
BACKS			
ENDS			

3. _____ to _____			
GUARDS			
TACKLES			
CENTERS			
BACKS			
ENDS			

4. _____ to _____			
GUARDS			
TACKLES			
CENTERS			
BACKS			
ENDS			

5. _____ to _____			
GUARDS			
TACKLES			
CENTERS			
BACKS			
ENDS			

FIGURE 5–15

about the opponent. It consists of a Fact Sheet, which identifies the opponent's outstanding characteristics and any features of the game that need to be emphasized. See figures 5–16 and 5–17 for an example and a reproducible copy.

The second page introduces your team to the opponent. It contains the name, year in school, height, and weight of each starting player by position on offense and defense. See figure 5–18. Next is the "Special Teams" page, as illustrated in figure 5–19, which identifies the personnel, statistics, and execution of the opponent's kicking game. As described earlier in this section, this information will be used later in the week by one or more prep teams to simulate the opponent's special teams.

This page is followed by the most important part of the report, the defensive and offensive information. First, the opposing team's basic defensive alignments are drawn, followed by drawings of the adjustments and stunts the opponent has used up to that time. See figure 5–20. This information is followed by drawings of the opponent's favorite passing plays. Figure 5–21 shows sample drawings and a reproducible copy of the format.

Finally, as illustrated in figure 5–22, the opponent's favorite formations and running plays are reported. The sample illustration shows a few formations, including a frequency count of the plays run at each hole from that formation. The frequency count reveals obvious tendencies and gives coaches and players an excellent idea of what has to be done to beat this team.

Just a cursory look at the illustration in figure 5–21 suggests the need to stop the power and the sweep plays when the opponent lines up in any of his favorite formations. It seems in the Pro Split formation, however, he favors the power to the tight end side. He also runs his fullback from the double wing but mostly from the fullhouse, which also is his favorite formation for the Crossfire action pass which has been very successful for him.

The Pro formation seems to be his favorite formation for the dropback pass, particularly the Pro spread, which reveals the obvious tendency to throw into the spread side. Such tendencies, particularly when they're so well-documented, instill confidence in your team when you organize and introduce defensive adjustments—which brings us to the final element of game preparation, the particulars of the practice schedule.

Figure 5–23 illustrates one day, probably mid-week, of the practice schedules developed at the end of the coaches' meeting. This particular schedule reveals the team's responses to the opponent's tendencies. Time is provided for individual drills and team activities that capitalize on the opposing team's predictability—which has grown considerably with the accumulation of the scouting reports.

Notice in the sample schedule such specifics as watching your secondary's coverage of the opponent's Crossfire action pass, which has been so successful for them, and such general emphases as avoiding any tackling below the waist. We discovered years ago in this regard that our first-string backs don't need prep teamers throwing themselves at the runners' knees. We can master our timing assignments and practice solid running technique without inviting unnecessary injury.

FACT SHEET

1. DHS has good size

2. #36, Tom Fullback, hard runner

3. #27, Bill Halfback, best ball carrier.

4. DHS likes the power & sweep plays

5. DHS likes XF action pass!

6. This play is a game-breaker!

7. #18, Jack QB, small but quick

8. We must eliminate mistakes

9. We must win to stay alive in conference.

10. <u>Refuse to Lose!</u>

11.

12.

13.

14.

15.

FIGURE 5–16

FACT SHEET

1.

2.

3.

4.

5.

6.

7.

8.

9.

10.

11.

12.

13.

14.

15.

FIGURE 5–17

OFFENSIVE TEAM

BILL END 6'1" – 180 SR.   TOM TACKLE 6'2" – 220 JR.   JIM GUARD 5'10" – 187 SOPH.   FRED CENTER 6'1" 190 SR.   JACK GUARD 5'11" – 182 SR.   HARRY TACKLE 6'2 – 250 SR.   LENNY END 6'2" – 195 SR.

JACK QUARTERBACK 5'8" – 165 SR.

BILL HALFBACK 6'0" – 190 JR.   TOM FULLBACK 5'10" – 190 JR.   JIM HALFBACK 6'1" – 180 SR.

DEFENSIVE TEAM

LENNY END 6'2" – 195 SR.   HARRY TACKLE 6'2" – 250 SR.   TOM NOSE 6'1" – 190 JR.   JIM GUARD 5'10" – 187 SOPH.   JACK END 6'1" – 192 SOPH.

TOM FULLBACK 5'10" – 190 JR.   JIM HALFBACK 6'1" – 180 SR.

BILL D. BACK 5'10" – 158 SR.   JACK QUARTERBACK 5'8" – 165 SR.   BILL HALFBACK 6'0" – 190 JR.   JERRY CORNERBACK 5'8 – 159 JR.

FIGURE 5–18

126

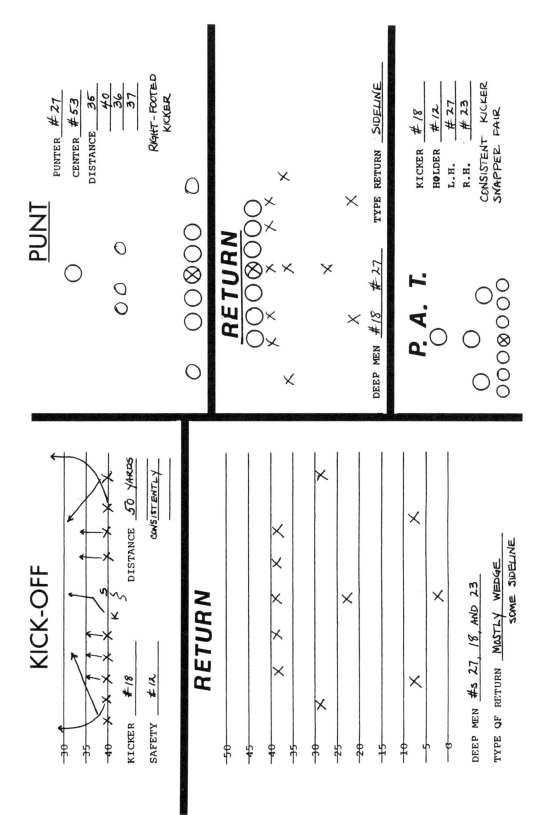

KICK-OFF

DISTANCE _50 YARDS_

KICKER _#18_

SAFETY _#12_ CONSISTENTLY

RETURN

DEEP MEN _#s 27, 18, AND 23_

TYPE OF RETURN _MOSTLY WEDGE_
SOME SIDELINE

PUNT

PUNTER _#27_

CENTER _#53_

DISTANCE _36_
_40_
_36_
_37_

RIGHT-FOOTED KICKER

RETURN

DEEP MEN _#18 #27_ TYPE RETURN _SIDELINE_

_P. A. T._

KICKER _#18_

HOLDER _#12_

L.H. _#27_

R.H. _#23_

CONSISTENT KICKER
SNAPPER FAIR

FIGURE 5-19

127

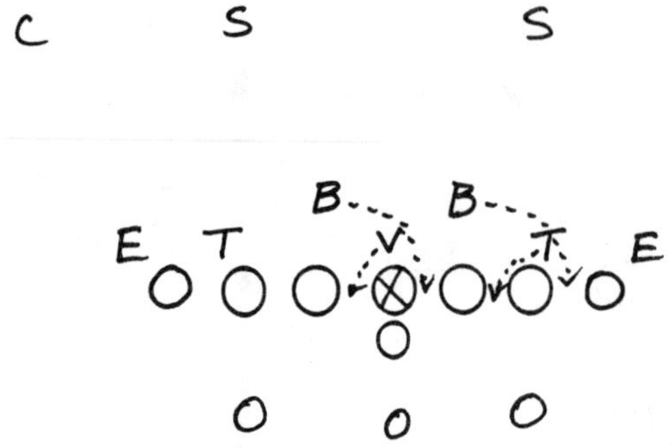

they will scrape the linebackers inside and outside.

5-2 tackles inside

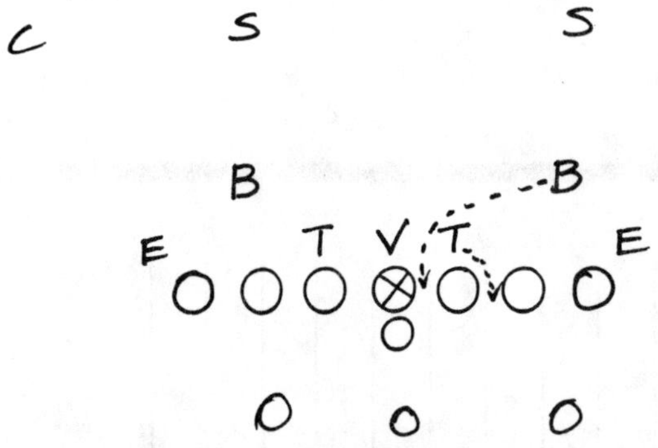

they scrape linebackers here, too.

5-3

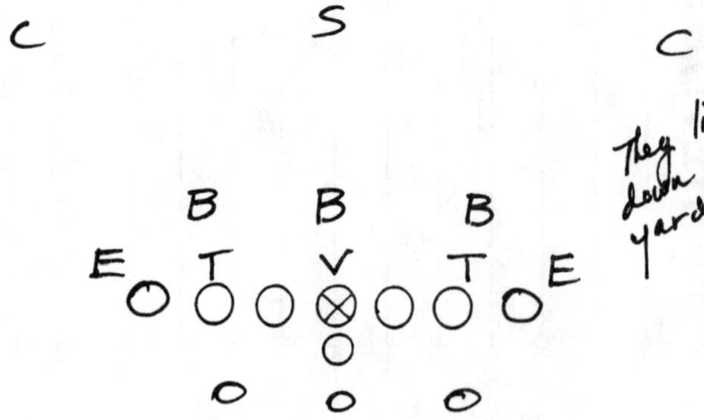

They like it on first down and any short yardage situation

FIGURE 5-20

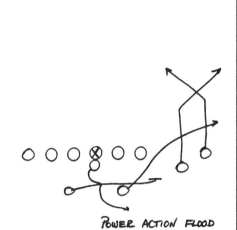

POWER ACTION FLOOD

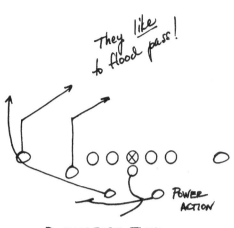

They *like* to flood pass!

POWER ACTION

DOUBLE POST FLOOD

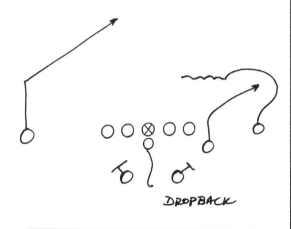

DROPBACK

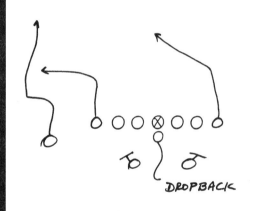

DROPBACK

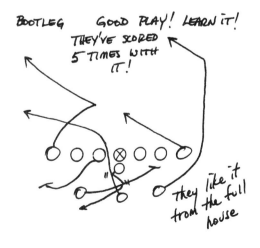

BOOTLEG   GOOD PLAY! LEARN IT!
THEY'VE SCORED 5 TIMES WITH IT!

They like it from the full house

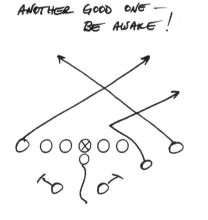

ANOTHER GOOD ONE — BE AWAKE!

FIGURE 5–21

129

RUNNING

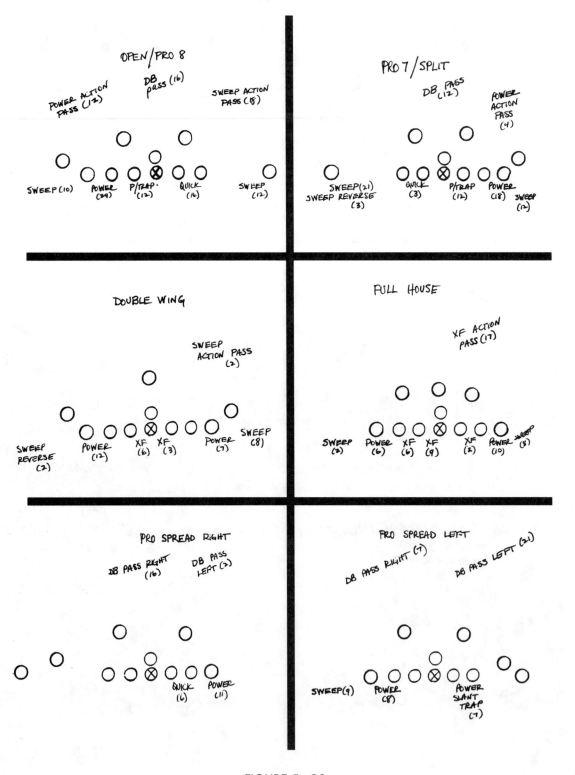

FIGURE 5-22

130

DAILY PRACTICE PLAN   DATE   Tuesday, Oct. 11

	ACTIVITY	EQUIPMENT	REMARKS
1. 3:00 to 3:10			
GUARDS			
TACKLES			
CENTERS	Team		
BACKS	calisthenics		
ENDS			
2. 3:10 to 3:30			
GUARDS	Defensive	4 air	Defensive ends
TACKLES	drills on meeting	flates for	concentrate on
CENTERS	the power and	outside backers	beating the
BACKS	stringing the		double-team
ENDS	sweep		block!
3. 3:30 to 4:00			
GUARDS	Team activity —	Cones to	Initial walk-
TACKLES	Introduce new	simulate	through followed
CENTERS	plays —	defense	by timing.
BACKS	running and		
ENDS	passing		
4. 4:00 to 4:45			
GUARDS	Defensive	Scrimmage	Watch the
TACKLES	scrimmage	Vests	secondary's
CENTERS			coverage of their
BACKS			crossfire action
ENDS			pass ——!
5. 4:45 to 5:30			
GUARDS	Offensive		Run new plays
TACKLES	scrimmage		twice as often
CENTERS			as regular offense.
BACKS			NO TACKLING
ENDS			BELOW WAIST!

FIGURE 5–23

We have observed that such general comments on the practice schedule, when added during the coaches' meeting, remind us of our good intentions during actual practice sessions. Similarly, the specific comments highlight elements of game preparation that require continuing emphasis during practice.

====== A FINAL WORD: TAKE A GOOD LOOK AT YOURSELF ======

Effective game preparation depends upon a well-conceived process for systematically and routinely watching upcoming opponents. The need for such a process and the process itself, as well as the uses of the information gained from it, have been discussed thoroughly in this section. A final word, however, involves scouting yourself, taking an objective look at your own tendencies in order to reaffirm your own unpredictability.

Learn to look at yourself as an opponent would look at you. Determine what you do from your favorite formations. Reviewing your own game films probably is the most exact way to determine your tendencies, but the scouting format outlined in this chapter is so precise and involves so little writing that we prefer to have a lower-level coach scout us on game days. By so doing, we can incorporate his information into planning for future games, in essence break our own tendencies when the opponent least expects it. We also can use the information at halftime to make possible adjustments for that particular game.

At the risk of sounding trite, we are reminded that knowledge is power, and football may provide the prototypical example of that fact. Less trite is the reality that self-knowledge may be the ultimate power. In football, therefore, we need to take a close look at what we're doing, both offensively and defensively. As Scotch poet Bobby Burns said, ". . . to see oursels as ithers see us." If you are the first among the "ithers," you will always be at least a few steps ahead of even your shrewdest opponents.

Practicing To Win

The team that is accustomed to winning, that takes the field expecting to walk off victorious, to do whatever is necessary to be victorious, is mighty tough to beat. You might have better personnel and a solid game plan, but you always know you have your hands full when you play a team that just doesn't know how to lose. You can also be sure that if the players don't know how to lose, they do know how to practice.

For one thing, they know why they're practicing. "Planned aggravation" on the practice field is one thing; purposeful activity is another. The coach who has been schooled in the Marquis de Sade Academy of Work for Work's Sake will field a team of well-conditioned but very frustrated athletes. The necessary repetition of the average practice session is tedious enough with an understanding of the reasons behind the drills. Without the reasons, players see drills as a monotonous routine that has only an indirect relationship to the team's performance on game days.

That's why it's generally a pretty good idea to meet with the team for about five to ten minutes before each practice session to explain the what, the how, and most of all the why of that day's drills. The meeting should be short and light, but it should identify the activities for the day and provide a sense of direction for the entire practice. Early in the week this meeting should summarize the high and low points of the previous game and give the players a general overview of what needs to be done in order to assure continued improvement for everyone.

It is at this point that individual players can be cited for their good or bad performances. Such mention should not be intended to punish or rebuke players but to highlight the need for a renewed commitment to hard work. It should also reaffirm the fact that football's a team sport and that the failure of just one player to do his job jeopardizes everyone else. The purpose of any constructive criticism in this meeting, then, is to refocus individual and team attention on the job at hand.

Comments from coaches during these meetings will not come as startling revelations to any of the players. That's why they need not be belabored. The players know who did good jobs, and, frankly, they probably don't care to hear anyone else, most of all the coach, singing the praises of individual players. A well-intentioned word or two is sufficient. Similarly, they know who "dropped the ball," so continuing criticism may anger or hurt certain players to the point where the coach's comments become counterproductive to what he hopes to accomplish.

It is wise, therefore, to let them know that you know and that you plan to do something about it. What you have planned won't come as a surprise anyway, particularly if you expect your team to evaluate its own performance with the form provided in Section Three. As a matter of fact, many of the players probably will be waiting to hear if your observations are consistent with theirs.

One year we had a team that was so in touch with what needed to be done to fine tune its performance, players told us during one of our daily meetings that they needed time to scrimmage some of the new plays. We had backed off scrimmaging during the previous two weeks because we were reluctant to get anyone hurt, and we had the perception that the team didn't need it.

The players told us the timing drills were getting boring and that they weren't getting a true picture of the plays against the bags. After we picked ourselves up and slapped the dust from our sweatpants, we told them what we had planned for that session but indicated that we could sneak in a 15-minute scrimmage in the middle of practice. They worked and hit each other so hard we had to shorten it to 10, but they—and we—got everything from that session we needed.

In addition to the work they needed, they learned once more that their opinions were important to the coaches. In addition, they reinforced in our minds that a good game plan may be born during a weekend coaches' meeting but that it's nurtured and strengthened during every practice session the following week. It becomes its strongest when everyone feels some ownership of it.

PRACTICE IN GENERAL

Practicing the Fundamentals.   Before we discuss the specifics of game preparation, let's say a few words about practice in general. The best place to start is with the fundamentals. The fundamental skills of football players must never be taken for granted. Not only do they enable players to execute the strategies that we feel are so important, but they do much to prevent injuries. These two products of practicing the fundamentals are often overlooked, particularly as the season progresses and the complexity of the offense and the defense increases.

As far back as October of 1932, in an article published in the *Athletic Journal*, a coach of growing reputation provided this observation: "A coach more often neglects to train men for their individual positions then he does the different phases of *team* play." It was as true then as it is now. The coach? Knute Rockne.

A balance between individual skills and team skills must be achieved if the team is to perform its assignments and minimize its injuries. The "Rock" was never wrong. Blocking a trap at 4 correctly is one thing; running the ball correctly through a poorly blocked trap at 4 is another. Ball carriers must drop the shoulder and drive the knees in order to protect both the ball and themselves when plays aren't executed correctly. Teams must set aside time to practice the fundamentals at least two or three times a week, if players are to develop and/or maintain good habits.

The Value of Repetition. The repetition of these fundamental skills is the only thing that will make them second nature during a game. Undoubtedly that's why our football forefathers called them "drills" when they practiced fundamentals. The constant repetition of a skill is the only way to integrate it into the body's memory. Players may have the need for the skill in their heads, but the thought process needed to translate it into action is an eternity for football players—for any athlete.

It's important to recognize, however, that drill reinforces the body's memory but hits a point of diminishing returns with the brain's memory. The single most important element in getting players to remember plays and blocking assignments is the validity of the initial learning experience. If their first exposure to the learning experience is well-structured and clear—and encourages and capitalizes on their motivation to learn—they will remember what to do with just periodic repetition. Drill, therefore, should be used more for the body's memory than for the brain's. This is an important point.

Pure repetition for its own sake may be counterproductive to what the coach hopes to accomplish, particularly if the drill sessions are live. After athletes have mastered their assignments, any attempts to reinforce their mastery with unnecessary repetition can result in a half-hearted effort from many of the players, and injury can result. That's why it's a good idea to influence the body's memory with short but frequent drills, some of which can be live. The reinforcement of assignment mastery, especially later in the week, should be accomplished in dummy scrimmages—with periodic diversions that break the monotony.

═══════════════════ MORE ABOUT DRILL ═══════════════════

The drills intended to influence the body's memory must be planned and practiced very carefully. During my first couple years in coaching, I recall having my backs practice lowering their shoulders by running through the bags each and every practice, sometimes for a half hour at a time. I also recall being upset at how infrequently they lowered their shoulders in games. My response? They ran through more bags during the next week's practices.

Talk about being in a rut. It finally dawned on me a short time later that one of my earlier educational psychology classes at Nebraska might have the answer. The attitudes created by an artificial situation (dropping the shoulder on the bags) sometimes persist longer than those generated by direct practice (dropping the shoulder in scrimmages or in a game). I had to resurrect a college textbook to get the answer, but it helped me then and has continued to help today.

If the initial learning situation is so boring or so poorly organized that players actually dislike the drill, not only will the skills they are expected to learn fail to transfer to game situations, but their attitudes will actually fight such transference. The creativity of good coaches, therefore, is not restricted to just X's and O's but to the design of practice sessions that are relevant and motivating to the team.

With that thought in mind, let's discuss a few more important principles to keep in mind when organizing practice plans:

- Coaches should rely on simulated drills rather than live practice (scrimmages) whenever the task to be learned is so difficult that the players can expect no success from the live practice. Consider, for example, our continuing demands on quarterbacks to read the secondary for weaknesses and openings rather than to find a favorite receiver and hope he gets open. Well, that may be a little extreme, but it's not far off, especially for the young quarterback who grew up watching his receivers and who never threw a ball to a friend who wasn't looking at him.

But that's precisely what we tell our quarterbacks to do, to find openings in the defense and we usually emphasize it most in a scrimmage situation when the heat is on the quarterback to perform. Such direct practice may fail to provide the kind of success we want our quarterbacks to experience, and if they experience little success in the initial learning situation, they aren't likely to transfer the expected skill to the game field.

Fundamental skills, therefore, are often best learned in fundamental drills. I discovered a long time ago, for example, that young quarterbacks learn to read the secondary if their first exposure is a simple drill that requires them to throw to one of two receivers, only one of whom is being covered by a defensive back. The quarterback's job is first to watch the defensive back's coverage, than to throw to the uncovered receiver. See figure 6–1.

Quarterbacks are very successful in this drill. They don't have to worry about different secondary coverages or a pass rush. All they have to do is watch the one defensive back's coverage. As the first couple weeks progress, we make the drill increasingly difficult by adding more receivers and defensive backs and by varying the secondary coverages. Eventually we add a pass rush. The point is, however, by that time the quarterbacks have experienced success, the kind of success that has ingrained good habits in them.

All players need similar opportunities. In your estimation, then, if direct practice might provide few opportunities for the players' initial success, develop a drill that will. Remember Lombardi's dictum: Great coaches don't simply know about football; they know how to teach football!

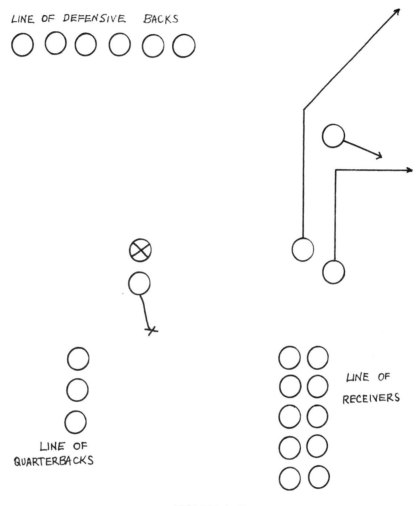

FIGURE 6–1

- The flip side of the previous principle is equally important: direct practice is preferable when a reasonable amount of success can be expected early in the season. As a backfield coach, I may want to use stand-up dummies early in the season to teach the relatively sophisticated art of spinning off tacklers, but I can emphasize high knee action the first time my players scrimmage. I also will practice high knee action in drills as a reinforcement, but that's a running technique that players can perform with some success almost immediately.

The same is true of certain blocking fundamentals. After an early explanation of how to execute the straight shoulder block, we want a one-on-one drill to be live as soon as possible because linemen learn such techniques best through the daily experience of executing them. This may not be as true when we teach stalking techniques or certain pass blocking fundamentals. Sometimes these techniques provide the greatest early success through simulated bag drills.

- Recognize as well that healthy competition can stimulate player motivation. Motivation involves a condition of readiness for all learners, including football players. Readiness improves learning and retention, which in turn improves transfer from one situation to another, especially if those situations are similar. That's why optimal levels of competition are important in fundamental drills of all kinds.

When teaching the spin technique, for example, set up three dummies to approximate a baseball diamond, with each dummy manned by a player. See figure 6–2. Then have every back hit each dummy with the appropriate shoulder,

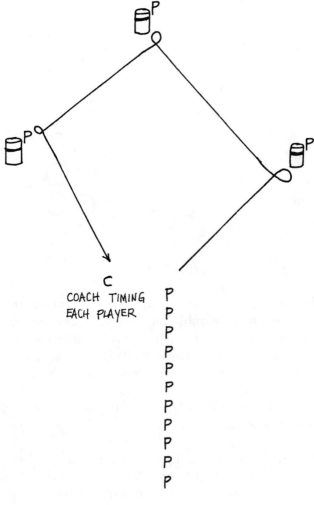

FIGURE 6–2

get the knees driving, and spin off the dummy, executing each maneuver as efficiently and as quickly as possible. To stimulate the appropriate levels of motivation, put the stop watch on each player and reward the quickest with fewer wind sprints at the end of practice.

Keep in mind that how each player feels about himself during the drill, his interest in the activity, and the nature of the corrective feedback he receives also will affect his levels of motivation. Coaches must do all they can to make each drill a positive learning experience for every player. Lesser-skilled players who embarrass themselves or who are embarrassed by coaches arouse the sympathies of their teammates and everyone loses motivation.

Contrived competition also reduces the occasional boredom that comes with the constant repetition of certain drills. All of us have our favorite drills; they just seem to us to get the job done the right way. If we introduce a little friendly competition, we usually can get more mileage out of them. For example, I like to put all our quarterbacks on the 10-yard line and have them practice the three-step drop simultaneously.

I like to have the quarterbacks throw to receivers who are executing seven-yard square outs. Each quarterback is expected to throw the ball before the receiver looks for it, and each is instructed to execute the exact number of drop steps before throwing. To spice things up, I put a stop watch on them to time the quickness of the first quarterback to get the ball off.

We then practice five and seven-step drops the same way, with the receivers executing intermediate to long pass patterns. The drill puts all the quarterbacks on the same line and demonstrates all too vividly the difference in the quickness of their drops. To work in quarterback drops individually, without the hint of competition provided by the simultaneous drill, would allow some poor habits to set in when quarterbacks may see no reason to get back and set up quickly, particularly in dummy scrimmages.

Competition, when held to optimal levels, creates the conditions for each player's motivation to establish the level of readiness he requires to learn not only fundamental skills but game-day strategies. It encourages the transfer of a skill learned in a drill to the execution of that skill in a scrimmage or, better yet, a game situation. Motivation and transfer, therefore, are important concepts for coaches to keep in mind.

- More about transfer. As desirable as it may be in most circumstances, it can be undesirable in others. It is bad when old learnings interfere with new. Let's use the quarterback once again as an example. The hands of a freshman aren't big enough to hold a football correctly throughout the entire range of motion when executing good passing technique. The early part of the motion requires the young quarterback to almost palm the ball as he rolls it past his ear prior to delivery.

Most freshmen, therefore, keep their hand under the ball throughout the delivery, in effect shot-putting it toward the receiver. Many of them get pretty good at it, but they never develop the quick delivery and the power that comes from rolling the ball through the range of motion, much like a pitcher throwing a fast ball. The transfer of old learnings, therefore, interferes with new.

Consider as well the young quarterback who holds the ball until his receiver is wide open, or who looks only for his best buddy to catch the ball. Such a strategy may have worked for Knute Rockne and Gus Dorais 75 years ago, but today's quarterback better do things differently, or he better learn to like the taste of pigskin, because he's going to eat a lot of footballs.

Such old learnings interfering with new learnings require a lot of attention. The development of good habits to replace bad habits needs a great deal of deliberate practice, another reason why drill in the fundamental skills is so important. Only the well-motivated repetition of proper fundamentals will get the job done.

- Consider as well the principle stating that any two similar learnings tend to merge. The more alike they are, the less the learner distinguishes between them. If similar learnings are to be executed differently, therefore, they should be taught separately of each other. The best example of this principle is the execution of pass routes in the dropback versus the play action passing attacks.

Many schools use the same receiver routes whether the pass is play action or dropback. Others make certain that play action pass routes closely resemble the blocking responsibilities of the running play. I prefer a format that requires similarity between blocking assignments and receiver routes. It is more confusing to the defense and is much more likely to capitalize on the element of surprise.

This is not to say that schools which use the same pass plays with play-action or dropback action are wrong. Some of them are very successful. They are wrong, however, if they fail to instruct the receivers to execute the routes differently. Smart receivers stalk defensive backs to simulate blocking responsibilities before breaking into play-action pass routes. They don't spring off the line like greyhounds out of a starting gate.

If they race through their patterns, they telegraph the play to the defense, and they usually fail to provide adequate time for the backfield to execute its fakes. At the time such pass routes are introduced to the team, therefore, the distinction between play action routes and conventional routes should be emphasized. The best way to make that distinction is to incorporate fundamentally different routes in the play action versus the dropback attacks. If the pass routes are similar, however, coaches at least should practice play action passes and dropback passes on different days.

The awareness that similar learnings tend to merge requires some kind of distinction when teaching these two passing attacks. The principle also is appropriate in other areas as well. Teach the cross block and the inverted cross block, for example, at different times. Teach your running backs at alternate times how to make a pocket when running to the right or to the left. Teach similar secondary coverages on alternate days. The needed awareness of their similarities can be taught to the players after the differences have been mastered by them.

- A final principle that is fundamental to athletic performance involves the spontaneous experience of talent. I have summed it up over the years with one suggestion to my players: "Trust your body!" I learned a long time ago that great runners don't think their way through holes and that great quarterbacks don't think the ball into receivers' hands. Once a runner starts deciding consciously where to run or the quarterback starts aiming his passes, he compromises his natural abilities.

The brain is a wonderful mechanism, but it has to be turned off once a running back or a quarterback is in the process of doing his thing. Each can think about assignments or likely lanes in the defense before the play starts, but once the ball is snapped, the kinesthetic connection between mind and body has to be made.

Basketball players don't think basketballs through hoops. They don't measure their shots. If they do, the miss. Good shooters feel the ball off their fingertips and allow their built-in instrumentation to measure distances. Once a basketball player overrides that instrumentation by consciously thinking the ball to the hoop, he runs into problems. So does a quarterback when he passes a football or a running back when he hits the line. Both must learn to trust their bodies to get the job done.

Coaches, therefore, must teach the offense and the defense and lead practice sessions with the awareness that players require the freedom to do their own thing as their bodies dictate. When we're discussing certain running plays against anticipated defenses before a game, for example, we can tell our players where the lanes are likely to be and how defensive personnel are likely to react, but we shouldn't tell them where to run. We compromise their abilities.

Some players have evaluated "coach pleasing" to a fine art. We grow to like such kids. But we also grow to admire, sometimes grudgingly, the bandit who listens to us but who is committed to himself and to the expression of who and what he is. He's usually a pretty good athlete—for obvious reasons. Trusting your coach's word, therefore, has its place in practice and game situations; trusting your body has an equally important place. Our job as good coaches is to make sure our athletes do both.

A FEW SPECIFICS

Now that we've looked at some general principles to keep in mind when organizing and executing a practice schedule, let's discuss some pre-game specifics. The first and perhaps most important element is being sure to integrate the scouting report into the week's activities.

================ **THE SCOUTING REPORT** ================

As indicated in an earlier chapter, once the season gets under way, the scouting report becomes the framework within which daily practices are planned. It is the instrument that points the way and makes each drill relevant and purposeful. For this reason, scouting reports should be available to each player after the first day's practice, and they should be mentioned recurrently during each practice, particularly the scrimmages.

Some coaches introduce the week's activities with a discussion of the scouting report, particularly with its information about the opponent's offensive and defensive tendencies. After such an introduction, coaches explain any new offensive plays or defensive adjustments that will be used against the opponent. The conclusion of this introductory session normally involves the team in the timing of the plays and the alignment and execution of the defensive adjustments.

The practice plan, therefore, may look like the one in figure 6–3. Notice that it's used for a variety of purposes. It describes the activities within specified time periods; it identifies the equipment needed; and it provides important remarks, even the assignment of one of the coaches to supervise wind sprints after practice. This particular practice plan reflects the kinds of activities that occur early in the week. Figure 6–4 illustrates a typical plan for mid-week.

Notice the emphasis on fundamentals before scrimmaging. This plan also suggests several other important considerations for an effective practice.

- It capitalizes on the kinesthetic learning of athletes. Explanation is followed by demonstration, which is followed by player execution. All those writers out there who have been emphasizing the need for modality learning in the classroom would be proud of us. As a matter of fact, they would find on any practice field in the country a superior example of teaching technique. Good football coaches spend their lives telling, showing, and having players DO.

Everytime a coach explains a play, demonstrates the blocking schemes and backfield action, and has the players execute it, he capitalizes on their auditory, visual, and kinesthetic modalities. He may not put it in those terms (this is the first time for me!), but he is engaging his athletes in a learning activity that is the envy of every academician who writes about effective classroom instruction. Tell, show, and provide practice; football coaches do it as well as anyone.

- It identifies equipment needs for the manager ("6 stand ups") and instructs him to have them in place, thereby saving precious time.
- It provides reminders to specific coaches and to all coaches in general regarding important elements of the practice. It indicates, for example, an emphasis on the routes in the belly pass, and it reminds everyone to instruct the defense not to tackle below the waist during the offensive

DAILY PRACTICE PLAN   DATE   Oct. 3, 1993

1. 3:30 to 4:15	ACTIVITY	EQUIPMENT	REMARKS
GUARDS	Entire team	Scouting	Meet on practice
TACKLES	together to	reports	field for
CENTERS	discuss scouting	available	demonstrations
BACKS	report	after	
ENDS		practice	

2. 4:15 to 5:00			
GUARDS	Team practice	Stand-ups	
TACKLES	to learn new	for prep	
CENTERS	plays and	team	
BACKS	defensive	defense	
ENDS	adjustments		

3. 5:00 to 5:30			
GUARDS		Stand ups	3 prep teams
TACKLES	Time new	and air	to run against:
CENTERS	plays	flates for	44 gap stack
BACKS		prep team	52 tackles inside
ENDS		defenses	53 straight

4. 5:30 to 6:00			
GUARDS	Run through		3 offensive
TACKLES	defensive		prep teams
CENTERS	adjustments		running (opponent's
BACKS			plays—run first
ENDS			then pass)

5. 6:00 to when-ever			
GUARDS	10 team		Tom, you take
TACKLES	hundreds		them tonight.
CENTERS			
BACKS			
ENDS			

FIGURE 6–3

143

DAILY PRACTICE PLAN   DATE   Oct. 5, 1991

		ACTIVITY	EQUIPMENT	REMARKS
1. 3:30 to 3:40				
GUARDS				
TACKLES		Team		
CENTERS	}	calisthenics		
BACKS				
ENDS				
2. 3:40 to 4:00				
GUARDS		Blocking		
TACKLES		assignments		
CENTERS	}			
BACKS	→	Running technique	6 stand ups	Near blaster—
ENDS	→	with line		
3. 4:00 to 4:20				
GUARDS		Pass protection		Work on picking up
TACKLES		blocking		stunting LBs
CENTERS	}			Live to ball
BACKS		Play-action		Emphasize pass
ENDS		passing—belly		routes in belly pass
4. 4:20 to 5:00				
GUARDS				Same 3 prep
TACKLES				defenses as
CENTERS	}	Offensive		Monday—
BACKS		scrimmage		No tackling below
ENDS				waist!
5. 5:00 to 5:40				
GUARDS				Emphasize running
TACKLES				plays with
CENTERS	}	Defensive		prep teams
BACKS		scrimmage		
ENDS				

FIGURE 6–4

scrimmage. I discovered a long time ago that we were wasting too many players on the practice field. It's bad enough when they get hurt in a game, but when they get injured in practice, I feel especially at fault.

So we decided to emphasize the no-tackling-below-the-waist principle in scrimmages, particularly when we got into the meat of the season. When we made the decision, we realized two quick advantages. One, we discovered that we were having fewer injuries during scrimmages. Two, we found that tackling above the waist forced the kids on defense to execute their fundamentals better than they had before.

They had to "face-up" to the runner and assume a good hit position before executing the tackle. If they failed to execute good fundamentals, they took the brunt of the hit and discovered quickly that tackling isn't something football players do half-heartedly. It became, therefore, a safety measure for the runner and a learning experience for the tackler. We continue to do it each year.

- The format also requires that we stick to a pre-determined time schedule. In meetings before practice, we allocate the appropriate amount of time for each drill, then try to stick to it during practice. We even tell our team manager to blow a whistle after each segment to keep us on schedule. It's easy when a drill isn't going well to tack on 10 or 15 more minutes to get the players' attention.

Such decisions usually are hasty and result more from frustration than careful planning. So I took a page out of my college coach's book. I use the Bob Devaney principle of staying with the time schedule. Now when I get frustrated I just schedule more of the same for the next day. The players get the message—just a I did so many millenia ago.

- Finally, the accumulation of daily practice plans provides a record of activities emphasized at various times in the season. Football players achieve success in the execution of fundamental skills incrementally. It doesn't happen overnight. The old saying reminds us that if you aim at perfection in everything, you achieve it in nothing. Football players, all learners for that matter, realize ultimate success through a progression of small but well-planned steps. The coach's job is to organize those steps in such a way that they eventuate in success for the players. A record of practice plans assures the continuity needed to guarantee that each of the necessary steps has been provided.

Continuity also requires daily meetings among the coaches to plan for the next day's activities. Nobody likes meetings, but they are necessary if practice each day is to achieve its purposes. Many coaches conduct such meetings, weather permitting, right on the field, usually when the team is doing wind sprints. Each coach indicates his needs for the next day, a little negotiation usually follows, and then one of them, often the head coach, takes the responsibility to write up the schedule for the following day.

SCRIMMAGING

Scrimmaging has been discussed at some length already, but its importance within the practice schedule warrants special treatment. Scrimmaging is as close to the real thing as a team can get before game day. As important as it may be to timing and the direct practice of fundamental skills, it can be harmful to the bodies of the players. That's why a conscious decision must be made each time a coach plans to scrimmage. The following criteria are helpful.

WHEN TO SCRIMMAGE

- Scrimmage when direct practice is the only way for players to develop their fundamental skills. Sometimes "the real thing" is needed if players are to block and tackle effectively. Such a need may not require a full scrimmage. Passing drills, for example, can be live to the ball on defense with no tackling after a reception. They can involve a live line every third or fourth play. They can be totally live every fourth or fifth play, or they can involve half-line scrimmages. A live line normally doesn't provide the potential for injury that a full scrimmage does, yet it involves the kind of pass rush the quarterback needs if he is to get the correct drop and release the ball at the right time. Another way to work with quarterbacks in a controlled situation is to have the first string quarterback, backfield, and receivers work with the second string line—against the first string defense. It involves a simple adjustment of personnel, but it challenges the usual security the quarterback enjoys during practice and may come closer to a game situation.

- Scrimmage when players require direct practice to execute their assignments correctly. Working against the bags may help with the timing of the offense plays and the mastery of assignments, but it doesn't provide the real-life circumstances that influence good execution. A live defense reacts to plays differently than a dummy defense. Most obviously, pass defenders on game days don't just stand in their positions or go through the motions of getting in the way.

Less obviously, defensive tacklers don't stand in their positions waiting to be trapped, nor do linebackers, particularly in attack defenses, wait to be blocked. That's why the beginning of the season requires more scrimmaging than the middle or the end. After football players have learned their assignments, they need some direct practice in executing them and in using the fundamental skills they have developed in all those drills.

Once they have learned their assignments, however, and are proficient in their execution, they require less contact work. It is at this point that the creative coach devises strategies to maintain players' motivation while enhancing their learning and execution. I learned a while back, for example, that one good way to sustain motivation is to bring out the chains during a mid-week practice and have alternating teams try to pick up consecutive first downs in two-hand tag passing drills.

Nobody gets hurt; the players refine their execution; I can liven up line play once in a while; the quarterback experiences the simulated pressure of a live situation; and the whole team gets excited about a little harmless competition. The team achieves quite a lot in the process. Players learn, have fun, and—again—not one gets hurt.

Well, try as I may I can think of no other reasons to have live scrimmages in practice. Certainly, scrimmaging early in the season enables you to identify the good players, but having done so, scrimmages should be used advisedly. That's it: scrimmage when players need work on fundamental skills and when they need to refine the execution of assignments. Live scrimmages for reasons other than these may not teach as well and can result in needless injury.

WHEN NOT TO SCRIMMAGE

- Do not scrimmage when players have mastered their fundamental skills and the execution of their assignments. The reason is obvious. Nothing much remains to be accomplished. The actual advantages to be gained are less important than the potential disadvantages to the program. A healthy player, hungry for a little contact and sufficiently rested and healed before a game, is a bigger plus than a hobbled player who knows where to go but can't get there.

- Do not scrimmage to punish the team. Players perform poorly in games for a variety of reasons—none of which requires contact drills as a punishment. Certain contact drills and some scrimmaging may be a reasonable consequence for the team that failed to execute assignments and/or fundamental skills correctly, but contact for the sake of contact is like pulling teeth for the sake of pulling teeth. It involves a whole lot of pain and doesn't resolve a problem. Pain for its own sake is the province of sadomasochists, not football coaches.

- Do not scrimmage (at least scrimmage advisedly) when your team is riddled with injuries. The few excellent players you may have become increasingly valuable to the team as others are injured. In the same sense, that good second or third-teamer becomes priceless when the great first-teamer goes down. An average player who's healthy is more valuable to the team than a banged-up All-American. Better yet, keep them both. Scrimmaging is not a habit.

- Do not scrimmage to make players tough. The toughness of a football player is a function of motivation, training, and the sense of belonging he feels with his teammates. Certainly some players are just naturally tougher than others. They enjoy physical contact and the challenge of a good fight. But the players who are not naturally tough are not going to become tough by banging heads with their more aggressive teammates.

Expecting them to do so is like teaching a child how to box by putting him in the ring with Mike Tyson. It is at best presumptuous, and at worst downright dumb. All an athlete learns in such circumstances are additional reasons why he doesn't like contact, in essence why he doesn't think of himself as tough.

No matter what we do, he may never think of himself as tough. But as his confidence increases, as he learns in controlled circumstances that he can play the game, maybe not as aggressively as certain teammates, but well enough to do his job, his self-perception will change. He will develop a tougher mind set and will be better motivated to make his contribution to the team effort.

We all have worked with scores of athletes who didn't like contact but who learned to tolerate it. In the process, they developed into excellent football players. I have worked with many, some of whom eventually played in college. I sometimes wonder what would have happened if someone had tried to pound toughness into them.

- Do not scrimmage to fine-tune the team's performance. Once the offense learns its assignments and proves it can execute them against even the most unpredictable attack defense, scrimmage becomes less a learning experience and more an invitation to injury. A good, hard timing drill against the bags, one that instructs the prep defense to react to backfield action, can accomplish a whole lot more than a live scrimmage.

Players can be pushed to work as hard as they can, thereby improving their conditioning while coaches watch their respective positions for assignment mastery. Movement from one set of bags to another, as illustrated in figure 6–5, encourages such conditioning while it tests players' knowledge of how to block several different defenses. They may be instructed to run 35 plays, each against a different defense. It's an excellent activity for late in the week when contact is avoided and conditioning is still important.

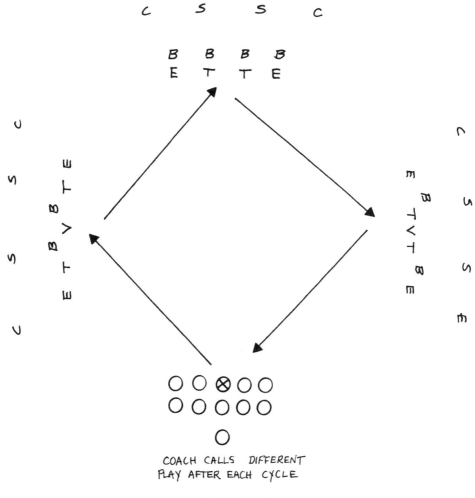

FIGURE 6–5

===== **LET'S WRAP IT UP** =====

My favorite definition of perfection is "something to be achieved by anyone who follows the advice he gives others." Well, I'm a far cry from perfect—just ask my wife—even on those rare occasions when I followed my own advice, but I have discovered that some of this stuff works. I have always believed, for example, in the importance of basic principles. I find that good ones are appropriate for a wide range of situations and that I can rely on them as guides for my behavior. The several that have been provided in this section are good guides to keep in mind when organizing any practice schedule.

Technology: Mirrors for Improvement

I didn't mind acting like a dinosaur as a player, but I sure didn't want to be one as a coach, particularly when it came to technology. Like everyone else, however, I had to battle the tendency. When computers weren't terrifying me, they were making beeping noises behind closed doors, enslaving hundreds of people who spent entire days feeding them, working them, and cooling them down. Remember, I grew up in the era of UNIVAC, that Star Wars mutant that filled up entire buildings and predicted not only brave but bizarre new worlds.

Well, the future is here, and UNIVAC is to computer technology what the Model T is to the automobile industry. It led the way but had to step aside as smaller, more powerful machines revolutionized an industry that has changed our ideas about knowledge. The flow of information and the creation of new knowledge has been accelerated to the point where future textbooks may be obsolete in a matter of months, even weeks.

If football coaches don't go with the flow of information, they risk obsolescence. Opponents who capitalize on any of several fine computer programs that coordinate scouting information from week to week and from year to year necessarily have a strategic edge on the rest of us who spend most of our time shuffling through papers trying to figure out why we're a dollar short and a day late on game days.

To secure such an edge, "high-tech" coaches generally consolidate scouting information in several different ways. They may use a commercially prepared format, or they may use the local computer whiz to develop one, but they soon discover that the computer reveals some very interesting facts within a few different categories:

- Down and distance tendencies. This category reveals a coach's tendency to play-action pass on short yardage, to throw conventionally on third and long, to run on third and long, to call certain favorite plays on first down, to run a draw on second and long, or to call any of a number of plays in certain game situations that have become habit to him.

- Field position tendencies. Many coaches sweep to the wide side of the field and power to the short side. They run only quick openers or inside fullback plays inside their own 20-yard line or become suddenly adventurous and prefer to throw the ball. They run the ball all the way down the field and invariably pass inside the opponent's 15-yard line. And, most importantly, they usually don't know they have such tendencies. When you know, good thing happen for you.

- Formation tendencies. The same is true of an opponent's formation and play-calling tendencies, probably the most revealing of all, especially in high school. Formation tendencies are revealing for several reasons. Formations necessarily restrict the number of plays a coach can call and usually the hole he can hit along the line of scrimmage. They also affect his passing capability and provide the quickest clues to his play-calling habits. A compilation of such tendencies, therefore, on a game-by-game, even a year-by-year, basis provides a very important defensive edge when you play an opposing coach.

- Personnel tendencies. What coach doesn't like to run his best horse behind his best mule? What quarterback doesn't find a favorite receiver, and what team doesn't have at least one player on defense who will find a way to hit anything that moves? How many teams try to sneak the second-string quarterback into the game at left halfback to throw the sweep action pass? Well, maybe not many in this latter regard, but coaches do develop tendencies with the ways they use their personnel.

Your task is to develop a record of those tendencies—all of them—so that when defensive decisions are made, they represent alignments, stunts, and strategies that counteract what the opponents like to do. Maintaining them in a computer program makes planning relatively easy.

━━━━ ANOTHER WORD ABOUT LOOKING AT YOURSELF ━━━━

Accept the possibility that your better opponents are doing the same thing with your tendencies. We all have them; we usually just don't take the time to determine what they are. The computer will make such record keeping easier for you and will provide the opportunity to scout yourself periodically in order to maintain a record of your own tendencies.

We already know that football is a modified chess match, made that much more fascinating by the unpredictability of human behavior. We can make the outcome more predictable, however, by establishing certain tendencies in easier games, then breaking them in big games. The strategy is to encourage the opponent to think we want to do one thing, get him to align himself accordingly on defense, anticipate his alignment as much as possible, and then do something else! Review Section five for more information on scouting yourself. But keep in mind that your opponents may be doing the same thing. A year-by-year record of their tendencies as well as yours will be very revealing.

=============== COMPUTERS AND WEIGHT TRAINING ===============

Computer and weight training have become almost inseparable among coaches and their athletes. Strength training and general cardiovascular conditioning have become so sophisticated within the past several years that computers have become necessary tools to coordinate player workouts. Most universities and some high schools use computers to provide individual workouts for their athletes, charting their progress and increasing their workloads as appropriate. In this way, activities can be designed and coordinated to meet the special requirements of individual players. Refer to figure 7–1 for an example of the program for one player.

Again, software can be secured commercially or developed locally. Coaches might also request programs from selected universities. College football programs are often willing to assist their high school counterparts. Not only are they anxious to help develop young players, but they are actually dependent upon them for their own programs. It's not uncommon, therefore, for colleges to work closely with high schools, particularly the schools they regularly recruit, to provide whatever they can to upgrade their programs.

=============== COMPUTERS AND PUBLIC RELATIONS ===============

Coaches have a responsibility to maintain and publicize their player and team statistics. Such information is important for several reasons. Some players, particularly in high school, play football because of the recognition they receive. And that's all right, so long as they're willing to pay the price for the PR. Our job is to provide the PR and, while we have them hooked, engage them in all the other learning activities that make football such a valuable experience for young people.

Players and fans also like to see team and individual records. They give some players something to shoot for, and they become important selling points during the recruiting process. Even if individual performances fall short of school records, they still have the potential to turn heads if used thoughtfully by coaches.

Well-organized statistics are a must for the coach who finds himself on the speaker's circuit or who simply wants coaches to give credit where credit is due during the team's post-season banquet. Parents are impressed by the coach who can provide a statistical breakdown of key games during the previous season. It provides well-earned recognition to certain players, and it reminds parents and others in the audience that the coach has done his homework and that he knows what he's talking about.

In addition, consider the self-assessment possibilities that well-organized statistics provide. Figure 7–2 illustrates a statistical breakdown of eight games for "DHS." Not only does such a format provide PR and communication value but it enhances the self-scouting process described earlier. Even a glimpse at

30. PLAYER Z   Week 1

EXERCISE DAY AND NAME	SET 1 WT × REP	SET 2 WT × REP	SET 3 WT × REP	SET 4 WT × REP	SET 5 WT × REP	SET 6 WT × REP
Monday						
HANG CLEANS	120 × 5	130 × 5	140 × 5	140 × 5	140 × 5	
PUSH JERKS	120 × 5	130 × 5	140 × 5	140 × 5	140 × 5	
SQUAT	300 × 5	325 × 5	350 × 5	350 × 5	350 × 5	
INCLINE PRESS	135 × 5	145 × 5	160 × 5	160 × 5	160 × 5	
Wednesday						
HANG CLEANS	110 × 5	115 × 5	125 × 5	125 × 5	125 × 5	
PUSH JERKS	110 × 5	115 × 5	125 × 5	125 × 5	125 × 5	
SQUAT	270 × 5	295 × 5	315 × 5	315 × 5	315 × 5	
INCLINE PRESS	120 × 5	130 × 5	140 × 5	140 × 5	140 × 5	
Saturday						
HANG CLEANS	115 × 5	125 × 5	135 × 5	135 × 5	135 × 5	
PUSH JERKS	115 × 5	125 × 5	135 × 5	135 × 5	135 × 5	
SQUAT	285 × 5	310 × 5	335 × 5	335 × 5	335 × 5	
INCLINE PRESS	130 × 5	140 × 5	150 × 5	150 × 5	150 × 5	

FIGURE 7–1

	DHS 20 RM 12	DHS 0 MS 28	DHS 21 NT 18	DHS 28 GBS 21	DHS 37 WS 27	DHS 28 WW 20	DHS 27 HP 10	DHS 35 NW 6
OFFENSE								
RUSHING								
YARDAGE	232	158	266	187	307	345	221	363
ATTEMPTS	43	43	43	44	44	55	46	56
AVERAGE	5.4	3.7	6.2	4.3	7	6.3	4.9	6.5
PASSING								
ATTEMPTS	5	17	4	8	13	10	8	6
COMPLTD	1	4	2	5	8	5	1	3
YARDAGE	15	39	12	47	197	58	22	66
TOTAL OFFENSE	247	197	278	234	504	403	243	429
TIME OF POSS.	25:37	25:35	25:59	23:36	26:53	30:25	26:17	29:00
FIRST DOWNS	18	8	14	16	19	25	13	22
RUSHING	14	8	13	13	12	20	12	19
PASSING	1	0	1	2	6	4	1	3
PENALTY	3	0	0	1	1	1	0	0
TURNOVERS	1	3	3	0	1	2	3	2
FUMBLES	1/0	1/1	2/2	0/0	1/1	2/2	2/2	1/0
INTERCEP.	1	2	1	0	0	0	1	2
DEFENSE								
RUSHING								
YARDAGE	119	87	− 2	127	109	178	45	125
ATTEMPTS	29	32	19	26	24	26	30	27
AVERAGE	4.1	2.7	− .1	4.9	4.5	6.8	1.5	4.3
PASSING								
ATTEMPTS	18	12	16	12	28	14	13	12
COMPLTD	9	7	8	9	18	5	7	3
YARDAGE	108	145	125	188	239	35	107	49
TOTAL YARDAGE	227	232	123	260	348	203	152	164
TIME OF POSS.	22:23	22:25	22:01	24:24	21:07	17:35	21:43	19:00
FIRST DOWNS	11	9	6	9	9	8	7	12
RUSHING	5	6	1	4	3	6	2	7
PASSING	5	3	5	5	4	2	3	3
PENALTY	1	0	0	0	2	0	2	2
TURNOVERS	0	0	0	1	2	0	4	1
FUMBLES	0/0	0/0	0/0	0/0	1/1	2/0	1/1	3/1
INTERCEP.	0	0	0	1	1	0	3	0

FIGURE 7–2

155

each week's team performance indicates that DHS is predisposed to run the ball and that its opponents are especially successful passing against the team.

During the off-season, an analysis of such statistics tells the DHS staff that they need to look at their passing attack because they don't seem to have much confidence in it. This appears to be a very successful football team that may be even more successful with certain strategic adjustments in both the offense and defense.

The final statistics of a single game, as illustrated in figure 7–3, further reflect DHS' preference to run the ball. Tough games such as this one force coaches to play their cards even closer to their chest and to stick with what they do and like best. Normally, what they do and like best is what works for them. That's why they like it best. But it does become a tendency that jumps out at opposing coaches when they analyze scouting reports of your games. That's why it's wise to beat them to the punch and immediately analyze your own game statistics for tendencies that jump out at *you*.

Finally, a look at the individual statistics of certain players reveals that two backs are carrying the running load. See figure 7–4. Numbers 22 and 33 have over 2,000 yards between them. The fact that the running game involves two players, however, makes the offense that much less predictable and reduces the need to throw the ball more often.

Number 22, however, has 27 touchdowns more than anyone else on the team. In playoff competition, he may be the exclusive key for opposing defenses when DHS is inside its own 15 to 20 yard line. The DHS staff may want to anticipate such a possibility from opposing defenses by decoying him and mis-directing the ball to someone else on goal line or near-goal line running plays.

Obviously, such a decision involves the running skills of the other starting backs and the relative unstoppability of number 22! The point, however, is that a look at game, individual, and cumulative statistics can be very revealing about your team's performance and tendencies. The information, therefore, is helpful not only for player recognition but for week-to-week planning activities.

One additional point: notice in the passing/receiving statistics in figure 7–4 the additional tendency to pass the ball to number 22. He is clearly an excellent athlete and a natural decoy in both running and passing situations in big games. Again, however, the skills of the other players in the finesse positions have much to do with the wisdom of such a decision.

TECHNOLOGY AS A MIRROR

Madeline Hunter, education's sage of El Segundo, California, emphasizes one of her basic concepts of effective instruction with the saying: "Show what you say and say what you show." Without confusing the issue with discussions of brain dominance and modality learning, let's at least acknowledge that seeing *and* hearing are better than just seeing or hearing. Seeing, hearing, and doing are

FINAL TEAM STATISTICS

	VISITOR DHS	HOME ETHS
TOTAL FIRST DOWNS	10	10
By Rushing	7	7
By Passing	3	3
By Penalty	0	0
THIRD DOWN EFFICIENCY	3–10–30%	4–12–33%
FOURTH DOWN EFFICIENCY	0–2–0%	0–0–0%
TOTAL NET YARDS	187	176
Total Offensive Plays (inc. times thrown passing)	47	47
Average gain per offensive play	4.0	3.7
NET YARDS RUSHING (Including Sacks)	140	120
Gross Yards Rushing	154	127
Total Rushing Plays	43	30
Times thrown—yards lost attempting to pass	2–14	3–7
Average gain per rushing play (inc. sacks)	3.3	4.0
TOTAL YARDS PASSING	47	56
Pass Attempts—Completions—Had Intercepted	4–3–0	17–3–2
Average gain per pass play	11.8	3.3
KICKOFFS Number—In End Zone—Touchbacks	2–0–0	1–1–1
PUNTS Number and Average	5–33.6	5–34
Had Blocked	0	0
FGs—PATs Had Blocked	0–0	0–0
TOTAL RETURN YARDAGE	73	102
No. and Yards Punt Returns	1–3	4–57
No. and Yards Kickoff Returns	0–0	2–45
No. and Yards Interception Returns	2–70	0–0
PENALTIES Number and Yards	5–35	6–50
FUMBLES Number and Lost	1–0	1–1
TOUCHDOWNS	1	0
Rushing	1	0
Passing	0	0
Returns	0	0
EXTRA POINTS Made—Attempts	0–1	0–0
FIELD GOALS Made—Attempts	0–0	0–0
SAFETIES	0	0
FINAL SCORE	6	0
TIME OF POSSESSION	26:16	21:44

FIGURE 7–3

157

Ind Stats

BALL CARRIER #	10	11	12	22	23	24	25	30
YARDS	2	85	129	1426	7	7	124	98
ATTEMPTS	3	29	37	185	2	4	34	23
AVERAGE	.7	2.9	3.5	7.7	3.5	1.8	3.7	4.3
LONG	6	19	19	97	7	5	21	8
TD'S	1	2	2	31	0	0	2	1
KO/PRTYD				210				

BALL CARRIER #	31	33	34	36	42
YARDS	210	859	100	48	2
ATTEMPTS	29	151	21	7	2
AVERAGE	7.2	5.7	4.7	6.9	1
LONG	40	35	20	12	1
TD'S	0	4	1	0	0

PASSING QB'S #	11	12
ATTEMPTS	14	62
COMPLTD	13	34
INTERCPT	0	2
YARDS	314	771
LONG	51	78
TD PASS	1	4

RECVRS #	22	25	33	35	81	85	87
YARDS	405	8	200	219	56	49	58
RECEPTION	15	2	11	9	2	4	2
AVERAGE	27	4	18.2	24.3	28	12.3	29
LONG	78	8	37	51	45	20	35
TD'S	3	0	0	1	0	0	0

FIGURE 7–4

even better. Research tells us that young people retain up to 90% of what they see, hear, say, and do. That's where technology, particularly video technology, comes in. I have been teaching educational administration and supervision at the graduate level in a local university for almost two decades, and I discovered long ago the value of developing "mirrors of performance" to help teachers with their professional growth. One of the most effective mirrors is the videotape, if used casually and appropriately.

It is every bit as effective for football players. Coaches have been using films and, more recently, videotapes to analyze game situations for decades. Most teams routinely watch films of previous games, among other things, to evaluate player and team performance. The purpose is not to immerse the players in a stream of planned aggravation but to observe mistakes, analyze them, and figure out ways to avoid them in the future.

Using the videotape for practice situations is just as effective. Many coaches videotape scrimmages early in the season to analyze player performance, to use as a training tool in team meetings, and to provide visual reasons for decisions regarding player placement. This is not to say that coaches must consistently defend their decisions; they can, however, show players their performance to give them something specific to work on.

INDIVIDUAL DRILLS

This same principle applies to individual drills. If "a picture is still worth a thousand words," then coaches should conserve both words and time by video-taping certain drills and showing them immediately to selected players to reinforce coaching points. How many times, for example, have backfield coaches told young players to get in a good hit position to use their legs to explode into a pass rusher, or to drop the shoulder and drive the legs into a potential tackler? I can recall early in my career wishing: "If he only could see what he's doing, he might be able to correct it."

Well, now he can. All I have to do is arrange to have a minicam on the field, (see figure 7–5) shoot certain players while they block or lower their shoulders, and then immediately show them what they have done right or wrong. Seeing the execution of the skill is reinforced by the immediacy of the feedback. Such feedback need not be constant. Once the minicam and a video playback unit have helped the player execute correctly and the skill has become a part of his body's memory, it need not be used any more.

There is another advantage as well. Visualization is now well-established as an aid to athletic performance. Researchers have discovered that athletes who visualize their performance benefit not only from the mental rehearsal it provides, but also from the conditioning impulses the brain sends to their nerves and muscles. In essence, thinking about the proper execution of a skill actually engages the nerves in the performance of that skill. The nerves don't know, for example, if the quarterback is actually throwing a football or just thinking about it.

It stands to reason, then, that if football players are to benefit from visualization, they had better think about proper execution. And what better way than to focus on their own performance after they have mastered a skill or a technique, have seen it performed, and have been praised by their coach for that performance? Watching Joe Willie Namath execute proper passing fundamentals in a training tape is one thing; seeing themselves do it is another. One is interesting but far-removed from their reality; the other is exciting and immediate.

REQUEST FOR AV SERVICES

The football team would appreciate your assistance in the development of a videotape of the following activities:

GAME:

    Date:

    Time:

    Location:

PRACTICE:

    Date:

    Time:

    Activity or drill:

    Additional equipment needed:

VIDEO PRESENTATION:

    Nature of the project:

    Purpose:

Thanks a lot for your help. Call us if you have questions.

FIGURE 7—5

══════════════ TAKE-HOME POSSIBILITIES ══════════════

Coaches never have enough time for practice. By the time the first game rolls around, every football coach wishes he had found more time to work on fundamentals or to sharpen up execution. Even in the pros, the level of competition requires practice time well in excess of the hours available. High school and college preparation are even more difficult, given the schooling and family demands on coaches and players.

What football coaches, therefore, hasn't dreamed of extending practice time beyond the field, of getting the most from every free moment available to his players? Video practice tapes can provide such an opportunity. You can make them or, better yet, can purchase them commercially. However you and your players get your hands on them, they can provide the kinds of experiences that provide the perfect complement to on-field practices. How do they work?

Well, imagine your middle linebacker early in the season hustling home from practice for dinner and homework. Following a feeding frenzy and the occasional battle with quadratic equations, he heads for the family room, pops a tape into the VCR, and assumes a hit position in front of the TV. Aside from the fact that it might provoke his parents into thinking that he finally took one too many forearms to the face mask, the experience in front of the TV has several benefits.

First of all, the tape provides several real-life blocking situations, each requiring a decision and a reaction from him. The television screen flashes a succession of blocking schemes involving the two guards, the center, and a full or partial backfield. Following each of the blocking schemes, the screen freezes and a graphic asks the middle linebacker what decision he made and why. Following that, a coach provides a brief explanation of the best reaction to each situation.

At the end of the tape, each of the decisional situations is repeated without the explanations so that players can watch them and react without interruption. The situations are similar to those illustrated in figure 4–22 and provide a representative sampling of most of the blocking schemes that middle linebackers will see in the course of a season. Their obvious value is that they provide not only initial learning experiences but ongoing opportunities to practice those experiences on the field and at home.

Every year, especially early in the season, I give copies of the tape to middle linebackers to take home if they've had a bad practice reading their keys. The additional practice they get at home invariably pays dividends during the next practice at school. Drill tapes don't explain certain phases of football and then gather dust in athletic offices. They are used repeatedly by athletes who can benefit from contrived scrimmages in their family room.

Such a use of video technology has other benefits as well. Coaches can use the succession of situations to quiz middle linebackers early in the season to see if any or all of them understand their keys and their reactions to them. In addition, the tape can be used by middle linebackers just before a game to reinforce their reactions to the kinds of keys they are likely to see in the game.

The same is true of drill tapes for quarterbacks who must read the secondary coverages to find the holes in the defense and for safeties and cornerbacks who must read their backfield keys through the line to identify run or pass action. In essence, drill tapes have a wide variety of applications and can transform a family room into a practice field for players who have done their homework and have some additional time to devote to something other than the movie of the week.

ANOTHER WORD ABOUT VISUALIZATION

To repeat: Visualization doesn't do much good if football players are creating mental images of the wrong way to perform a skill. Such a practice simply perpetuates the bad habit that you and I are working so hard to correct. It also doesn't work if players don't know what images to mentally rehearse before they take the field. Drill tapes provide the pictures that they can retrieve from their memories to visualize their reactions to game situations.

In essence, the repetition provided by drill tapes, whether they be for the middle linebacker, the safety, the cornerback, or the quarterback, ultimately influences the body's memory as well as the mind's. When that happens, reaction time to real-life situations is necessarily faster, and players gain the knowledge and the confidence needed to grow accustomed to winning. And think of it—at least some of this can happen in front of the TV. Readers who are interested in securing such tapes are encouraged to contact the author.

VIDEOTAPES OF GAMES

Post-Game Uses

- Team meetings—Meetings to review game films (tapes) are as firmly etched in football tradition as pre-game jitters and halftime pep talks. Coaches wouldn't know what to do with themselves if they couldn't chew an occasional tail or appeal in their own unique way to the collective conscience. After all, we all seem to accept the fact that the will to win is useless without the will to practice, and the will to practice is sometimes impossible without a well-orchestrated review of last week's game film!

- Parent meetings—Booster Clubs, Pep Clubs, and plain old parent get-togethers provide great PR, a sense of unity, and the weekly opportunity to unseat the few armchair quarterbacks who were certain that you should have quick kicked on third and one. Such meetings are a whole lot more enjoyable than some coaches think, and they provide the setting for mutually reinforcing relationships with the parent community that can result in welcomed equipment for your program!

- Take-Home Possibilities for Players—Anyone who has been on the business end of a lesson plan for more than a few weeks realizes that peer evaluation has more lasting influence than those "words from on high." We just naturally want our colleagues to respect us and to offer the sense of belonging that is so critical to our motivation. Peer evaluation among football players is no less influential. That's why it's a good idea to have the players meet at a teammate's house once in a while to watch the film/tape and to share the kinds of spontaneous observations that only teammates can provide. Obviously, the personality of the team has much to do with this decision.

POST-SEASON USES

- Recruiters—You may have a storehouse full of credibility, but recruiters, be they college or professional, still prefer at least a glimpse of the real thing. Normally they prefer to see recruited players perform against the team's toughest competition, so it's generally a good idea to make multiple copies of selected game tapes, particularly if they are likely to be mailed to recruiters. It's also wise to accompany each tape with relevant information about the player. See figure 7–6 for a reproducible.

- Selected highlights—Football coaches are among the select few professionals in our society who can pack an inspirational speech with something other than hot air. That's why they find themselves so often in front of audiences, all kinds of audiences: parent groups, Rotary Clubs, Chamber of Commerce groups, junior high school activities programs, conventions, and a full range of media presentations.

In addition to the anecdotes that coaches always share, such audiences also enjoy highlight tapes of past seasons. Videotapes of outstanding plays and players provide a dramatic and entertaining complement to speeches for parents, students, and community groups. When talking with other coaches, they illustrate the strategies that are the focus of the presentations. All that is required is some minor editing and a graphic or two, and the tape becomes a valuable supplement to any speech for almost any group.

To the Recruiter:

The tape which accompanies this letter involves one of this year's tougher games and illustrates the performance of (player's name). Following is pertinent information about him:

Color of jersey:

Jersey number:

Position on offense:

Position on defense:

Relevant game statistics: (As appropriate)

      Yardage gained:

      Passes completed:

      Receptions made:

      Unassisted tackles:

      Interceptions:

Additional important information:

      ACT/SAT scores:

      Class rank:

      Educational objectives:

You may require additional information regarding athletic or academic performance. Feel free to contact me at your convenience. When you have completed your review of the tape, please return it to:

                    Coach's name
                    Coach's address

Thanks for your interest in our program and players.

                                   (Signed)

FIGURE 7–6

======================================= **LET'S WRAP IT UP** =======================================

Just a cursory glance at *TV Guide* supports the notion that your TV is one tube that is best left unsqueezed—unless you have filled it with the ideas we've discussed in this section. The TV can become not only an aid to recruiting or to the evaluation of team performance, but a practice field for individual players to work on their fundamentals.

The use of such drill tapes is revolutionary in football, for that matter in any sport. They represent a practical use of technology that has immediate and lasting value for football players at all levels of competition.

The computer provides complementary advantages. It may not have the visual impact of videotape, but it provides a process for the organization of information about you and your opponents that strengthens your entire program.

Sammuel Johnson indicated long ago that there are two kinds of knowledge. Either we know the answer or we know where to find information about it. With each day, football becomes more sophisticated; technology is one of the reasons. Either we control such influences on the evolution of the game, or they control us.

SECTION 8

Game Day

To most football teams, an eternity is a finite period of time. It's usually the few days before a big game. Even then, those days involve an obvious contradiction: they take an eternity to pass, and they still don't provide enough time to get everything done. So we wait forever for the game to arrive and when it finally does, we usually wish we had just one more day to get ready.

What we do on game day must be two-fold. One, we must not compromise what we already have done. Two, we must somehow provide for what we haven't done. Provision for what we haven't done generally is made by adjusting our personnel and/or the game plan. Assuring what we have done is the primary focus of this section. As the old saying goes: "Mighty are the preparations!" We don't want to compromise all those preparations by slipping up at the last minute.

But first, a word about adjustments in personnel or game plan. A brief pre-game meeting with the coaching staff to make a final assessment of the game plan is an excellent way to remind everyone of what you plan to do and why. On occasion these meetings will identify or reaffirm one or two perceived weaknesses in the plan. Last-minute changes, however, are ill-advised. They will confuse the players and cause a lack of confidence in all the preparations.

The coaches must focus on suspected weaknesses, especially during the first half, in order to make necessary halftime adjustments. Confidence in the game plan is essential before and during the game, but blind adherence to it inhibits the kind of flexibility that all teams need to adjust to the inevitable surprises good opponents prepare for you. A brief pre-game meeting with the coaching staff provokes the mind set that coaches need to respond effectively to such surprises. It can be arranged conveniently while the team is getting dressed for the game.

PRE-GAME

Pre-game activities for the players start the night before the game. Football players need a good night's sleep if they are to perform effectively on game day. They should be home early—usually by 10 PM—and should be in bed by 11:00.

They may not sleep very soundly, particularly before a big game, but they should stay in bed for a good seven or eight hours, maybe more depending upon their individual sleep needs.

They must be well-rested and appropriately nourished prior to reporting to the lockerroom and pre-game meetings. The time before the game can sap a lot of psychic energy from even the most confident football player. How players are handled by their coaches before the game, therefore, will influence the level of intensity they bring to the game. The food they eat may have the same effect.

- *Diet*—First of all, it's important to recognize that the pre-game meal is designed primarily to make players comfortable during the contest, not to supply their energy needs. As a matter of fact, too much food even two or three hours before the contest can cause indigestion and possible vomiting. It generally takes the body about four hours to digest a meal, unless the meal is mainly carbohydrates, which are digested faster than proteins and fats.

That's why a good pre-game meal should include primarily grains and fruits. See figure 8–1 for a reproducible to use with your team. It should not consist of that rare piece of beef that coaches recommended back in the Stone Ages. The proverbial taste of blood is not the spur to action that many coaches thought. More likely, it does to football players what it does to feasting lions—makes them tired. So if you encourage your players to eat a big lunch of beef before the game, expect a team of very docile lions who will spend most of their time looking for a comfortable place to lie down.

The same is true of any big meal. Remember, it takes the stomach approximately four hours to process food into the small intestine. The larger the meals or the closer to game time the meal occurs, the longer it will take to digest. I've known some players over the years who react to nervousness by increasing the size of the feedbag. What they don't realize is that during the game their blood is rushing to the stomach to digest food instead of into their muscles to provide strength.

Players, particularly two-way players, should be instructed to load up on carbohydrates at least three to four hours before the game. Orange juice, bananas and cornflakes, skim milk, wheat toast and jelly provide everything players need before even the most rigorous game. Such a meal will make them comfortable and will be easily digested before the game, unlike proteins and fats which take longer.

Obviously, and as indicated in the reproducible, players with certain physical conditions requiring medical attention should see their family doctor for a specific diet to meet their unique nutritional needs.

Football coaches have been asserting for decades that football is a game of inches. Smart football coaches realize as well that those inches apply as readily to the foot-long hot dog players eat an hour and a half before the game as to the

POINTS TO KEEP IN MIND:

The pre-game meal that is most important to you is the one you have the night before the game. Because of the energy you will require the next day, it's always a good idea to eat a meal high in carbohydrates: milk, yogurt, navy beans, pinto beans, bananas, carrots, grapes, corn, raisins, pasta, whole wheat breads, crackers, bagels, and so forth. These will provide the energy you need to perform to the best of your ability on the following day. The actual pre-game meal really won't provide that much energy, considering the amount of time it takes to get into your system, so eat a light meal designed to make you comfortable during the game. Carbohydrates are again a good idea because they are easily digested. A good breakfast of orange juice, cornflakes with sliced bananas, whole wheat toast with jelly, and skimmed milk will provide everything you need to play a good game. Pancakes are also a good source of carbohydrates.

REMEMBER:

1. Eat your pre-game meal three to four hours before the game. Eat nothing up to one hour before the game. A full stomach during the game brings blood to your stomach to help digest food and away from your muscles—where you most need it.

2. Don't eat candy bars for quick energy just before the game. They may produce low blood sugar, which may leave you tired and weak.

3. Water is always available on the field and sidelines. Drink as much of it as you can—in moderation. Be sure to replace the moisture you lose through perspiration. Don't bloat yourself, but also be sure to drink a healthy supply of water before the game.

ALSO:

Any athlete with a physical condition requiring medical attention may require a modified diet for training and competition. In such instances, we encourage you to meet with your family doctor to secure his or her input regarding your nutritional needs.

FIGURE 8–1

fourth down on the one-foot line. Both situations influence and depend upon player intensity, so learn to tolerate those few times when they *act* like hot dogs—never when they *eat* them just before a game. The same is true of the candy bar myth. Contrary to the worn-out idea that they provide quick energy, candy bars actually may lower blood sugar and sap energy. All coaches, therefore, are well-advised to tell their players to eat a well-balanced, moderately high carbohydrate meal three to four hours before the game, then about an hour before the game do nothing but head for the water fountain when they feel like swallowing something. We will talk more about water in a later section of this chapter.

- Arrival Time—Arrival time for away games obviously is determined by the distance the team must travel, but pre-game preparations tend to be standard regardless of home or away situations. Generally, it's wise to have the team arrive approximately two and a half to three hours before game time. Players must get taped; the team must review its game plan; they must find a moment or two to relax while getting dressed and to visualize their upcoming performance; they must receive a pre-game talk; and they must have an adequate amount of time to stretch out and loosen up before kickoff time.

- The Initial Meeting—It's usually a good idea to have the team meet in a large classroom or auditorium as soon as players arrive. The purpose of this meeting is to reintroduce them to the purpose of the day's activities and to review elements in the game plan that may have caused them problems during the week. This meeting also provides a good time to take a final look at a videotape/film of the opponent. Such an activity provokes the right mind set for the upcoming game. This meeting, therefore, is informational and purposely low-key.

- Training Room and Lockerroom—Following the initial meeting, the team is instructed to get taped, dressed, and in the right mind set for the game. This part of the pre-game preparation takes time because some of it is devoted to relaxation and visualization. Once dressed, the players should be encouraged to lie down, shut their eyes, and visualize their performance.

Some programs even separate the linemen and the backs at this point and place each in separate rooms. A few even direct them to colored rooms, red/intense for the linemen and linebackers, blue/mellow for the backs and receivers. Well, that may be the ultimate in psychological conditioning and a bit extreme to some of us, but a legion of pragmatists out there insist that if it works, do it. I'll leave that up to you.

- Pre-Game Meeting—Before taking the field, the team should meet one more time to develop the right mind set for this particular game. Every team has its own distinctive personality and reveals it in obvious ways to the discerning coach. Obviously, the importance of the game will determine the coach's approach with the team in this meeting. His perception of his players' level of intensity, however, is equally important.

Both these factors must be determined by the coach to decide on the approach he will take with the team. A team that has gone flat—for whatever reason—doesn't need an informational, laid-back, it's-up-to-you kind of pre-game talk. The players need someone with blood in his eyes to get their level of intensity where it ought to be. Conversely, the hyped-up team doesn't need more hype. When it's overloaded, any system shuts down, including football teams. It's wise, therefore, for coaches to assess the team's level of intensity before this meeting. Oftentimes, just a short stroll through the lockerroom is all that's required.

- What About Prayer?—We are sometimes as diverse in our religious beliefs as we are in our shoe sizes. But each of us, regardless of our religious preferences or affiliations, enjoys the chance to pursue these beliefs in ways that are appropriate for us. For that reason, I have always believed that a few moments at the end of the pre-game meeting should be devoted to silent prayer for most, meditation for some. The best way to initiate that time is with the words: "A few moments of silence—each in his own way."
- Pre-Game Workout—The facilities available to the team will determine the "what" and "how" of the pre-game workout. I have always liked to have the team do most of its calisthenics and some of its agility drills on a nearby practice field or in a fieldhouse. It also is a good location to do some of the kicking and passing warm-ups. It's generally a low-key location, and it represents a fitting place to conclude preparation for the game. It also provides for an impressive team entrance to the game field.
- Taking the Field—Sometimes the way a team takes the field sets the tone for the whole game. I remember one year, for example, watching our players doing calisthenics in the end-zone at an away game and seeing the opposing team run onto the field through our players. It was an attempt at intimidation that not only failed, but actually put fire in our players' eyes before the kickoff. We won the game—handily. Be careful about loading your opponent's gun.

Another example stands out in my mind as well. It was another away game and we were working on selected drills when we heard the dramatic repetition of a drum beat approaching the field. Players and coaches alike couldn't help but look as the opposing team marched very deliberately behind its band, all silent and purposeful, the only sound the beat of the drums. It was a team with a great tradition and the reputation for clean but tough football. Its way of taking the game field was also an attempt at intimidation, and I'm here to tell you it worked. It was all we could do to get a couple of our players onto the field!

I've become convinced over the years that the class you and your team reflect in your behavior, more so than anything else, provokes in your opponents a genuine respect for you that at times can be intimidating. You may not intend it to be intimidating, but it is. It doesn't involve the kinds of hot-dog antics that simply anger your opponent. I don't want my opponent angry at me; I want his respect.

So take the field deliberately and seriously, almost mechanically. Sell your intention: "We are here to do a job—and we're about to do it!" For example, we always have our team march in two columns from the back practice fields to the game field. Players are instructed to walk slowly and look straight ahead, showing no emotion.

Then, when they get alongside the end zone, they run in single file from the end zone to the near 40-yard line, across the field, and back to the end zone to complete their pre-game calisthenics. The march from the practice field and the single-file entrance usually takes about five minutes, just enough time to get the opponent's attention and give him something to think about.

- On the Field Workout—After calisthenics, the team has a prescribed routine to follow. It never varies, so early in the season, prior to the first game, we give the players a description of the pre-game workout. See figure 8–2. It details everything from their entrance onto the field to their approach to the sideline. Sometime before the first game, we also give the whole process a dry run to make sure the players understand what we expect.

An important component of the whole process is how all this is done. A good friend, quite a successful businessman, used to remind me that "presentation is half the sell job." I learned quickly that the principle applies equally to the sale of cars, toys, and football teams. We sell ourselves every time we take the field and, later, every time we approach the line of scrimmage.

If we cascade through the opponent like the local fringe element, the tactic is likely to backfire by angering opposing players. If we jog randomly onto the field, we don't do anything one way or the other to get our opponent's attention. But if we sell ourselves by taking the field in a disciplined and orderly fashion, we draw attention to ourselves and cause the opponent to give us some thought. What he thinks can often give you the momentum in the early stages of the game.

- Equipment considerations—A final pre-game preparation involves the tools of the trade. If you're like me, you need a checklist of some kind to make sure you have enough towels, water bottles, extra chin straps, ammonia capsules, and so on. Figure 8–3 provides a reproducible copy you can share with your team's manager. It is comprehensive, easily adopted, and serves as a substantive reminder each week to have the right materials on hand.

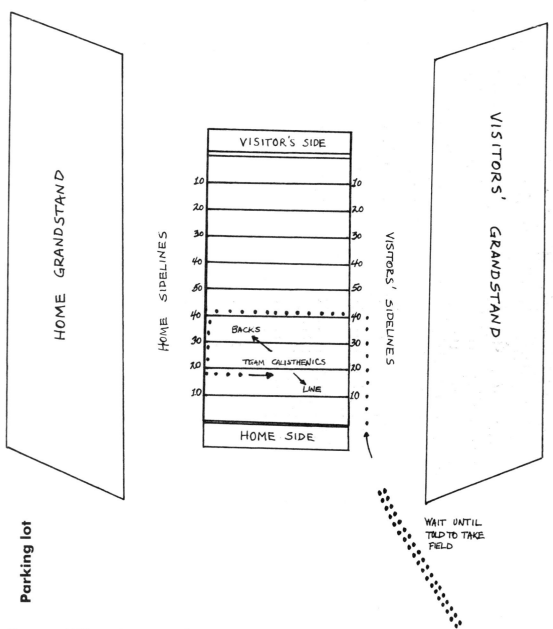

Team —Will march in two columns from practice field, will circle field in single file and line up in four or five waves for calisthenics. After calisthenics, break down into:

Backs—Do agilities, then go to passing

Line —Do agilities, stance and starts and shoulder bumping

Team —After drills, get into teams and run plays from the ready list. Line up on goal line for national anthem; after anthem, sprint through cheerleader hoop and come to sideline. Gather around head coach.

WIN GAME!

FIGURE 8—2

MASTER CHECK LIST

GAME DAYS

Legend: V—Varsity   A—Away games only
         S—Sophomores   W—Weather related
         F—Freshmen

ITEM	CODE	EQUIPMENT	QUANTITY	COMMENTS
BALL BAG				
1	VSF	Footballs	12 + 2 game	_____
2	VSF	Kicking T's	2 ea	Orange + Black
COOLERS				
3	V	Cooler, large	1 ea	for ice cubes
4	VS	Cooler, styrofoam	1 ea	for ice cups 5 ea
5	VS	Cups	30 ea	drinking
6	VS	Jugs, water	2 ea	_____
7	VSF	Water bottles	6 ea	_____
KIT				
8	VSF	ACE Bandages	All sizes	_____
9	V	Air pump	1 ea	for helmets
10	VSF	Ammonia Capsules	1 box	_____
11	VSF	Antiseptic	1 tube	_____
12	V	Aspirin	1 bottle	with Doctor's consent
13	VSF	Band-Aids	1 box	_____
14	VSF	Chalk	1 box	halftime briefing
15	V	Cotton	1 roll	_____
16	V	Eye-Black	1 tube	No glare
17	V	Firm-Grip	tube-jar	Stickum
18	VSF	First aid chart		_____
19	VSF	First aid cream	1 tube	_____
20	VSF	First aid spray	1 can	_____
21	VSF	Gauze Bandages	1 roll	_____
22	VSF	Gauze Pads	All sizes	_____
23	VSF	Heat Jelly	1 jar	for back ailments
24	VSF	ICE Packs	2 ea	_____
25	V	Insect Repellent	1 can	_____
26	V	Med Flash Light	1 ea	check battery
27	VSF	Mole Skin	1 roll	for blisters on heel
28	V	Mouth Guards	2 ea	_____
29	VSF	Pencil + Paper	1 ea	coaches' notes
30	VSF	Pen, Permanent	Red or Black	for labeling
31	VSF	Cotton Swabs	1 doz	long size
32	V	Salt Tablets	1 jar	_____
33	VSF	Scissors	1 pair	_____
34	V	Skin Freezer	1 can	_____
35	VSF	Shoelaces	4 pair	_____
36	VSF	Stretch rolls	1 ea	for taping
37	VSF	Tape (white)	10 rolls	_____
38	V	Tape (brownstretch)	4 rolls	_____

© 1992 by Michael D. Koehler

FIGURE 8–3

174

MASTER CHECK LIST (*Continued*)

ITEM	CODE	EQUIPMENT	QUANTITY	COMMENTS
KIT				
39	VSF	Tape Cutters	1 ea	
40	VSF	Tape Prep	1 can	
41	VSFW	Tough Depressor	1 doz	for mud removal, cleats
42	V	Triangular Bandage	1 ea	for head injuries
PAD BAG				
43	V	Belt	1 ea	
44	V	Chin Strap	1 ea	BIKE
45	VA	Complete Issue	1 ea	Jocks + Socks
46	V	Pads	5 extra pr.	tape on injuries also
47	VSF	Towels for sideline	10 ea	keep QBs, backs, balls dry
TOOL BAG				
48	VSF	Cleats	20 ea	
49	VSF	Helmet Parts	All kinds	2 face masks
50	VSF	Pliers	2 ea	
51	V	Pocket Knife	1 ea	manager's tool
52	VSF	Screwdrivers	2 ea	Reg. + Phil
53	VSF	Shoulder Pad Straps	5 ea	
54	VSF	Shlder stp connector	8 ea	
TOWEL BAG				
55	VSFA	Towels for showers	60 ea	
MISCELLANEOUS				
56	VW	Capes for sidelines	25 to 30 ea	Cold and wet days
57	VW	Hand Warmers for QB	1 pair	Cold days

FIGURE 8–3 (*Continued*)

THE GAME

Team discipline and organization are as evident during the game as any time preceding it, probably more so to the fans. A sense of order and purpose must influence the behavior of players and coaches alike. It's important, therefore, to establish the processes that encourage both to focus on the tasks at hand. One of the most obvious and the one that can sometimes involve the greatest confusion is sideline control.

- Sideline Control and Substituting—Nothing looks worse from the stands or can cause more confusion on the field than a football team that creates a mob scene on the sidelines. Players may be waving to girlfriends or family in the stands; they may be clowning around with each other and ignoring the game; or they may be so into the game that they are crowding the coaches onto the game field. Whatever they're doing, if it lacks the discipline and orderliness that we've already identified as so important, it can negatively affect the outcome of the game as well as the impression we've worked so hard to create.

Coaches, therefore, are well-advised to condition their teams to behave appropriately on the sidelines from the first minute of the first game. Too many of us fail to give this aspect of team behavior the attention it deserves early enough in the season. By the time our frustration levels reach an all-season high—about the time of the third or fourth game—and we start shouting for a little order on the sidelines, it's generally too late. So distribute copies of figure 8–4 to the team before the first game.

Addressing such issues before problems arise makes it a whole lot easier for everyone involved. Attaching a natural consequence to inappropriate behavior influences positive behavior that much more. Players who persistently misbehave on the sidelines don't dress for the next game, and subs who are not sitting at their designated spots on the bench in the third or fourth quarter don't get into the game.

None of this takes much time to organize, and it can save a whole lot of confusion on game days.

- *Who Watches What and From Where?*—At this point, it might be a good idea to review part of Section 4, particularly Figures 4–7 through 4–10. Communication among coaches is critical if good ideas and effective strategies on the sidelines are to become reality on the field. Obviously, the better the coordination, the better the communication. It's wise, therefore, to establish a process that provides the "who," "what," and "where" of effective sideline communication.

- *Who*—Much of the "who" is determined by internal program decisions regarding the coach who actually calls the plays. Offensive plays, for example, may be called by the head coach or the offensive coordinator; defensive signals by the head coach or the defensive coordinator. Regardless of which coach calls the play, however, he should receive some feedback regarding the play's execution and some input regarding sequencing alternatives.

Such feedback need not be immediate and it should not be lengthy. Oftentimes the play caller has a sequence in mind when he calls a particular play, usually determined by the ready list prepared during the previous week. Any immediate feedback through a head set or from an assistant coach can be disruptive to the play caller's train of thought.

As a matter of fact, most big-time coaches use the sideline phones only to request information. They may be used as well by assistants to communicate

SIDELINE BEHAVIOR

We have spent a lot of time, coaches and players alike, working hard to develop a program we can be proud of. Class is very important to us and should be reflected in everything we do on and off the field. This includes how we behave on the sidelines. We as coaches try to follow these guidelines. We expect you to follow them as well.

DO cheer for the team on the field.

DO follow the progress of the game.

DO be ready to assist injured teammates off the field.

DO provide moral support to teammates coming off the field.

DO stand up for kickoffs.

DO sit at or near your designated location on the bench—most of the time.

DO NOT wave to friends in the stands.

DO NOT stand on the benches.

DO NOT horse around with teammates.

DO NOT crowd the coaches.

DO NOT stand most of the time.

LEs	LTs	LGs	Cs	RGs	RTs	REs	QBs	LHBs	RHBs	FBs

B E N C H

These guidelines have been developed to enable all of us to concentrate on the primary reason for this football game—to win it. Without teamwork, we don't win, and good teamwork includes appropriate sideline behavior.

FIGURE 8–4

177

each play call to coaches upstairs in the press box, but they are generally used by head coaches only for suggestions when they need them. In addition, they expect the feedback to be brief but substantive.

When a head coach, for example, is stymied by a particular secondary coverage and he asks for a suggestion from the coaches upstairs, he doesn't expect a listing of alternatives or a dissertation on the merits of the play-action pass. *He wants a play*. And the next time the coach wants a play, he doesn't expect detailed explanations of why the previous suggestion didn't work. *He wants another play*. Brevity, therefore, is the key to effective use of the phones.

That's why it's advisable during a pre-season coaches' meeting to establish and discuss procedures for the effective and efficient use of the phones. When used intelligently, they may often spell the difference between victory or defeat. The same is true of sideline communication without the phones. Assistants should make input only when it's requested or when an observation is *so* important that it has to be shared with others.

- *What*—Obviously, sideline communication involves much more than input into play calling. It may involve information regarding:

    —The physical condition of players: "Tom's hamstring is acting up again: he's still our best blocker but don't expect him to run the ball very well."

    —The performance of players: "Tom, shake it off! That fumble is ancient history; just start running the ball the way you know how!"

    —The needs of players: "Tell the manager to get a supply of towels to the backs so they can keep their hands dry."

    —The physical condition of opponents: "Their left corner is hobbled. Let's send Billy at him."

    —The performance of opponents: "Russ is destroying the player on his head. Stay at his hole."

    The point is, sideline activities require proper coordination to assure that such observations are shared with play callers. Generally, it's a good idea to filter the observations of players and coaches through one coach. He can make the input when the time is right and with an economy of words. Any head coach is going to start foaming at the mouth if coaches and players are throwing ideas at him randomly. Even if the ideas are good, even critical, coaches will ignore them because they may seem so intrusive at the time.

- *When*—As already discussed, the best time to communicate needed information to the head coach or the play caller is when he requests it, unless the information is critical to the outcome of the game. This is a good principle to keep in mind.

- *Where*—Where to communicate observations involves two general locations. Obviously, much of it is shared on the sideline during the game.

The other location is somewhere in the lockerroom or enroute to the lockerroom for halftime activities.

HALFTIME ACTIVITIES

Among the many and diverse skills requested of a coach is the ability to make halftime adjustments in his game plan. Such adjustments often determine the difference between winning or losing. Obviously, any adjustments result from the ability of the staff to give dimension to the problems confronting them. Observations like "we just can't run the ball" are useless because they are defeatist in nature. Better is a comment that identifies the pattern of stunts the opponent is using that seems to be causing the problem.

Best is a comment that identifies the scope of the problem and identifies a strategy to counteract it: "Their inside scrape into the home halfback is killing us; we're going to have to start lead blocking it in order to pick up the offside linebacker." Obviously, such observations not only provide dimension for the problem but suggest at least one solution to provoke reaction from colleagues. An excellent way to start such a discussion among coaches at halftime is to have the assistants upstairs with phones or on the sidelines jot down reactions to the questions on a form such as the one in figure 8–5. It will provide something substantive for the head coach or the play callers to think about.

The form is necessarily simple. It seeks specifics about the team's offensive and defensive successes, and it requests solutions regarding second half strategies. Responses to the third question can range from "keep doing what we're doing offensively and defensively" to "start stunting more on the inside to get to their quarterback" to "get back to more short traps up the gut" to any kind of specific that provides a sense of direction.

"Well, what do you think?" wastes too much time. Time during the halftime intermission is at a premium. Discussions among coaches must be anticipated just before the end of the first half to make them profitable. Then, when coaches get together with players, they can seek reinforcement of their observations and their decisions. "Where is the tackle lining up most of the time and what is he doing to you?" "What's the best way for you two to block that hole?" "What if we lead block the four hole? Will that handle it?"

- *Player Input*—Such questions answered by the people most directly involved—the players—provide either reinforcement or reason to reassess the solutions we as coaches have suggested. That's why a blackboard is so critical in the lockerroom at halftime. Players should tell coaches where their opponents are lined up and exactly what they're doing at the snap of the ball. The accumulation of the observations of players and coaches should then result in the team's adjusted strategies for the second half.

HALFTIME ADJUSTMENTS

Answer these questions just before the end of the first half:

1. What were our most successful plays during the first half?

    WHY??

2. What were their most successful plays during the first half?

    WHY??

3. What must we do in the second half to win this game?

FIGURE 8–5

- *Before Taking the Field*—One thing remains before the team returns to the field. The pre-game pep talk is often less important than a good half-time speech. Before the game, player adrenalin handles most of the hype. During the halftime break, many players are sore, tired, and hoping for an end to the hostilities. They may need a boost before taking the field. The kind of boost delivered, however, depends upon the status of the game at that point.

If the team is winning or is tied, the coach's exhortations can involve challenge, criticism, and all the fire and brimstone he can muster on short notice. Winners can absorb all kinds of heat. They expect it, and they have the confidence to transform it into energy. Occasionally, such winners may be on the losing end of the score at halftime. With such a team, any decision by the coach to heat up the lockerroom before the start of the second half is a judgment call.

Obviously, any time a coach applies heat, he makes a judgment call. Although tradition dictates that we lose our tempers as often as we find the practice field, reality reveals that football coaches plan very carefully, even when to lose their tempers. Such coaches have learned as well that losing teams haven't developed the ability to transform heat into energy.

Too much heat saps what little energy they have left. The excess criticism that is exciting to the winning team provokes indifference in the losing team. The players don't accept it as a challenge but as a reminder of their inability. As a result, they see the coach not as a source of inspiration, but of recrimination and blame. Sometimes they need a hand on the shoulder instead of a fist in the face. It takes a conscious decision by the coach to decide which option to choose.

POST-GAME

- *On the field*—Class is evident in everything we do. We win with humility; we lose with resolution. We approach the opponent after the game with the same equanimity whether we have won or lost. John Wooden asserts that balance is important in everything an athlete does, whether he's in a solid hit position or in the right frame of mind before or after a game. Coaches influence this sense of balance more than they realize.

- *In the locker room*—The lockerroom after a game is not the place to focus on the specifics of performance, unless they were good. Even then, any recognition should be brief. The more we dwell on individual performance, the more we contradict our claims that football is a team sport. Even the greatest performance is in some part dependent upon the assistance of teammates. We reinforce that position when we acknowledge a superior performance but keep it in proper perspective.

"Proper perspective" is the guideline for dealing with the end of every game, regardless of the outcome. Unless it's the final game of the season, it must be celebrated or mourned quickly, and before the players leave the lockerroom it must become ancient history. The focus must shift as quickly as possible to the next game. Any tendency to dwell on a previous game, either in satisfaction or frustration, causes a team to lose some intensity. Even the later review of the game film should focus on the need for improved performance for future contests. The team that isn't anticipating every opponent soon falls for a sucker punch from one of the them.

After players are reminded to show their bumps and bruises to a coach or the team trainer, the coach's final emphasis should involve training rules. The end of a game often signals the start of the festivities, and you and I as coaches learned long ago that the cry to "let the games begin" drowns out any attempt on our part to stop them. Our role, therefore, is to reaffirm the value and the inevitability of the training rules and to hope that the self-discipline we talked about in chapter four leads the players in the right direction now.

- *Final game of the season*—The final game of the season can be a real letdown for the players, especially the seniors. If it happens during a play-off situation, it can be especially hard on the team because it probably involves a loss and concludes the season suddenly. The loss of the game itself is a small part of the letdown; the primary letdown involves the loss of friendships, relationships, the daily routine, the activity, the weekend excitement, even the smells of cut grass and analgesic balm.

That's why it's a good idea to conclude the season with a team meeting that focuses on the following:

—Introductory comments from the head coach. Because this involves such a personal reaction, such comments will be unique to the coach. They should, however, announce the conclusion of the season and serve to introduce the comments from the assistant coaches and from any others who over the past several months have worked with and grown close to them.

—Comments from assistants and others. Generally, coaches have special feelings for every team they coach. Often, the distinctive personality of a team will provoke strong feelings in anyone who works with it. Such feelings should be shared with the team after the season's final game. The emotion that fills the room at such times reinforces the claim that football is much more than blocking and tackling. It is relationships, closeness, caring, and commitment to one another. That's why the final game is such an emotional experience for everyone. The thoughtful expression of those emotions reinforces not only the values of the program but the kinds of traditions that transform families into winning programs.

—A thank you and a challenge. Usually the meeting concludes with the head coach's feelings about the team, his hope that the friendships will continue, an official thank you from him, a commitment to help players with college, and

_____ HIGH SCHOOL ATHLETICS

CONTEST RESULTS

Sport _____ Date _____

Site _____ Opponent _____

	<u>Win/Loss</u>	<u>Scores</u>	
Varsity	_____	____HS _____	OPP _____
JV	_____	____HS _____	OPP _____
SOPH	_____	____HS _____	OPP _____
FROSH A	_____	____HS _____	OPP _____
FROSH B	_____	____HS _____	OPP _____

COMMENTS (i.e. individual awards, tournament placement etc.):

SIGNATURE _____

Please return prior to 8:30 a.m. the day following the contest. Thank You!

FIGURE 8–6

183

handshakes all around as just the seniors leave the room. Returning players stay in the room to receive their thank you and their challenge for the coming year. Training rules and hard work, including classwork, are re-emphasized as the mantle of responsibility is passed to next year's squad.

This final meeting obviously is a whole lot more fun if the season concludes with a win. Regardless of the outcome of the final game, however, the meeting is important as a transition to next year and should be memorable in its own right. It sustains continuity in the program and emphasizes the coach's commitment to each young man as someone much more than a football player.

- *Post-Game Interviews*—It's obvious that post-game interviews should accentuate the positive. As coaches, we can eliminate the negative later in meetings and practice. The negatives are problems that require work and that, frankly, are no one else's business. The positives involve publicity for player and team accomplishments that we want everyone to recognize. They may provide the needed coverage to earn All-State honors for just one more player and to encourage two or three more athletes to join your program next fall.

It's a good idea to develop a process that gets all your scores to the athletic director and papers as soon as possible. A simple form such as the one in figure 8–6 takes care of the scores; you take care of the message, either by meeting with reporters after the game or by calling or mailing a media release such as the one in figure 8–7.

- *Player Interviews*—Generally it's a good idea to meet with potential or actual blue chippers early in the season to introduce them to the fine art

MEDIA RELEASE

Copies to: (Names of local papers)

For immediate release

James Smith
Head Football Coach
Anywhere High School
1111 South Street
Anywhere, Iowa 75648
709-868-1234

(Specifics of media release)

FIGURE 8–7

Reporters from local newspapers or radio stations may contact you at home before or after a game to get your reactions. This is an exciting time for players but can at times result in someone saying the wrong thing. In order to help you when you are asked for reactions, we want you to read and remember the following points. See any one of the coaches if you have questions about any of the guidelines.

DOs	DON'Ts
DO give as much credit as possible to your teammates.	**DON'T** load your opponent's gun with provocative comments.
DO take a few moments to think about each question before answering it.	**DON'T** be critical about your teammates or opponents.
DO find positive things to say about your teammates *and* your opponent.	**DON'T** miss an after-game meeting in order to hold an interview. Have reporters wait until after the meeting.
DO maintain a positive attitude throughout the interview. You are representing your team.	**DON'T** give away strategies in pre-game interviews.
DO remember that parents and other students will be reading your comments.	**DON'T** speak for your coaches or anyone else. Give only your positive reactions.
DO keep your comments brief.	**DON'T** volunteer information.
DO refer reporters to coaches when they ask questions that make you uncomfortable.	**DON'T** help reporters "make stories" by sharing ill-advised comments. *You* are the story, not the comments you make.

FIGURE 8–8

185

of handling reporters. You might even discuss with them the ins and outs of the handout which is illustrated in figure 8–8, a form which should be given to the whole team early in the season. It really isn't wise to leave such things up to player discretion. With one ill-chosen word, some of the smartest and otherwise most discreet players can alienate teammates or load an opponent's gun.

LET'S WRAP IT UP

The game day is the culmination of all our efforts. We don't want to resolve any potential problem on this critical day simply by re-arranging the deck chairs on the Titanic. Too much is riding on our decisions and on the processes we've developed to help make such decisions. If specific processes have been well-designed and well-oiled, every game day should proceed as planned. You may not win them all, but you'll lose those few only because your opponent capitalized on his strengths, not your mistakes.

SECTION 9

Conditioning and Weight Training

We all realize that strength is primary to successful execution on the football field. It promotes quickness, confidence, improved coordination, and endurance. As any athlete knows, or soon learns, fatigue is the football player's worst enemy. Vince Lombardi once said that fatigue makes cowards of us all. A tired athlete simply can't do his job. Fatigued football players don't pick up critical first downs or make late-game goal line stands. They lose.

They also get injured. Football players who don't commit themselves to good weight programs suffer far more sprained ankles, twisted knees, and separated shoulders than players who lift weights regularly. More importantly, they risk serious head injury. Football players don't build up their necks to snap collar buttons. They build up the muscle pad in the back of the neck to absorb shock.

I ended my football career at Nebraska with a cerebral hemorrage that could have been avoided. My motivation to lift weights at that time in my life related more to appearance on the bench than to performance on the field. Nor was weightlifting as high a priority in school as it is today. The advances in both technique and technology have strengthened many athletes to the point where they probably hit harder than I did, yet experience fewer injuries, especially career-ending injuries like mine.

Many high schools and some colleges and universities fail to realize these benefits because of their inability to stay on top of new developments in the field. Usually, they're busy enough maintaining their programs, let alone continuing to improve them. Plus, the weight of tradition doesn't allow for much change, nor does the lack of resources and equipment.

Inadequate resources and equipment, however, are no longer a sufficient excuse to short-change the strength and conditioning needs of football players. Weight training and general conditioning programs don't require sophisticated equipment or facilities, just the right kinds of activities at the right times. The development of a top-notch football player, including his strength and conditioning, requires a series of well-conceived activities and player self-discipline much more than mirrored walls and chrome-covered machines.

Consider, for example, the four basic characteristics of any effective conditioning program: strength training, flexibility, cardiovascular efficiency, and proper nutrition. The absence of any one characteristic in the school's conditioning program can seriously compromise the effectiveness of the other three. We learned that lesson only too well a few years ago. Our strength training program was meeting only a part of the conditioning needs of our players.

The players were working hard enough; don't get me wrong. And they were physically very strong. Few of our opponents could muscle with us up front—except late in the fourth quarter. The muscle mass so essential to good performance in the line provoked oxygen demands in many of the players that literally exhausted them in the fourth quarter of several games. We couldn't help but observe how tired they were.

Our response? More wind sprints on Monday and Tuesday. However, several players still ran out of gas late in the game. So we went in search of alternative solutions, and we discovered that wind sprints don't necessarily meet the aerobic needs of athletes. They improve speed and running efficiency, but the term wind sprint relates much more to "sprint" than it does to "wind."

Our new response was to have the entire team run laps around the field at a pace that was within the aerobic range of most of the players. The few who lagged behind inevitably found their own aerobic ranges and began to show signs of improvement. A few of them even caught up with the group in a few weeks. We also required them to jog during the summer and in the off-season when they weren't involved in another sport. When most of them began showing up for the first day of practice aerobically fit, we began to combine wind sprints and laps. The combination works very well. It works well because the wind sprints develop explosive energy and a tolerance for the lactic acid that causes muscle fatigue following strenuous exertion, and the laps develop the cardiovascular endurance that football players require late in the game. That's why a combination of aerobic and anaerobic exercise is so important for football players. We'll discuss the specifics of such exercises later in the section.

Another example? Consider this combination—the relationship among water, flexibility, and muscle strength. Every so often we run into the athlete who is wound so tight he snaps muscle fiber like worn-out rubber bands. His willingness to pump iron strengthens and hardens his muscles, but his failure to maintain flexibility results in injuries that compromise all his hard work with the weights. Add to this problem the failure to drink enough water to prevent muscle cramping, and you have a young man who has real problems on hot days or after rigorous exertion. Then add the relatively common practice of someone giving this athlete salt tablets when he starts to cramp up, and his problems complicate even further. Any water in his body will be trying to get to his stomach, where the salt is, instead of to his muscles, where he needs it.

Good conditioning, therefore, requires a range of activities that provide for all four components: muscle strength, proper nutrition, flexibility, and cardiovascular efficiency, including both aerobic and anaerobic activity. Such is the focus of this chapter. We will look at each of the four components as they relate to in-season and out-of-season activities.

══ OUT-OF-SEASON WEIGHT TRAINING AND CONDITIONING ══

The goal of every football player during the off-season is to get bigger and stronger. It's that simple. Players want to increase body mass while they strengthen skeletal and cardiovascular muscles. All it requires is the knowledge of what to do and the self-discipline to do it. Football players can develop all kinds of self-discipline when they have a real handle on what's expected of them. When left to their own devices, they forget a day now and then. When the workout regimen is outlined specifically and program expectations are clear, players are more motivated to get the job done. That's why it's wise to provide handouts to the entire team whenever possible. The chapter will provide several.

- Nutrition—We already have dispelled a few myths involving candy bars/quick energy and salt pills/water retention. Let's dispel a few more. What about the idea that water consumption during exercise/practice upsets the stomach? Or that more protein develops bigger muscles?

  Well, not only does a reasonable amount of water during exercise not upset the stomach, it is potentially harmful not to drink water. Athletes should consume as much as a half cup of water every 10 to 15 minutes during exercise to replace body fluids. In fact, it's wise for coaches and athletes alike to remember the word CUBS regarding water during exercise.

  "C"—cells. The body's cells require water to do their job.

  "U"—urine. Water consumption stimulates the urination that eliminates toxicity from the body.

  "B"—blood. Water increases the volume of blood in the body, which in turn carries more oxygen to the brain and muscles.

  "S"—sweat. Water consumption stimulates perspiration, which is the body's cooling mechanism.

  Protein and muscle? Excess protein, like other excess nutrients, is stored by the body as fat. A well-balanced diet will provide appropriate levels of protein and other nutrients to develop muscle. The four food groups (milk, meat, fruit, vegetables and grain) will provide all the nutrients football players need to get stronger. Most players require only a half gram of protein for each pound of body weight. Sufficient amounts of hamburger and pork chops daily, for example, combined with an occasional egg, orange juice, fruits and vegetables, milk and ice cream, will supply adequate protein for the development of muscle. Players should be encouraged to see their family doctors for a diet that meets their specific nutritional and health needs.

- Daily Diet—As with pre-game meals, football players, especially early in the season during double sessions, require diets high in carbohydrates. They must continue to resupply muscles with the glycogens required for strenuous exercise. The football player who fails to replenish such reserves compromises natural talent—as well as all those hours he spent with the weights. Again, however, it's always wise to encourage players to discuss their unique nutritional needs with the family doctor.

- Flexibility—Football players generally fail to understand the importance of good flexibility, probably because guys like me don't remind them often enough. And I should know better. I have more indentations on my hamstrings from pulls and tears than Wyatt Earp had notches on his gun. Just a few more minutes of stretching before exercise and competition would have eliminated a lot of pain for me and increased my playing time by several quarters.

It also would have made me faster and quicker. To minimize injury, therefore, and to maximize physical potential, coaches should emphasize a regular program of stretching activities for every player on the team, particularly before and after rigorous exercise—and sometimes during. A handout to be used during the off-season is important if players are to integrate stretching activities into their workout schedules. See figures 9–1, 9–2, 9–3, and 9–4 for the basic principles of stretching and illustrations of selected activities. Reproduce them for distribution to your team.

STRENGTH TRAINING

Every football player should be familiar with the three basic principles necessary for strength building.

- Specificity—Refers to the specific muscle to be developed. Work on biceps, for example, might involve barbell curls, dumbbell curls on an incline, chin ups, reverse curls, concentration curls, or any of several other exercises with dumbbells or on a machine that concentrates on that specific muscle. Obviously, bicep strength is critical for ball carriers but also is important for all positions. For that matter, it's hard to think of one muscle or one muscle group that isn't important to football players. The range of exercises, therefore, should be comprehensive enough to provide a broad workout but specific enough to provide work on the muscles which are most important for certain positions on the team.

- Overload—Refers to the muscle working harder than normal to become stronger. Players don't have to be rocket scientists to understand this principle, but they do need a few guidelines to do it correctly. See figure 9–5 for a reproducible. Unncessary strain during a weightlifting workout can damage muscles. That's where the final principle comes in.

- Progression—Refers to a gradual increase in the work load. If an athlete, for example, is working on his biceps (specificity), he should work with a

Good flexibility will provide you a full range of motion in most everything you do in football, whether it involves throwing the ball or running with it. Good flexibility enables you to perform with less energy and reduces injuries. Recognize, therefore, that stretching exercises should become an important element in your off-season *and* in-season conditioning program. Read each of the following basic principles of stretching, study the diagrams, and perform them regularly.

BASIC PRINCIPLES

1. Stretch for comfort, *not pain*. Don't strain when stretching.

2. Think about how good the muscle feels when it stretches.

3. Progressively stretch the muscle more and more, with *time* and with *no* pain.

4. Stretch *without* bouncing. Such ballistic stretching can cause injury and may actually tighten the muscle.

5. Always stretch the tight side of a muscle first.

6. Stretch before and *after* each workout. As a matter of fact, stretch any time of the day. It will relax you and will make each stretching episode easier.

7. Breathe slowly and normally while stretching. There is no reason to hold your breath.

8. Remember that stretching is a critical part of any conditioning program, as important as weight training and good nutrition. Do it regularly.

FIGURE 9–1

191

BENT
LEGS

STRAIGHT
LEGS

FIGURE 9–2

192

FIGURE 9–3

193

FIGURE 9–4

194

Weight training is another important element in your off-season conditioning program. Obviously, the bigger and stronger you are when you return next fall, the greater the contribution you will make to the team. Follow these three principles when designing your particular workout schedule. They will enable you to maximize your strength gains without risking injury.

1. *Specificity*—This refers to the specific muscle you plan to develop. You might work on your biceps, for example, by doing chin ups, curls with your back against the wall, cheat curls, incline curls, concentration curls, or any of the others we have discussed during workout sessions.

2. *Overload*—This refers to working the muscle more than normal. Arm curls on the attached Football Off-Season chart, for example, indicate a weight of 100 pounds repeated 10 times. Obviously, you will adjust the amount of weight to reflect your current bicep strength. It might be 60 pounds 10 times, or it might be 120. The point is, you should work with an overload that you can repeat 10 times.

3. *Progression*—As the overload becomes easier, increase the amount of weight—*minimally*. Don't overdo it so that you strain yourself and risk possible injury. Continue to increase the amount of weight as the specific muscle becomes stronger.

Remember as you continue with your strength workout that flexibility continues to be important and that proper nutrition will assist you with the proper strength gains. It's also important to work a specific muscle only every other day to provide time for the muscle to grow. Don't work the same muscle every day. Talk to one of the coaches if you have specific questions.

FIGURE 9–5

weight that he can curl correctly 10 times in three sets (overload). As the sets become easier, he might add five pounds (progression) to maximize his workout, in essence to maintain the overload. The continuation of these three principles, three times a week, working specific muscles on alternate days to provide for growth inbetween workouts, will result in noticeable gains within a four-to-five-week period.

Some schools provide a general program for their players to follow during the off-season, such as the one in figure 9–6. Obviously, the program is modified by the player to reflect his specific needs, but it continues to accommodate the principles of specificity, overload, and progression. In addition, many schools strongly encourage football players to attend summer conditioning programs. These programs are ideal because they provide additional motivation, individual attention, and the team and family concepts that are so important to football programs.

- Cardiovascular Efficiency—During the off-season, players should work on both aerobic and anaerobic activities that will give them the zip they need when the season starts. Heredity already has given them the combinations of fast-twitch and slow-twitch fibers in their muscles that in large part determines the position on the team they will play successfully. Proper exercise during the off-season, however, can improve both fibers. It's important, therefore, to emphasize a training program for football players that combines sprinting (fast-twitch fibers) with distance work (slow-twitch fibers) that accommodates both their aerobic and their anaerobic needs.

Figure 9–7 explains the principles underlying the training program and refers to a second handout (figure 9–8) you should develop to meet the age appropriate needs of your players. Figure 9–8 explains one college's interval training during weeks one, eight, and 14 of the summer. The distances and frequencies are adjusted each week to provide for both aerobic and anaerobic exercises. This information is designed to just get you started. Do a little research on the subject to develop a program that is appropriate for your players.

The important thing to keep in mind during the off-season conditioning program is that your players will be on their own most of the time. You may have a summer program for them at school, but most of them will continue to lift and run at other times of the day—at least we hope they do. To give them the boost they need, provide some handouts that prescribe the specifics of their at-home exercise programs. The mere expectation of such conditioning without the proper direction ultimately excludes all but the most motivated athletes. This chapter will help get them all motivated.

IN-SEASON WEIGHT TRAINING AND CONDITIONING

The goal of every football player during the in-season is to win football games. He makes his contribution when he performs to the best of his ability. He performs to the best of his ability when he maintains an optimal level of good physical

Football Off-season

MONDAY   1) Bench—cycle
          2) Overhead jerk 3 × 5
          3) Dumbell military 3 × 6–8
          4) Dips (weighted) 3 × 6–8
          5) Abs

TUES-   1) Squat—cycle
DAY   2) Back 3 × 6–8
          3) Biceps
          4) Neck
          5) Abs

THURS-   1) Incline—cycle
DAY   2) Close grip bench 3 × 8 @ 70%
          3) Power cleans 3 × 5
          4) Shrugs 3 × 8
          5) Triceps 3 × 6–8
          6) Abs

FRIDAY   1) Leg extension 2 × 8–10
          2) Leg curl 2 × 8–10
          3) Back 3 × 6–8
          4) Biceps 3 × 6–8
          5) Neck and Abs

BACK LISTS
Front Chins
Behind Neck Chins
Wide Grip Lat Pulls
Close Grip Lat Pulls
Incline Rows
Seated Rows
Bent Over Rows
Reverse Grip Chins
One Arm Cable Rows
One Arm Dumbell Rows

TRICEP LIFTS
Tricep Pressdown
Lying Cable Extensions
Overhead Cable Extensions
Overhead Tricep Press
Lying Tricep Press
Incline Tricep Press

BICEP LIFTS
Barbell Curls
Reverse Curls
Preacher Curls
Cable Curls
Concentration Curls
Incline Dumbell Curls

FIGURE 9–6

Football players who want to perform to the best of their ability throughout the entire game, particularly in the fourth quarter, have to be in good cardiovascular condition. You may be the strongest player on the field, but if your heart and lungs aren't strong enough to pump oxygen into your muscles at key times in the game, you won't get the job done! The following information, therefore, is very important for you. Read it carefully and be sure to use it during the off-season, especially in the summer, to keep you in good physical condition. If you have questions, be sure to talk to one of the coaches.

WORKLOAD

First of all, consult your family doctor before you begin any conditioning program. You will want to provide for special needs as he or she identifies them. Once you get his or her OK, follow these guidelines:

When running distances to improve your aerobic needs (the endurance you require in the fourth quarter), be sure to maintain a pace that is within your target range. Here's how you do it.

Take the number 220, subtract your age, then subtract your resting pulse (your heart rate when you first wake up in the morning), multiply the number you have left by .70 up to .85, depending upon how hard you want to work, and finally add your resting pulse. The number you have left is the number of beats per minute you should maintain to get a good aerobic workout. Look at the following sample:

220 − 17 (your age) − 65 (your resting heart rate) × .70 (a good workout for any 17-year-old) + 65 (your resting heart rate) = 161.6. This number equals the number of beats per minute you want your heart to achieve during a 20 to 30-minute run.

The best way to determine this heart rate is to stop periodically and place two fingers across the underneath part of your wrist. Count the beats within a 10-second period of time. Then use the following chart to determine your heart beat within a minute.

Number of beats within ten seconds	Beats per minute
22	132
23	138
24	146
25	152
26	158
27	164

Again, be sure to see your doctor to secure approval for your target heart range, then refer to the attached program for specific distances to run.

FIGURE 9–7

INSTRUCTIONS WITH EACH SET

When engaged in interval training, football players must exercise and rest at appropriate times to maximize the benefits of the program. For that reason, they must be instructed to follow certain directions in their running program:

Heart Rate—Any time players see this instruction, they should check their pulse rate to make sure it returns to 120 before running again.

1 to 3—This term instructs them to rest for three times the amount of time it took them to run the prescribed distance. For example, if the player ran the 440 in one and a half minutes, he should wait three minutes and ten seconds before he runs the next 440.

1 to 2—This instruction tells the player to wait twice as long as it took him to run the prescribed distance before running again.

SAMPLE WEEKS

Week One

Day 1
Set One 1 × 880 (Heart Rate)
Set Two 2 × 220 (1 to 3)
Set Three 6 × 110 (1 to 3)

Day 2
Set One 1 × 880 (Heart Rate)
Set Two 2 × (440 (1 to 2)
Set Three 6 × 55 (1 to 3)

Day 3
Set One 1 × 880 (Heart Rate)
Set Two 6 × 55 (1 to 3)
Set Three 6 × 110 (1 to 3)

Week Eight

Day 1
Set One 1 × 880 (1 to 1)
Set Two 4 × 220 (1 to 2)

Day 2
Set One 4 × 440 (1 to 2)

Day 3
Set One 4 × 880 (1 to 1)

Day 4
Set One 1 × 3500

WEEK FOURTEEN

Day 1
Set One 8 × 110 (1 to 3)
Set Two 10 × 55 (1 to 3)
Set Three 10 × 55 (1 to 3)

Day 2
Set One 10 × 55 (1 to 3)
Set Two 10 × 55 (1 to 3)

Day 3
Set One 8 × 110 (1 to 3)
Set Two 10 × 55 (1 to 3)

Again, these are sample programs. Coaches are encouraged to research the topic of interval running and to develop specific programs which are appropriate for their players.

FIGURE 9–8

199

There's nothing strange about being tired during two-a-days. If you're not tired, you're not working hard enough! But you can help yourself with the proper diet. Recognize that you draw on energy stored in your muscles as carbohydrates. During one day of double sessions, you can use up all your carbohydrates. If you don't replace them that night, you won't have any for the next day's practices. So read the following information and use it during double sessions as well as when the season gets underway. We will be providing similar information later regarding your pre-game meal.

FOODS HIGH IN CARBOHYDRATES

Be sure to eat a lot of cereals, breads, pasta, muffins, pancakes, rolls, and other grain products. Fruits and vegetables are also high in carbohydrates. Yogurt, milkshakes, milk, cocoa, and ice cream also have lots of carbohydrates. Cakes, pies, cookies, soft drinks, and other sugary foods are high in carbohydrates but low in most other nutrients. Be sure, therefore, to use these only as supplements to your diet.

OTHER FOODS

Recognize that foods from the Meat Group are relatively low in carbohydrates, but they are important in your overall diet. So eat a variety of foods from each of the four food groups (Milk, Meat, Fruit/Vegetable, and Grain) in order to provide all the nutrients your body requires.

WATER

Drink a lot of water! It will prevent cramping and will maintain the flow of oxygen to your brain and muscles. Research indicates that the loss of even 5% of your body fluids can result in a significant loss of your mental capacity. Some of us can't afford that! So drink a lot of water. We'll take care of your water needs on the field; you take care of them at home.

A REMINDER

Be sure to see your family doctor regarding your unique nutritional needs or to identify the best possible diet for you while you are participating in football. This handout is designed to provide general information to get you started.

FIGURE 9–9

condition. Our job is to make sure he remains in good shape. In addition to everything else we do regarding motivation, discipline, scouting, game plan, record keeping, budgeting, and heaven knows what else, we have to oversee each of the components of a good conditioning program during the in-season. No one said that coaching was easy.

- Nutrition—Early in the season, especially when the team may be tackling the terrors of Hell Week, players' nutritional needs are pronounced. Two-a-days tend to sap the energy of even those few who ran their way through the summer. That's why it's a good idea to give players some information about their nutritional needs at the very first meeting. The proper diet in relation to the right attitude will do wonders for their energy levels when they feel as if the sun is sitting on their shoulders. See figure 9–9 for a reproducible.

Section eight provides a reproducible for the team regarding pre-game meals. Much of the information is similar—which is OK. It bears repeating, particularly as the lack of water is potentially very harmful to players' health.

- Strength Training—Obviously, in-season activities don't provide as much time for weightlifting as off-season. That's not to say that we can't find a few extra minutes during the day at least to maintain present strength levels. Some schools schedule weightlifting activities before school and provide individual computerized programs for each player to chart strength gains and to increase work loads.

See figure 9–10 for a sample program. Notice the progressive weight increases as well as the relatively few exercises required of this particular athlete. The physical demands on football players during the in-season preclude any possibility of rigorous weight training programs. Some time, however, must be devoted to strength maintenance and/or improvement. Individualized programs such as the one illustrated provide the best process. There are several which are commercially available or which can be secured from a local university program.

If computers are as scarce to you as 4.3 forties, get your players to lift the good, old-fashioned way. Get five or six sets of barbells exclusively for the practice field. Position them in as many stations in the end zone and have the team lift every other day after practice. This kind of activity is particularly good during double sessions. The team can run sprints or distances after the first practice and lift after the second. A simple routine of curls, French curls, butterflies, military presses, behind-the-head presses, and upright rowing will require only 15 to 20 minutes of practice time and will maintain or enhance strength.

In-Season Weight Training

PLAYER X   Week 2

EXERCISE DAY AND NAME	SET 1 WT × REP	SET 2 WT × REP	SET 3 WT × REP	SET 4 WT × REP	SET 5 WT × REP	SET 6 WT × REP
Monday						
HANG CLEANS	135 × 5	155 × 5	175 × 5			
SQUAT	330 × 8	355 × 8	380 × 8	405 × 8		
Tuesday						
PUSH JERKS	135 × 5	155 × 5	170 × 5	170 × 5	170 × 5	
BENCH PRESS	155 × 5	180 × 5	210 × 3	210 × 3	210 × 3	
INCLINE PRESS	150 × 5	170 × 5	190 × 5	190 × 5	190 × 5	
Thursday						
HANG CLEANS	125 × 5	145 × 5	165 × 5			
SQUAT	315 × 8	340 × 8	360 × 8	385 × 8		
Friday						
PUSH JERKS	125 × 5	145 × 5	160 × 5	160 × 5	160 × 5	
BENCH PRESS	165 × 5	190 × 5	220 × 3	220 × 3	220 × 3	
INCLINE PRESS	140 × 5	160 × 5	180 × 5	180 × 5	180 × 5	

FIGURE 9–10

- Cardiovascular conditioning—Some teams substitute distance running before practice for daily programs of calisthenics. Fifteen minutes of calisthenics before practice is a tough habit to break for most football teams—until coaches begin to realize the conditioning advantages of periodic distance running. The same 15 minutes allows most of the players to run at least a mile and a half at a pace which is humane for most athletes and well within their aerobic ranges. Follow it with five minutes of stretching to promote flexibility and to restore normal pulse rates, and regular practice can begin. A mile and half before practice at a 10-minute mile pace will barely break a sweat for most players, and it will provide the aerobic activity they need to enhance their endurance late in the game. Occasional wind sprints after practice will meet their anaerobic requirements; periodic distance running, before or after practice, will keep them in good cardiovascular condition, an aspect of general conditioning for football players that has been overlooked by many programs.

If we provide a comprehensive program of off-season conditioning for our teams and most players report on the first day in good shape, the cardiovascular component of the in-season conditioning program need only maintain their current levels of fitness. One way to assure players' compliance with the off-season program is to borrow a page from the Bob Devaney Book of Effective Expectations.

I wasn't the greatest conditioner during my playing days, particularly in college. I'm old enough now to let the truth be known. But I always showed in shape for Coach Devaney's first practice at Nebraska, a little affair that required all the backs to run a mile in full pads in under six minutes.[1] If we took longer than six minutes, we knew we would receive additional and generous portions of wind sprints after every practice for the first week in the fall. It was sufficient inducement to keep us in shape during the off-season.

Similar "traditions" will work for you. If the team returns in the fall in good cardiovascular condition, our jobs are much easier. We worry less about fourth-quarter endurance, and we can devote more practice time to fundamentals and strategy. It's important to realize, however, that even then, some maintenance activities are required to keep the team in peak condition.

- Flexibility—This aspect of general conditioning is absolutely critical during the in-season. Some teams lose more players to non-contact muscle pulls and tears than to contact injuries. In their mad dash to bulk up, many players forget to loosen up. The result is needless injury for players who are wound the tightest, often the team's strongest players, the ones we need the most.

---

[1] I talked to Coach Devaney about this recently. He is still as helpful as ever and as deserving of respect.

Effective stretching activities before and during practice are essential if players are to maintain the needed flexibility to avoid such injuries. Eight to ten of the stretching exercises illustrated in figures 9–2, 9–3, and 9–4 that increase the flexibility of the major muscle groups will not require a lot of time, usually only 10 to 12 minutes, but they will help prevent costly injuries to team members.

In addition, coaches are well-advised to tell their players to inform them any time they feel tightness or cramping in a muscle. It may lead to potential injury. Obviously, we don't want to hear from every player with a bruise on his forearm, but we do want to know if the calf or hamstring is tightening up to the point of restricting movement. Five minutes out of the scrimmage to drink a little water and to stretch out the muscles can prevent a lot of lost time in the future.

Smart players realize as well that they can stretch out their muscles anywhere and at any time. Time outs or even moments between plays allow the 15 seconds required to stretch out a hamstring or a groin. Players will develop these habits only if they are encouraged to do so. If coaches tell them to stretch in practice, players will start doing it in games.

LET'S WRAP IT UP

Fortunately, the real world doesn't have to fit the stereotypes we create. All football players, even the linemen, don't have to be the Goliaths that everybody thinks they are. My experiences in high school and college included a lot of players who spent their evenings drinking milkshakes to put on pounds but who played a whole lot of football—and played it well.

Every football coach dreams of the young giant with a heart so big it fills his chest cavity. Sometimes we get him; usually we don't. So we go with the players who compensate for their lack of size by being in excellent physical condition. Lynn "Pappy" Waldorf, one of the game's great coaches, put it this way: "I was a college coach for 33 years, and I never believed a boy was too small. If he could play, I'd find a spot for him. You can't have too many good players. Good players win games for you, not big players."

Good players are invariably in excellent physical condition. During my 30 years of coaching, I've worked with a good many players who didn't hit *harder* than their opponents, just *longer*. "Longer" wins more games.

SECTION 10

Athletic Scholarships

Voltaire said it: "In a long dispute—both parties are wrong." What better way to explain the misunderstandings and the vested interests that define intercollegiate athletics today? The dispute certainly has been long. An official of Princeton University once questioned ". . . whether evils may not arise from sports in no way under control of the college authorities." The official? James McCash, president of Princeton in 1874. He made the comment only five years after history's very first American college football game.

Are all the parties in the dispute wrong? Maybe not, but one wonders why reasonable and enduring solutions have not been forthcoming from the people responsible for college sports. President McCash sounded his warning well over 100 years ago. Others have written and spoken volumes since then, and many of the abuses have continued, fundamentally unchanged, to the present day.

High school coaches, athletes and the parents of athletes, therefore, must be aware of what others are seeking from high school and college athletics. Such is the purpose of this section: to look at the history of player eligibility in order to better understand current trends and decisions, to re-explore the needs of athletes, to identify and discuss parental expectations, and to present reasonable approaches for coaches and other school personnel.

The history of player eligibility has been influenced profoundly by money and the pressure to win. This may be no startling revelation to you. Exactly how it happened, however, is revealing and an important piece of knowledge for coaches at all levels. Following, then, is a brief history of player eligibility.

A LOOK AT THE PAST

Long before the turn of the century, when Harvard, Yale, and Princeton were writing the first few pages of American football history, Harvard president Charles Eliot argued for the elimination of freshman eligibility. Prompted by the rising number of "ringers," itinerant athletes who attended school only during the football season, Eliot argued for students to prove themselves academically before being allowed to represent the school on the football field. Fourteen years later, in 1903, Harvard made freshmen ineligible.

The Big Ten preceded Harvard by eight years when in 1895 it established itself as a conference that prohibited freshman eligibility. Amos Alonzo Stagg, then the head coach of the University of Chicago, a charter member of the Big Ten, wrote: "One year's residence and a full year's work were required of all candidates for teams, with playing limited to three years. . . . The good old days were gone, and none mourned them long. Football's greatest growth dates from that housecleaning." (Stagg, 1924)

Though Stagg played end for the University of Chicago while on the payroll during his first two coaching seasons, he became one of the game's most outspoken proponents of amateurism and led the way for several changes that influenced player eligibility. Freshmen remained ineligible in many major schools until 1968, when the NCAA declared freshmen eligible in every sport except football and basketball. Then, in 1972, freshmen became eligible in all sports.

The decision was made to save money by eliminating separate freshmen squads and enabling smaller schools to be more competitive by using freshmen. The issue of athletic parity asserted itself and ultimately led to the decision in 1973 to require of athletes a 2.0 grade point average in all high school subjects to be eligible for an athletic scholarship.

Prior to that decision, prospective college athletes had to be able to predict a 1.6 grade point average in college in order to receive a grant-in-aid. The prediction was based on a set of tables that computed class rank and admissions test results. The predicted 1.6 was tougher for many high school athletes to achieve than the expectation of Bylaw 14.3 (Prop 48). By comparison, any high school athlete achieving a 700 on the SAT, in order to predict a 1.6 in college, would have had to earn a 3.0 grade point average in high school. Bylaw 14.3 requires only a 2.0 in 11 core academic units.

The elimination of the predicted 1.6 GPA in college struck a blow for athletic parity among NCAA teams because it made college admission easier and enlarged the pool of eligible high school athletes. Freshman eligibility gave athletic parity a further boost by allowing freshmen to compete immediately on the varsity level. As athletic parity improved, however, academic integrity seemed to suffer.

Concerned about the image of intercollegiate athletics, a group of college presidents united under the banner of The American Council on Education (ACE). Under the leadership of President Jack Peltason, ACE introduced Proposition 48 at the 1983 NCAA Convention in San Diego and held its ground until Prop. 48 ultimately became written into the NCAA bylaws.

══════════════ A LOOK AT THE PRESENT ══════════════

One of the most obvious results of Bylaw 14.3 is the need for football coaches at all levels to make its provisions known to their athletes. That high schools meet periodically with athletes and their parents to highlight the requirements of

Bylaw 14.3 is essential. As important, coaches must acknowledge several realities the NCAA conventions have not addressed over the years: money, watered-down courses, winning, TV contracts, recruiting violations, or pressures on coaches to produce.

Fortunately, a good many college coaches play within the rules and have their players' best interests at heart. Pressures to produce, however, provoke a different reaction in other college coaches. Many of them see their athletes only as so many means to an end. They are the ones who provoke all the media hype and cause parents and high school coaches so much concern during the recruiting process.

As mentioned in an earlier chapter, ongoing communication between parents and coaches is critical if the athlete is to make college decisions which are in his best interests. Much of the early communication should focus on getting parent/ student expectations in line with the realities of athletic scholarships. Many high schools are engaging parents in fall meetings designed to address this issue.

ATHLETIC SCHOLARSHIPS: FACT AND FANTASY

How many high school athletes and their parents realize that major universities mail as many as 5,000 to 8,000 questionnaires each year to prospective high school football players? How many of these families realize that NCAA rules allow each school only 20–25 scholarships? In essence, a high school football player who receives a questionnaire from a college expressing interest in him as a player may encounter odds as high as 300 to 1 *against* his receiving a scholarship. How high are the odds if a player receives no questionnaires?

These are the kinds of statistics parents must recognize if they are to look at intercollegiate football realistically. The best way to introduce parents to such statistics is in a fall meeting with a coach, a representative of the counseling department, and the athletic director—maybe even the college consultant, if the school has one. The purpose of such a meeting is to review the expectations of the NCAA, to re-emphasize the importance of academics, and to discuss the realities of athletic scholarships.

My frequent appearances in high schools to discuss these topics have taught me that the best way to get the attention of parents is with a brief quiz. A copy of the one I use is provided in figure 10–1. See how many of the questions you can answer correctly. The answers are at the bottom of the next page. Several of the answers are eye-openers; they invariably provoke worthwhile discussions.

For example, statistics indicate that 106 major colleges and universities (NCAA Division I schools) award approximately 2,600 football scholarships each year but mail just under a half *million* questionnaires. Of the approximately 265,000 high school seniors who play football each year, therefore, only 1% will receive a scholarship to play for a major university. Another 2% will receive scholarships—most always partial scholarships—to play for Division I and Division II schools.

WHAT DO YOU KNOW ABOUT SPORTS IN AMERICA?
TAKE A MOMENT TO TEST YOUR KNOWLEDGE

Place a check mark before the best answer. We'll discuss the results in a minute.

1. An approximate total of 876. ... This number represents the Division I basketball scholarships awarded yearly in

   ___ A. Illinois ___ B. New York ___ C. The Midwest ___ D. The nation

   ___ E. None of the above

2. If a student receives a questionnaire from a school like Notre Dame or Michigan expressing an interest in him as a football player, what are his odds of eventually receiving a scholarship to that school?

   ___ A. 2 to 1 ___ B. 5 to 1 ___ C. 10 to 1 ___ D. 20 to 1 ___ E. 200 to 1

3. Which of the following involves more athletes in football or basketball than any of the other three?

   ___ A. Division I ___ B. Division Iaa ___ C. Division II ___ D. Division III

4. What percentage of high school athletes eventually receive a scholarship to play basketball in college?

   ___ A. 1 ½ ___ B. 5 ¼ ___ C. 10 ½ ___ D. 13

5. Approximately what percentage of NFL players failed to graduate from college?

   ___ A. 15 ___ B. 30 ___ C. 50 ___ D. 66 ___ E. 90

6. Approximately what percentage of high school senior basketball players eventually play professionally?

   ___ A. 4 ___ B. 4 tenths of one per cent ___ C. 4 one hundredths of one per cent

   ___ D. 4 one thousandths of one per cent ___ E. 4 in every 1,000

7. How many major college basketball programs (Division I) are there in the United States?

   ___ A. 103 ___ B. 152 ___ C. 205 ___ D. 292 ___ E. 376

8. Each of these schools annually awards the following number of athletic scholarships to *incoming freshmen*:

   ___ A. one ___ B. two or three ___ C. five

   ___ D. seven ___ E. nine or ten

9. How many major college football programs (Division I) are there in the United States? Approximately

   ___ A. 106 ___ B. 127 ___ C. 151 ___ D. 178 ___ E. 231

10. Approximately how many athletic scholarships does each school award annually to *incoming freshmen*?

    ___ A. 20 ___ B. 25 ___ C. 30 ___ D. 35 ___ E. 40

FIGURE 10–1

208

Most schools are fortunate, therefore, if one of their seniors—in every two- or three-year period of time—receives a scholarship to play in college. Parents who watch Junior score the winning touchdown against a cross-town rival and celebrate his All-Conference honors at the end of the season deserve the vision of watching him punch one across in the Rose Bowl. Expecting it, however, is a different thing.

Over 100,000 high school players in this country earn All-Conference honors every year, and an approximate maximum of 7,000 scholarships, mostly partials, are available to the seniors within that number. Parents and athletes must understand such statistics in order to plan realistically for the future and to impose reasonable expectations upon you and me when we work with their kids.

(Answers to quiz: 1-D, 2-E, 3-D, 4-A, 5-D, 6-D, 7-D, 8-B, 9-A, 10-B.)

WHAT ABOUT THE PROS?

Unfortunately, to many disadvantaged high school athletes, professional football is the only road to a better life. Such a misconception is a double-edged sword. It creates a dream that is not only unrealizable but deceptive. It obscures the importance of an education and the broad opportunities that it has to offer for the future. A quick look at the facts can help turn a few heads in the right direction.

Professional football makes room each year for approximately 215 rookies. When we take the time to compare that number to the 265,000 high school seniors who play the game each year, we realize that only 7/1,000th of 1 percent will play professional football. Even if these few players beat the odds and join a pro team, they will realize an average career of only three years.

In the face of such facts, even the most intransigent student thinks twice about the value of a classroom education. Our job is to share such information and whenever possible reaffirm the value of an education. A previous chapter emphasized the power that high school coaches have to curb abuses on the college level. We also have the power to influence players to study. Meetings with their parents in the early fall will help.

MORE ABOUT THE MEETING

Once you have made your pitch for academics and have shared relevant statistics regarding scholarships and the unlikelihood of a professional career, you should emphasize the importance of the Coalition (see figure 10–2) and discuss a few of the rules and regulations that determine eligibility to participate in college athletics.

═══════════════════ **THE COALITION** ═══════════════════

1. The student-athlete
2. The parents
3. The counselor
4. The coach
5. The Athletic Director

. . . working together to assure a positive educational experience for all athletes at all levels.

FIGURE 10–2

- A Little About Bylaw 14.3—Few athletes and their parents understand the provisions of the NCAA's Bylaw 14.3. Most NCAA regulations are foreign to players and their families, even the regulations that receive so much media attention. Athletes and their parents need to listen to an explanation and take something home for future reference. See figure 10–3 for a reproducible. It will provide the reminder that most people need to plan ahead, and it will preempt those few who get into trouble and then claim, "no one ever told me."

Even if such people fail to attend your meeting, the fact that you held it and that you distributed valuable information will avoid a lot of trouble for you if one of your players fails to meet the requirements of Bylaw 14.3. Another good idea is to make a tape available in the athletic department, the guidance office, and the library which explains the ins and outs of college eligibility and the recruiting process.

You may want to make such a tape yourself, or purchase one. I developed one recently that contains all the NCAA requirements, addresses the issue of academics and athletics, discusses many of the statistics mentioned in this section, provides exciting shots of NCAA competitions and interviews with athletes and coaches, and explores the recruiting process and the kinds of questions that should be asked before a young man makes a decision to attend and play for a certain school.[1]

---

[1]Copies can be secured by writing Department R 62, College Board Publications, Box 886, New York, New York 10101–0886, or calling 1-800-323-7155. The cost is $49.95.

SO YOU WANT TO PLAY IN COLLEGE?
WORK IN HIGH SCHOOL!

To be eligible to practice, play, and receive athletic aid at a Division I institution as of the fall of 1995, student athletes must:

1. Earn a grade point average of 2.5 on a 4.0 scale and score a minimum combined score of 700 on the SAT or a minimum composite of 17 on the ACT.

   OR

   Earn a grade point average of 2.0 on a 4.0 scale and score a minimum combined score of 900 on the SAT or a minimum composite of 21 on the ACT.

2. The NCAA has developed a sliding scale to accommodate variations in grade point average and SAT and ACT scores. See your coach or counselor for additional information.

3. Complete a core curriculum of at least 13 academic units (full-year courses), including:

   —3 in English

   —2 in social studies

   —2 in math

   —2 in science (at least one lab course, if offered by your school)

   —2 more in any of the above or in computers, philosophy, or non-doctrinal religion.

   —As of 1995—2 more from among English, math, and natural or physical science.

NOTE: NCAA Division II schools will require the same 13 academic units but will not use a sliding scale. They will require a 2.0 grade point average on a 4.0 scale and a combined score of 700 on the SAT or a composite of 17 on the ACT. Contact your counselor or coach for additional information about NCAA Division III schools.

FIGURE 10–3

===================== **ADDITIONAL SPECIFICS** =====================

Figures 10–4, 10–5, and 10–6 provide additional specifics to complete the information for parents. They provide as much information about the requirements of regulatory organizations as parents and athletes need in order to plan their academic programs and to acknowledge the importance of good grades. Parents and athletes also enjoy the quotes from prominent names in sports. Several are provided as additional reproducibles in figures 10–7 and 10–8. The reproducible entitled "What Is (Was)?" in figure 10–7 provides quotes from prominent figures that date back as far as 1874 and history's first college football game between Rutgers and Princeton.

The game at that time really didn't resemble what you and I watch every fall, but it did begin to reflect some of the same problems and abuses that currently receive so much media attention. The purpose of these handouts is to indicate that many of our problems really aren't new and the solutions to some of them can be found in quotes that go back over 100 years ago!

The reproducible entitled "What Should Be" in figure 10–8 provide conflicting ideas about the current picture of intercollegiate athletics. They range from Stagg's quote about the abolishment of athletic scholarships to Denlinger's assertion that college athletes should be paid. The purpose of these quotes is to highlight the diversity of current opinion across the country and to underscore the difficulty in finding one best solution.

The message to be communicated to parents at this meeting, therefore, is that high school football coaches and other school personnel must work closely with athletes and their parents to maintain an educational focus throughout the athlete's playing career in high school and college. Too many people out there have their own interests in mind when it comes to football: winning, money, prestige. Your interests are consistent with the needs of your players; this meeting and the materials you provide prove it.

========= **MORE TO SHARE IN THE MEETING—OR ELSEWHERE** =========

More needs to be said about athletic scholarships. You might share this additional information in meetings with parents, in a weekly newsletter you share with the community, in a column you provide the local newspaper, in periodic press releases, or in any of several additional ways.

- NCAA Divisions—Remind parents that the NCAA consists of four divisions in football: I, Iaa, II, and III. Tell them that only Divisions I, Iaa, and II give scholarships and that such scholarships are often partials— granted for only one year but renewable. Most often they are renewed; on occasion they are not. The question of renewability often becomes an issue

1. A "unit" equals one full year of study, approximately 180 hours of instruction.

2. Courses taken after the eighth semester (correspondence, summer school, et al.) do not meet the core requirements of Division I schools. They *may* meet the requirements of Division II schools.

3. Certain eighth grade courses may satisfy core requirements if considered equivalent by the high school.

4. The GPA may be calculated based upon the student-athlete's 11 best grades (*22* best semester grades).

5. Repeated courses may be calculated only once, but the better grade may be used.

6. Correspondence courses may not be used to satisfy core requirements.

7. Pass/fail grades may not be used.

8. One-year courses that are spread over two years will be considered one course.

9. The principal of the high school decides what constitutes a core course, verified by the college.

10. Courses for LD and handicapped students have been approved by the NCAA Council. The NCAA should be contacted for additional information.

THE NCAA
6201 COLLEGE BLVD.
OVERLAND PARK, KANSAS 66211
913-339-1906

FIGURE 10–4

1. For Division I schools, minimum required scores must be achieved by July 1 prior to the first year of enrollment.

2. For Division II schools, the minimum required scores must be achieved prior to the first full-time enrollment.

3. Both divisions require that tests be taken under national testing conditions on a national testing date.

4. For the SAT, the highest subtest scores achieved on different test dates may be combined to achieve the 700.

5. For the ACT, the highest scores of the individual subtests achieved on different test dates may be combined to determine the highest composite score.

6. Non-standard administration of the ACT and/or SAT for learning disabled or handicapped students is possible—under specified conditions. See your counselor, coach, or AD for information.

FIGURE 10–5

ELIGILITY REQUIREMENTS FOR
THE NATIONAL ASSOCIATION OF
INTERCOLLEGIATE ATHLETICS (NAIA)

Student-athletes must meet two of the following three requirements:

1. Achieve an 18 on the ACT OR a 700 on the SAT

2. Earn an *overall* high school grade point average of 2.0 on a 4.0 scale.

3. Graduate in the top half of the class.

FIGURE 10–6

"You've got to cheat in recruiting to win. Competition is fierce."

Coach of Boston College
Bob Cousy

"It's a nice question whether evils may not arise from sports in no way under control of the college authorities."

President of Princeton/James McCash
1874

"Approximately 80% of all players in the NFL did not graduate from college."

Dr. Harry Edwards—1982

"Reality is where rumors of professional sports teams paying the bill for college athletes scholarships have become so common, they're hard to refute."

Blowing the Whistle on Intercollegiate Sports—
Bob Evans

"The evil in current football rests not on the hired men, but in academic lying and in the falsification of our standards as associations of scholars and of honest men."

President of Stanford
1905

"At a third of American colleges and unviersities with major men's basketball programs, fewer than one in five players ever graduate."

General Accounting Office
1989

"In 1988, 35.5 million spectators watched football games at 680 four-year colleges. According to a study by the College Football Association, $17.3 million were spent in one community solely from fans attending football games during the season."

Chicago Tribune/1989

"Most of the evils that have beset the game from time to time have been the direct result of student and alumni management, but the blame lies on the faculty doorstep."

Amos Alonzo Stagg
1927

FIGURE 10-7

"This is what college football should be: the most rewarding experience in a young man's life."

Bo Schembechler/1989

". . . the abolishment of the so-called 'athletic scholarship' indicates an awakening conscience to a much-needed reform."

Amos Alonzo Stagg/1927

"Some athletes generate ten to twenty times as much income as their scholarship is worth to a school. . . . Why not pay them their worth?"

Ken Denlinger/Athletes for Sale

"There is no valid reason why even the most worthy athlete should receive any consideration that is not available to the general body of undergraduates."

Carnegie Foundation Study/1929

"Millions of dollars just went to Michigan and Notre Dame last Saturday. It's a shame to think that the only ones who weren't paid were the players."

Amateur sports official/1989

"The basic purpose of education is not to provide a convenient springboard to lucrative contracts in the NFL or the NBA, but to teach people how to think . . . how to enable people to come into possession of all their powers."

Norman Cousins/1989

"The reasonable response to the apparently inevitable professionalization of big-time college sports clearly is to accept professionalism. Pay the athletes a decent salary and provide them with adequate fringe benefits. . . ."

Allen Guttmann/Amherst College/1988

"Play not for gain but for sport.
Who plays for more than he can lose with pleasure,
Stakes his heart."

Walter Camp/"Athletic Extravagance"/1885

FIGURE 10–8

during the recruiting process. This topic will be discussed at length in a future section.

Underscore the fact that Division III schools do not grant athletic scholarships. Some commercial organizations that find athletic scholarships for high school athletes will claim that Division III schools "find a way" to come up with money for players. Perhaps some do, but my experience has been that most of them play by the book, primarily because they have much more to offer than a few bucks.

- Selective Schools in Division III—First of all, consider the fact that more athletes participate in Division III football and basketball than in either of the other two divisions. Whereas Division I football involves some 13,000 athletes and Division II about 11,000, Division III football provides playing opportunities for over 17,000 athletes. It also provides opportunities for high school student-athletes to get into schools that normally might not accept them. This is an important piece of information, particularly for students and parents seeking admission to selective schools. Opportunism in intercollegiate athletics is a two-sided coin. Coaches sometimes use players, and players often use coaches—in reasonable and legitimate ways.

Coaches in all three NCAA divisions need good football players to win games. It's not surprising, therefore, that many of them seek minor concessions from the office of admissions for good athletes who also are good students, if not quite good enough to gain admission without football.

Intercollegiate athletics, therefore, involves some bad news and some good news for your football players and their parents. The bad news, which you share with them in the early fall meeting, is that scholarships are not as available as many of them believe. The good news is that hundreds of hard-working athletes who have invested themselves equally in classwork can use their abilities to gain admission to some of the nation's most selective schools.

Remind your parents and athletes that selective schools make no guarantees for such concessions, just as there are no guarantees for athletic scholarships to major universities. In fact, and this is a key point to be made with football players and their parents, the only guarantee available to all high school athletes is that participation in college sports is at best an uncertainty. What is certain is that high school football provides excitement and self-fulfillment in its own right. No more can be expected of it.

- Walking On—This brings up a related issue. Someone once called love "the tie that blinds." As true as it may be for couples, it's equally true for the love of football. Some high school players love the game so much and want to play it so fervently in a major college, they consider the prospect of "walking on" if a scholarship is not offered. Athletes and their parents must recognize several important characteristics about walking on.

Following are names selected randomly from a roster of football players. What do you notice about them, and what school do you think they represent?

Name	Position	Height	Weight
Rob _____	Running Back	6'4"	225
Brock _____	Running Back	6'1"	200
Brady _____	Tight End	6'4"	220
Bill _____	Tight End	6'7"	240
Chet _____	Guard	6'3"	250
Ninet _____	Guard	6'4"	240
John _____	Linebacker	6'3"	232
Darren _____	Linebacker	6'2"	230
Kevin _____	Tackle	6'4"	270
Tim _____	Tackle	6'6"	280

If you guess the correct school, we will provide the souvenir of your choice from any of this year's football equipment.

FIGURE 10–9

One, college coaches give preferential treatment to scholarshipped players. They may sound happy that a certain player plans to walk on, but they're still happier to see their scholarshipped players on that first day of practice. Two, they had good reason for not offering a scholarship in the first place. Walk-ons invariably bump into a group of outstanding college athletes. Three, walk-ons often end up playing on prep teams against first stringers, and their love of the game is severely tested. And four, although they may be allowed to use the same training tables as scholarshipped players, walk-ons usually don't have access to tutors or receive the same kinds of concessions from professors. In essence, they put in the same time, get more bumps and bruises in practice, for considerably less compensation.

If players and their parents consider walking on as an option, they need another piece of advice. Have them contact you before deciding on a school or schools. Students who walk on at schools that are far from home or that normally don't recruit your high school are simply not given the same treatment as from schools with which you are familiar. The college coach who wants to recruit your players tomorrow has to be kind today to a walk-on from your school. If he's unfamiliar with you and your school, he is less likely to be loyal to one of your players.

================================ LET'S WRAP IT UP ================================

The odds indicate that high school players are more likely to be hit by lightning than to play professional football. Their chances are better to receive a scholarship to college, but not nearly as good as most of them think. "Student" is still the key word in student-athlete and should remain the focus of all discussions regarding college.

Another way to encourage athletes and their parents to focus on academics and to look at college football realistically is to share figure 10–9 with them during one of those meetings in the fall. It's been a good attention-getter during my presentations at high schools and national conventions. As you probably have guessed, the names were not selected from a college roster but from a listing of the top high school football prospects in a major metropolitan area.

You and I realize that college football, even in Division III schools, is probably tougher than it has ever been. The players are bigger, faster, and stronger every year. Our job is to develop those players. We also are responsible for the players who can't play in college. We must encourage them to accept their limitations and to acknowledge the realities of football beyond high school. In spite of the expectations of some players and their parents, only a select few can play for Notre Dame or Michigan—or for a good Division III program! Our job is to help them accept that fact. Meetings, videotapes, and other means of communication will help. They will help parents and players understand more about college football, and they will help *us* at the end of the season when family expectations occasionally run contrary to the real world.

Player Recruitment

The Marines apparently get the job done with "a few good men." But it's not the answer for football teams. Football coaches want the good ones, too, but we also want as many others as we can "get our pads on." That's not to say that we want to direct the mob scene from Ben Hur every day on the practice field, but we do want enough players to enable us to run against a number of defenses and to alternate offensive and defensive prep teamers frequently enough to prevent injury.

Some schools today are particularly hard hit by declining student enrollments. Such schools are affected in a number of ways, only one of which involves the number of players on the football team. Reduction-in-force problems require creative problem solving from both administrators and coaches. Coaches must devise new strategies for attracting players—or they must create alternative ways to practice.

Frankly, it's easier to attract players. Alternative ways to practice are rarely improvements. Most often, they are ineffective compromises with reality. The focus of this section, therefore, is on attracting athletes to your program, a process that has several advantages.

The Need for Bodies

Many football programs refuse to cut players. They establish such a policy for two primary reasons:

- *Player Development*—High school boys can work up an appetite by opening the refrigerator, and some of them add not only pounds but inches, often three to six in one summer. The boy who rattles when he runs to the freshman field because the smallest pair of shoulder pads in the equipment room are too big for him may be starting as the varsity outside linebacker as a senior—even a junior. We won a state championship and a mythical national championship in 1975 with at least seven starters who barely made the "B" squad as freshmen.

221

Had we cut them as young players, we not only would have denied them the opportunity to play a game they came to love, but we would have denied ourselves a state championship. The '75 team would not have been the same without them.

- Everyone Gets a Chance—If we genuinely believe that football teaches valuable lessons to young men, then it's our job to provide the opportunity to as many of them as possible. Too many schools perceive "making the team" as some kind of an elitist accomplishment and not the chance to learn the values of self-sacrifice and team membership. If coaches eliminate the fear of being cut and emphasize the right values, growing numbers of parents in the community will desire to have their kids play for them.

It's one thing to attract young men to the program; it's another to attract their parents. It's unfortunate but true that even conscientious parents need help establishing positive values within their children. It's unlikely that such parents are simply falling down on the job because of their interests and responsibilities outside the home—although that is true for a significant number of parents.

What is more likely is their growing inability to stand toe-to-toe with social forces such as television, hard rock, movies, peer pressure, and the army of daily temptations that scream for self-indulgence instead of self-reliance. Parents, therefore, come to depend on coaches and other persons in the school who can counteract these forces by guiding their children toward many desirable values, the kind that result from a growing sense of self-satisfaction.

Do what you can to share your program goals with the parent community. They are not the enemy, seeking only recognition and scholarships for the their children. That kind of parental narcissism does prevail in some communities, but it does not reflect the behavior of most parents. Treat them as allies, and your program will grow in direct relation to the support they provide.

SUPPLY LINES

Coaches have other supply lines available within the school and community. Feeder schools, park district programs, community organizations, and in-school programs such as PE classes and intramural activities all provide excellent sources of football players. All of them require some of our time. One in particular warrants ongoing attention. Just as we want parents to be allies, we want excellent working relationships with feeder schools.

- Feeder Schools—Elementary schools (K-8), middle schools, and junior high schools are almost exclusively responsible for the number and quality of the athletes we receive in our football programs. It's surprising, therefore, how few high school coaches establish ongoing relationships with feeder school coaches, particularly given their knowledge. Feeder school coaches can routinely share:

—The names of promising athletes who are apprehensive about trying out for high school football.

—Information about the behavioral needs of selected athletes.

—Strategies to be used with certain athletes to maximize their performance.

—Information regarding the best positions for certain players.

—The specifics of players' academic performance and needs.

Certainly high school coaches can discover such information about their players, and they are likely to learn much more as the season progresses. But the communication between high school and feeder school coaches before the season starts accomplishes at least two important things: one, it prevents high school personnel from reinventing the wheel; two, it convinces feeder school coaches that their judgment is valued and that the success of the high school program is to some extent dependent upon them.

All coaches involved in the process must be careful not to share confidential information that violates trusts with parents, but a great deal of helpful information can be articulated at a relatively brief meeting, perhaps at the local bistro over lunch paid for by the high school. It is time well spent.

Such a meeting provides information and paves the way for ongoing interaction among all the coaches involved. Much of that additional interaction involves help and/or courtesies extended during the season. The help can come when you invite feeder school coaches to accompany you or your staff on scouting assignments or to attend staff meetings involving game preparation. My experience has been that feeder school coaches enjoy such experiences, learn from them, and provide another set of eyes during the actual scouting.

They also enjoy and appreciate invitations to be on the sidelines with you on game days, particularly for big games. They enjoy watching many of their former players, getting a bird's eye view of the game, and generally being in on the action. Obviously, they won't join you for every home game, perhaps just one, usually early in the season.

The point is, feeder school coaches make a sizeable contribution to high school programs; their hard work and knowledge should be recognized whenever possible. The closer we cooperate the better job each of us will do in developing our athletes and our programs. The mutual respect that results will provide the continuity so necessary for program development, which includes player recruitment. Everyone benefits.

- Park District Programs—Questions of continuity are as important with park district programs as with feeder schools, particularly because park district programs in many communities provide youngsters their first and sometimes only early experience with football. The impact of these early experiences often has far-reaching consequences, not only for the players but for their parents, at least one of whom probably questions quite seriously the value of physical contact!

Feeder school and high school coaches, therefore, are well-advised to work closely with park district programs and personnel, most of whom are knowledgeable and responsible people. Many of them do a great job introducing youngsters to the hard work and the pleasures of athletic competition. Some few, however, have a misguided perception of what football is all about. They sometimes push too hard, expect too much, yell too loud, and generally understand too little about kids and football.

Such people need our help; even the most short-sighted eventually will respond to the advice and modeling we provide. A few, however, will remain as inflexible as they are short-sighted. Because they're in it for themselves, they provide little for the children and ultimately threaten your program. They must be replaced by people who understand the game. That's one big reason why you need an ongoing relationship with the park district.

- Frosh, Soph, and JV Coaches—Lower-level coaches may not be a pipeline for players, but they perform an important role in recruiting. Good lower-level coaches possess two very important characteristics. First, they have a thorough knowledge of football fundamentals. Performance habits are developed early in a player's career. They must be good habits; bad habits become increasingly difficult to break as players gain more experience. Lower-level coaches also have a knowledge of strategy, but sophisticated offenses and defenses are considerably less important to young players than a simple but well-sequenced set of plays and the opportunity to learn and enjoy the skills of blocking and tackling.

This suggests the second characteristic required of lower-level coaches. They attract players. Then they have holding power. A big turnout of freshmen who bump into a drill sargeant for a coach soon find something else to do in the fall. It's wise, therefore, for head coaches to select lower-level coaches more for their ability to establish relationships and to teach fundamentals than to mold football teams.

Winning is still the primary goal of every football game, but having a good time doing it is critically important, particularly when youngsters are first introduced to the game. Experienced players have learned and usually accepted their limitations. Their satisfaction is most often realized within those limitations and by capitalizing on whatever strengths they possess as young football players. They maintain their fantasies, but with each passing year such fantasies are circumscribed by the realities they can no longer deny.

The younger the player the greater the fantasy. Satisfactory performance is as motivating to beginners as to experienced players. But it doesn't feed their fantasies as readily as their imaginations do. Football to them is an opportunity to walk the same stage with Barry Sanders and Joe Montana and to dream of their own starring role. As their skills develop—or fail to develop—and as they realize the real-world pleasures of playing football, their fantasies will be less important as motivators.

The point is, beginning players need the guiding hand of a coach or coaches who can transform fantasies into real experiences that nonetheless provide the same drama and the same excitement that caused Sanders and Montana to love football. Young athletes will eventually accept their limitations when they realize they are sharing the same stage with such football immortals. They may not throw as well as Montana, but they can share the same pulse-quickening experiences and further the same traditions. Only a coach who likes kids and who loves the game of football can make this happen.

COORDINATING EXPERIENCES

Sequence and continuity are important throughout the entire developmental process of young athletes. The park district program or feeder school that teaches good fundamentals is heaven-sent to the high school coach. He can then move on to the development of more sophisticated skills and the refinement of his offense and defense. Linemen who can simulate run action by fire-out blocking and effectively preventing the penetration of the defense make a play-action passing attack that much more possible. Refined skills do influence the range of strategies available to a coach.

Share your knowledge of fundamental skills, therefore, with park district and feeder school coaches. Provide information for them as illustrated in figure 11–1 and volunteer your services during practices or meetings to help with drills and strategies. Your time commitments may not allow for such assistance during the season, so you may want to meet with coaches sometime during the summer as your respective schedules allow.

My experience has been that park district coaches welcome input from colleagues. It is most welcome when it is requested by them, but it can also be welcome when such input is offered discreetly. No one wants to be told what to do, but all of us want to know what to do. Figure 11–1 offers helpful information and assistance without telling coaches what to do. It also opens the door to improved continuity among different programs and to joint meetings to discuss strategy.

During the meetings you will undoubtedly have the opportunity to suggest offensive and defensive strategies, the kind that are consistent with your program. When the athletes join you as freshmen, their knowledge of the basic plays in your offense will enable your lower-level coaches to spend that much more time on fundamentals. The principles of continuity and sequence, as described in chapter four, apply as well to the consistency of program elements among the park districts, feeder schools, and high schools.

Football coaches have been emphasizing teamwork for a long time, so we at the high school want to work with you. You perform an extremely important role with young football players, and we appreciate all that you have done. If you can think of anything we can do to help with your program, we'd like to return the favor. And, to be honest, we have a selfish reason or two. If we teach similar fundamental skills, the easier each of our jobs will be as players move from one program to another. We would appreciate your reactions, therefore, to the following descriptions of the football fundamentals that each young player must learn now and then build upon each year. If you like the descriptions, please feel free to use them. If you don't like them, please tell us why so we can learn from your coaching techniques.

Thanks, and if we can help in any other way, please give us a call.

BASIC SKILLS FOR YOUNG PLAYERS

The Football Stance—A good football stance always emphasizes the three Bs: base, balance, and bull-neck. The base starts with feet approximately shoulder-width with the toes on the right foot intersecting the arch of the left foot if the player is right-handed. Reverse the instructions if the player is left-handed. The back should be approximately parallel to the ground when the player puts his hand down. He may rest on his fingers or knuckles, whichever is more comfortable. His weight distribution should be approximately 60% on his legs and 40% on his hand, depending upon the play call. If he's running straight ahead for crucial yardage, he may want more weight on his hand; if he's running obliquely into the off-tackle hole he may want more weight on the legs. He should bull his neck in order to look straight ahead. Good ball carriers *must* see where they are running. Lazy or tired players who drop their heads in their stances hardly ever get them up in time to make a critical cut in the hole.

BASE—foot positioning, knees wide in the stance, feet slightly pigeon-toed, tail up.

BALANCE—Weight distribution depending upon the play call.

BULL-NECK—Head up at all times, always alert for daylight.

Starts—Players should be relaxed in their stances with the off arm resting on the knee, their tails up and their necks bulled. Once they hear the snap count, they must explode out of their stances, driving their arms and emphasizing high knee action. Like a good sprinter, the initial movement must be forward. That's why the tail must be up in the stance. If down, the player's first movement is *up*, not *forward*. Coaches must emphasize the first five to ten yards of the start. They are the most critical. Emphasize low, forward movement, high knees, and hard arm drive just prior to receiving the hand-off.

Receiving the Ball from Center—The quarterback's stance when receiving the ball from center must be as comfortable as possible. Like his running back counterpart, he must have his feet about shoulder width and be balanced on the balls of his feet. His back must be relatively straight with a slight forward lean. The stance should approximate a good hit position: legs slightly bent at the knee, back relatively straight, head erect, and arms relaxed in front. The quarterback's arms should be straight, bent slightly at the elbows. His right hand (or left, if left-handed) should be positioned firmly against the center's crotch just behind his testicles. His hand must remain in that position throughout the snap, following the center while the center snaps the ball and initiates his fireout block. If the quarterback keeps his arms relatively straight, he will be in a much better position to follow the center until he receives the ball. Notice the following illustrations.

The 3-Step Drop—Once the quarterback receives the ball, he should drop step with his right foot at a 90 degree angle away from the line of scrimmage. His second step is a long one away from the line of scrimmage, and his third enables him to stop his backward momentum in

© 1992 by Michael D. Koehler

FIGURE 11–1

order to set up in his passing position. The drop should be executed as quickly as possible, and it should conclude with the quarterback, his feet firmly planted, in a solid passing position.

The Handoff—A good handoff is the primary responsibility of the quarterback. He must *always* look the ball into the running back's pocket. The quarterback must always keep his weight low, in effect shielded behind the offensive line. His arm must be relatively straight. The ball should be presented in front of the ball carrier, and at the moment of exchange should be "wristed" into the ball carrier's stomach. The ball carrier should feel the ball hitting his stomach so that he knows where it is at all times. It should not just be held in front of him with the expectation that he will find it and take it from the quarterback. The quarterback must wrist the ball gently but firmly into the ball carrier's stomach, being careful not to hit the front part of the ball carrier's shoulder pads where the ball carrier is unlikely to feel it.

The Pocket—The ball carrier should make a pocket by raising the elbow of his arm nearest the quarterback to a position roughly the same height of his chin, with the near hand almost in front of his own mouth. The arm away from the quarterback should be bent at a 45 degree angle with the forearm roughly parallel to his own belt. The elbow should be tight to the body to prevent the ball from being pushed *through* the pocket. Once the ball carrier feels the ball hit his stomach, he should nestle the ball with the arm away from the quarterback and drop the arm nearest the quarterback over the ball to secure it. The ball carrier must seek to cup his hands over the tips of the ball in order to secure it with both arms. "Get the tips" is the coach's frequent command when teaching ball carriers how to receive a handoff. Finally, the ball carrier must *never* look for the ball. His job is to find the hole and run to daylight; the quarterback's job is to get the ball in his pocket.

The Hit Position—Finally, the hit position is critical to every football player. It is the primary position for blocking, warding off blockers on defense, and facing up to make a tackle. The hit position involves a balanced stance with the feet approximately shoulder-width and the player's weight on the balls of his feet. The back is straight with a slight forward lead, the arms dangling in a relaxed manner in front of the player. With slight variations for different positions on offense and defense, the hit position is fundamental for every football player and should become a habit on every play. Notice the following illustrations:

These fundamentals are important for every young football player. If executed correctly within the framework of a well-conceived offense and defense, the team is going to win a lot of football games.

FIGURE 11–1 (*Continued*)

ATTRACTING PARENTS

Some high school coaches have little to do with the parent community. A few see themselves as Robin Hood and the parents as so many Sheriffs of Nottingham, natural adversaries, good seeking the triumph over evil. What a mistake! Certainly there are some parents out there who seek life's pleasures through the accomplishments of their children, but they are definitely in the minority. The coach who disagrees with this statement is certain to lose one of the best resources available to him—those genuinely concerned parents who are quick to support a coach and program that stand for something.

Parental support will not determine the success or the failure of the program, but the absence of it will provoke a lot of uphill battles. Successful football coaches see parents as colleagues with a common goal, namely whatever is best for the kids. Parents know as well as the coach does that a well-supported program, morally and financially, is best for their children. Think of parents, therefore, as allies and friends. Disregard the exception to the rule who qualifies his or her support with ulterior motives, and focus instead on the good people who will encourage their sons to play for you and who will work with you to guarantee the success of your program.

Every community has several ways for coaches to address groups of parents. A few moments sequestered in your office to organize a speech, letters sent to the right people, and only a night or two away from your favorite chair will do much to attract parents to you and your program. Consider the following as opportunities: junior high graduations, junior high and elementary school banquets, fraternal and service organization luncheons (Jaycees, Rotary, Optimist Club, Knights of Columbus, Chamber of Commerce, Kiwanis, and so forth), park districts events, and local interest group luncheons and evening meetings (League of Women Voters, anti-drug groups, and church or temple group activities).

A coach's increased visibility can do much to sell the benefits of student participation in the program. The additional time commitment is minimal, and the responses of the parent community will provide increased support for the program, particularly in the face of dwindling resources and declining student enrollments. Use the reproducibles in figures 11–2, 11–3, and 11–4 to initiate contact with the right people.

ATTRACTING ATHLETES

If you wake up one day and find yourself in charge of a great football program, you haven't been asleep. Great football coaches do a whole lot more than diagram X's and O's when everyone else is in bed; they devise ways to motivate and discipline players and, equally important, to *get* them. Attracting gifted athletes to your program is not as easy as it sounds.

LETTER TO FEEDER SCHOOLS

Dear (Name of principal):

Just a quick note to volunteer my services for any banquets, graduations, or parent meetings you have planned for the future. I have been a long-time admirer of your school and have appreciated the quality of the students you send to the high school. I would like to return the favor. You know as well as I do that the NCAA and other regulatory organizations across the country have done a great deal to re-emphasize the importance of academics in the lives of athletes. I am in complete agreement with them and would like to do what I can to influence the thinking of young athletes and their parents.

I also share the concerns of many citizens in our community about the use of drugs among adolescents. I have revealing statistics that will interest parents and students alike. In addition, I have a great deal of information regarding college athletics, scholarships, and the unlikelihood of professional sports careers. I realize that such topics may not be appropriate for all students, so I will await your invitation for the most suitable forum.

Thanks, (name of principal), and feel free to contact me at your convenience. I look forward to working with you.

Sincerely yours,

Tom Smith
Head Football Coach

FIGURE 11–2

LETTER TO LOCAL ORGANIZATIONS

Dear (Name of President):

I know that your organization is always looking for speakers for luncheons or other occasions, so I would like to volunteer my services. Groups like yours do a tremendous service for this community, and I would like to do what I can to make my contribution. Fortunately, a wide range of topics is available, any one of which might interest your membership.

Intercollegiate athletics is filling the sports pages and the television commentaries and remains one of the key issues in society today. I have some interesting information on the topic. I also have revealing information about athletic scholarships to college and the unlikelihood of a career in professional sports.

Obviously, drugs (steroids in particular) remain an issue. I have additional statistics on that topic. And, of course, we can always talk about the high school football program, a subject which obviously is near and dear to my heart. Just give me a call at your convenience; I'm sure we can find a time that's mutually convenient.

I look forward to hearing from you and your fine organization.

Sincerely yours,

Tom Smith
Head Football Coach

FIGURE 11-3

LETTER TO PARK DISTRICT

Dear (Name of President):

Our mutual responsibilities to the young people of this community give us a common goal, so I would like to offer my services as a speaker at the appropriate park district function. Obviously, the most relevant topic is the high school football program, but I have considerable information as well about drugs, intercollegiate athletics, and the value of academics. Each of these topics has merit and could be appropriate for one or more of your functions.

A strong relationship between the park district and the high school will benefit both of us and, most importantly, will provide the kinds of programs our children and parents need. I am anxious to work with you and look forward to hearing from you at your convenience.

Thanks, (Name of president), for your time.

Sincerely yours,

Tom Smith
Head Football Coach

FIGURE 11-4

The best way to get them is to win—a lot. A winning program guarantees attention, and most gifted athletes like attention, or at the least, recognition. Everyone wants to be associated with a winner. But not everyone can be a winner, at least consistently. So most coaches must rely on other ways to attract athletes. If they don't find such athletes, they seriously jeopardize their chances to develop a winning program. Some of the other ways?

- Beat the Bushes—"Beating the bushes" is one of the most obvious and one of the best ways to find athletes for your program. We all enjoy the compliment of being asked to do something because we're good at it— even if we're not really good at it. The person who recognizes our potential, however, becomes significant to use because he's meeting one of our ego needs. And teenagers have more ego needs than pimples.

That's why it's equally important not to shame them into playing football. Sharp-edged instruments can get the job done, but they can also cause a lot of pain. For that reason it's usually best not to use them. The best tool to use when attracting athletes is the one that builds, not destroys. Stick with the compliments; they work better than sarcasm.

Be careful as well that when you encourage a young man into coming out for football you aren't destroying a relationship within the school. Some athletes commit themselves to other sports and choose not to risk injury by playing football. You may disagree with this decision in principle, but you should honor it until you have had the chance to speak to the athlete's coach. We'll speak more of the "specialist" in a later section of this chapter.

- Newspaper Column—A few years ago the editor of a local newspaper joined me for lunch to discuss a mutual venture. We ended up discussing several different ideas, one of which involved the creation of a column for his paper that invited letters from the community and provided responses from me. I agreed to do it and discovered that it really didn't take much of my time, yet provided the opportunity to communicate a range of important issues to the parents and children within the community.

I discovered that I was able to provide revealing information about drugs (steroids in particular), Bylaw 14.3 (the old Proposition 48), conditioning, nutrition, coaching pointers, and a range of related sports topics. The columns that dealt with drugs received a great deal of positive response from people within the community, most of whom saw my stance as further reinforcement of the significant work they had been doing to stop the use of drugs in our schools.

The column gave me a great deal of pleasure, involved only minimal research, was relatively easy to write, and addressed several very important topics that influenced the thinking of athletes and parents alike. It enabled me to focus on the value of academics, the requirements of the NCAA, the statistics regarding athletic scholarships, and the unlikelihood of a future in professional sports.

Because it was so well accepted, it also did much to sell our football program. Parents and athletes alike were impressed by our emphasis on academics and on the possibility of using football to get into a highly selective school. That alone brought out a couple of students who I'm sure would have been doing something else in the fall, one of whom turned into a very important player on defense.

- Have Fun—Fun is not a reward; it is a consequence of purposeful and well-conceived activity. Give an athlete something to do—no matter how hard—something to be proud of, and something to look forward to, and you have a young man who is having fun. Having fun doesn't involve the silly, undisciplined kind of activity that characterizes some football programs. Kids need a sense of direction. When young football players are told what to expect and when the program capitalizes on their internal motivation, they are more likely to have fun.

Coaches who believe they have to browbeat players into playing hard do much to kill their own programs. If enjoyment on the football field is not a reward, the absence of enjoyment on the football field is not a punishment. It is a result—usually of a coach's inability to involve his team in activities that are inherently satisfying. When that happens, players don't have fun, and they don't come out in the fall. Recruiting players, therefore, usually is a function of offering a worthwhile experience for them.

- The PE Pipeline and Intramurals—When you decide to beat the bushes, head immediately for the PE teachers and the school's intramural program. Each is a resource for the finest athletes in school, and the persons involved in such programs often have the kinds of relationships that can result in the sudden willingness of certain kids to play football.

A WORD ABOUT "THE SPECIALIST"

Most freshmen in high school can select their best sport as reliably as they can determine their future vocations. Some few who want to be doctors become doctors; most don't. Some few who want to play basketball in college receive scholarships; most don't. Athletes should be discouraged, therefore, from specializing in one sport, particularly early in their high school careers.

Coaches of certain sports who encourage specialization often do a disservice to young athletes. The young man who is 6'4" as a freshman and is encouraged to think only of basketball may not grow beyond 6'6" or 6'7" and may never develop the feel required of highly recruited basketball players. His avoidance of football because of its potential for injury may deny him the perfect opportunity to use his size and speed in a sport for which he is best suited.

Specialization in athletics, like the decision to select a course of study in college, is determined best after experience has had a chance to influence the player's thinking. Early educational experiences for students should emphasize foundational knowledge, and early playing experiences for athletes should emphasize foundational skills and a broad range of activities. Specialization is appropriate only after all possible alternatives have been explored. That hard-nosed little guy at safety who is in the middle of every pile may love football, but he may be a potential All-State wrestler. Encourage him to try both.

Obviously, the question of specialization for athletes is an all-school issue. Football coaches who agree with the philosophy that athletes should experience a broad range of sports are well-advised to suggest the topic as an agenda item during an all-school coaches' meeting early in the fall. A consensus opinion of all coaches is a school's best way to resolve the issue. Better yet, coaches should encourage the athletic director to develop or write such an opinion into the school's athletic code/philosophy. See figure 11–5 for a sample statement. "Black and white" now is always better than "black and blue" later.

SAMPLE STATEMENT OF PHILOSOPHY

"We believe in the value of athletic participation in all its forms. Such participation fosters the qualities of team membership, individual commitment, and personal excellence. Because every sport offers opportunities to develop these qualities, we are philosophically committed to a range of sports activities for every athlete who has the time and the desire to play them, and we are opposed to recommendations that athletes restrict participation to a single sport, unless that athlete is competing professionally."

FIGURE 11–5

================ LET'S WRAP IT UP ================

Effectively recruiting football players is not simply a matter of luring them onto the practice field. It will work only if you can keep them there by providing valuable and satisfying experiences. The strategies outlined in this chapter work; they are excellent ways to communicate the merits of your program and to encourage participation in it. The single best recruiting element available to you, however, is your current team. Make your players' experience worthwhile, and each of them will sell the program to parents and to other students. "Selling by telling" is always your best strategy.

Drugs

One of the biggest problems in high school and college athletics today is that the formula for success is the same as for a nervous breakdown. It has led to amazing athletic accomplishments *and* to a widespread abuse of steroids. One of the causes is stress—and constant stress destroys. It can crumble the foundations of historic institutions, including the cherished traditions of competitive athletics.

The good news is that the destruction is far from complete. Amateurism may have given way to big paychecks for Olympic athletes, but the principle of athletic competition for its own sake is alive and well in high schools and many colleges across the country. The graduation rates of student athletes in many major universities may be abysmal, but the NCAA, university officials, and football coaches at all levels across the country are seeking ways to make it tougher for such schools to recruit athletes and to avoid public scrutiny. Steroid abuse may continue to be an issue, but—with the help of folks like you and me—athletes now seem to better understand the dangers of such illicit drugs.

Stress, however, continues to take its toll. If we are to prevent it from destroying what is important to us in American sport, we must recognize its sources and devise ways to combat them. This is a mighty tall order. Stress in our society is a complicated issue and involves much more than the equally complicated issue of steroid abuse. Like drug abuse, stress has become so common in our society that we tend at times to accept it as a condition for our accomplishments and progress.

The values of American sports, as well as the problems that confront them, are a reflection of the larger society. Stress for many of us has been accepted as an unavoidable problem, just as steroid abuse for many athletes has become an unavoidable solution. Not much will be done to change either until we recognize stress not as a problem but as the symptom of a problem—and steroid abuse as a solution of that symptom. Good doctors don't treat symptoms; they acknowledge them as elements in a diagnosis. Treatment is suggested when the diagnosis is complete and the problem is identified.

We as coaches must take the time to recognize the problem confronting us, not the symptom or one of its solutions. Then we must sustain a focus on it in order to find workable solutions, the kinds of solutions that reduce stress and eliminate the need for steroids. Again, a tall order. But it won't start until coaches really look at our society's preoccupation with winning—often at all costs.

════════════ KEEPING THINGS IN PERSPECTIVE ════════════

OK, the suggestion that winning at all costs is our problem may not be a startling revelation. But the problem is much more insidious than many of us realize. After all, winning is a goal of every competitive activity. "Winning," however, is one of our society's most misunderstood and misinterpreted goals, and we as coaches must develop our own interpretations of it before we can hope to seek solutions.

Misinterpretation? One of the most obvious involves the comments of one of our profession's greatest winners. He was originally quoted several years ago as saying, "Winning isn't everything; it's the *only* thing." And he meant it, but, as often happens, we accepted his comment at face value and missed the essence of what he intended. You see, Vince Lombardi *also* said, "Winning isn't everything. The will to win is everything. It is more important than any event which occasions it."

"The will to win is everything," and, to paraphrase Vince, it is more important than any game we try to win. Those are powerful words, and they reflect a philosophy of competitive sports that has existed in this country for centuries. They emphasize the commitment of personal excellence in competitive athletics, not a blind conformity to winning. They seek the best we can be as athletes and individuals, not the worst we can become as cheaters and steroid abusers.

Consider these words: "Play not for gain but for sport. [He] who plays for more than he can lose with pleasure—stakes his heart." The author? Walter Camp, the father of American football. He wrote that in 1885. To what extent have some among us "staked our hearts" since Camp struggled before the turn of the century to have football reflect the positive values of American society? The answer is found in our goals.

If for businessmen the exclusive goal of free enterprise is to make as much money as possible, then cheating is an answer. If for students the exclusive goal of a classroom education is to get an A, then cheating is an answer. If for coaches the exclusive goal of athletic competition is winning, then cheating is an answer. And if for athletes the exclusive goal of playing football is to beat the other guy, cheating is an answer. The situation is similar for businessmen, students, coaches, and athletes.

If beating the other guy is what this society is all about, then it's relatively easy to find excuses and reasons to justify anything we do. If on the other hand the businessman seeks pride in his product or service, the student seeks intellectual fulfillment, and the coach and athlete seek a sense of personal excellence, than our goals involve a whole lot more than merely winning, and we realize that cheating is not just a violation of the rules but an abuse of ourselves.

Put another way, if the exclusive goal of educators (coaches included) is to reflect the values of society, then we must fall in line with the expectations of our constituencies. If the goal, however, is to influence the positive development of social values, then we must resist the pressure to emphasize just winning. You see, once we do resist, we will have started to solve the issue of steroid abuse.

I am not suggesting that coaches who commit themselves and their players to a maximum effort to win are inducing stress or provoking steroid abuse. Certainly they are risking it, given the misguided goals of some athletes and parents. Fortunately, however, our profession is blessed with a great number of dedicated people who understand what Vince Lombardi meant by "the will to win" and who manage to sustain a focus on the importance of personal excellence in competitive athletics.

WHAT COACHES AND PARENTS
NEED TO KNOW ABOUT STEROIDS

Even then, problems persist. Consider the recent story of a major college football player who told *Sports Illustrated* of his fight with steroids and how they almost drove him to suicide. Or what about the 17-year-old high school senior in Ohio who recently died of an apparent heart attack during football practice? The county coroner indicated that the young man died of arrhythmia, a condition caused by a diseased and enlarged heart. He connected the condition to excessive steroid use.

What about the former pro football player who recently admitted to using steroids and now is suffering from cardiomyopathy, the result of a dilated and enlarged heart? The player's cardiologist has not ruled out steroid use as a possible cause and is considering a heart transplant for the athlete.

Most striking is Lyle Alzado's own story. The former All-Pro for the Oakland Raiders admitted to excessive use of steroids and human growth hormone. In a sensitive and courageous account of his life in professional football, Alzado admitted in *Sports Illustrated* to years of drug abuse, abject denial of potential health problems, and disturbing mood changes that contributed to his success as a player and to disruption in his personal life. He was convinced that steroids were also responsible for his biggest problem—inoperable brain cancer.

In addition consider the well-documented stories about athletes and body builders like Alzado who experience depression, hallucinations, and illusions because of their illegal use of steroids. Even non-athletes, using steroids legally, experience psychological imbalance. A recent story involves an adolescent who took Anavar and Deca-Durabolin, both anabolic and androgenic steroids, for three or four months to rehabilitate his knee following a traffic accident. One afternoon he put a shotgun in his mouth and pulled the trigger. His mother links his suicide to steroid use.

"Roid rages," the unrestrained aggressiveness that often results from steroid use, underlie scores of media accounts involving sudden and unexplainable violence. None was more graphic than the story of the 30-year-old prison security guard who started taking steroids to enhance his strength building. He started with 20 mg. of methandrostenolone a day and gradually increased to 30 mg. a day with added weekly doses of testosterone and one injection of methenolone.

Happily married for several years, the young man began to experience obvious irritability, depression, and finally paranoia. Six to seven months after starting the steroid cycles, he shot a woman in the back because of a harmless remark she made regarding a phone in her store. Now in prison and denied access to steroids, he has returned to his normal personality.

Other documented stories involve a body builder who experienced such dramatic mood changes from using excessively high doses of steroids that he planted a bomb under his girlfriend's car, a sailor whose steroid use transformed his excellent naval record into a criminal record involving burglary and arson, and a young woman who became so uncontrollable she lost her job and severely beat her boyfriend. These are frightening stories, particularly in light of the relatively high incidence of steroid use.

WHAT DO THE STATS SAY?

When we consider that one in ten U.S. citizens last month used an illegal drug, we realize that drug use in this country is challenging far more than our athletic traditions and is prevalent within all levels of our society. In athletics, it prevails from high school, maybe earlier, to collegiate and professional football, to the most elite levels of world competition.

When Canadian track star Ben Johnson lost his world record in the 1988 Olympics after testing positive for steroids, his coach testified at the inquiry that he had encouraged the athlete to use steroids as early as 1981. He justified his recommendation with the claim that as many as 80% of the world's elite track athletes use steroids. The accuracy of his comment is subject to continuing debate, but when one considers the reports of national magazines that as many as 85% of all professional football players have used steroids, one can hardly question the prevalence of their use.

Although less prevalent in high school, steroid use by adolescents is nonetheless dramatic. A recent report published in the *Journal of the American Medical Association* indicates that one in 15 high school seniors has used steroids, with approximately one-third of the users starting at or before the age of 15. The half million teenaged boys who use steroids also pay black market dealers anywhere from $50 to $400 for pills and/or injections.

A recent NCAA study reported that anabolic steroid use is more prevalent in high school than in college, where only one in 20 athletes admit to using them. Although the difference between the two is not especially significant, the higher incidence of drug use among high school athletes highlight the pressures of adolescence: to look good and perhaps to perform well enough in football to receive a scholarship.

OTHER DRUGS/METHODS

Such pressures provoke the use of other performance enhancements as well. Some atheletes believe that supplementing their diets with extra vitamins and minerals will enhance athletic performance. Nothing in medical literature, however, substantiates this position. Sports nutritionists emphasize repeatedly that a well-balanced diet provides everything athletes require to improve strength and endurance.

Many athletes also load up on baking soda before a strenuous contest, believing that it reduces the lactic acid in the muscles that cause fatigue. Whether or not this practice enhances athletic performance is still debated, but it has been known to cause gastric distress and diarrhea, two conditions that could give new meaning to the term "running back!"

Amphetamines may still be a problem in high school athletics. Developed in the '30s and used by both American and German soldiers to combat fatigue in WW II, amphetamine use in the United States was especially high in the '60s and prevailed among college students and truck drivers as well as athletes. Amphetamines enhance speed, endurance, and reaction time but are now easily detected by drug testing procedures. For that reason, they are virtually non-existent among Olympic athletes but may still be used in colleges and high schools.

Yet another drug used to enhance endurance is Erthropoietin (EPO), a hormone that increases the number of oxygen-carrying red blood cells in the system. Used primarily by distance runners, EPO is not expected to be a problem for high school football coaches.

Finally, special mention should be made of the availability of the human growth hormone (HGH), which went on the market in 1985 as a treatment for shortness. HGH not only has the potential to make athletes taller, it also builds muscle and burns off fat. Because of its expense, however, and its potentially serious side effects, HGH is not widely used in the United States, rarely by high school athletes.

WHAT DRUGS ARE DOING TO ATHLETES

Most obviously, anabolic steroids and other illicit drugs are enhancing personal appearance and athletic performance. Why else would so many adolescents risk hair loss, more pimples, a serious dent in their budgets, and a needle in their rear ends up to once a week? Let's face it, these consequences normally are on the low end of their list of druthers. Unfortunately, however, the consequences can be far more serious.

The potential physical effects of steroid use are well-documented but still subject to considerable research. Claims have been made by some sports doctors that steroids' side effects can be devastating: burst tendons, sterility, kidney damage, liver cancer, and heart problems. Frankly, such claims are still being extensively researched.

Less dramatic and less publicized are the potential problems with steroid use that are more immediate. Most obviously, any drug purchased on the black market suggests possible health problems. The use of steroids may lead to the use of other illegal drugs. The legal implications can be significant. And finally, the psychological problems that result are well-researched.

Consider the research of two psychiatrists from the Harvard Medical School who interviewed 41 athletes using steroids and discovered serious depression in nine of them and psychotic symptoms, including auditory hallucinations, in five others. Fortunately, such symptoms usually disappear when use of the drug is discontinued. In another study, a noted sports psychologist discovered that athletes who use steroids can experience significant depression and paranoia during off-training cycles.

Such findings underscore the need for all football coaches to recognize the signs of steroid use in order to prevent potentially serious problems for their athletes. Fortunately, many of the signs are easily observable.

WARNING SIGNALS

Figure 12–1 can be distributed to your team early each season. It accomplishes two primary objectives. Because it identifies the telltale symptoms of steroid use, it enables players to detect it in each other and it lets them know that *you* know how to detect it. This latter reason is one of the strongest for distributing such a list to the team. It also provides graphic evidence for parents that you are opposed to performance-enhancement drugs and that you are a knowledgeable resource within the community. It also suggests you are willing to do something about player use of illicit drugs.

TAKING A STAND

We already have discussed the pressures to win in competitive athletics and what the football coach must do to maintain the proper perspective in his program. As with some good parents, however, even the most thoughtful practices fail to provide for the developmental need of all children. Some are inclined to go astray no matter how positive the environment.

The _____ football program is opposed to the use of any illegal drug, including anabolic and androgenic steroids. The medical community has proven beyond a shadow of a doubt steroids' damaging physical effects, and we as football players and coaches are opposed to the artificial enhancement of performance. That is why Section I, subsection A-4, of the Athletic Code expressly forbids the "use of or possession of tobacco (all forms), alcohol, marijuana or any illegal drugs or related paraphernalia, look-alikes, or abuse of prescription/nonprescription drugs."

Athletes will arouse the suspicions of their coaches and teammates if they are observed exhibiting any of the following signs:

1. Obvious behavioral changes, especially extreme aggressiveness on and off the football field.

2. Significant increases in weight and size over a brief period of time.

3. Physical changes, including puffiness around the eyes, acne, hair loss, or breast development in males.

Athletes are reminded that anyone found guilty of steroid use will be subject to the consequences which are outlined in Section II, subsections A, B, and C, of the Athletic Code.

As important, players using steroids will reflect by that behavior a lack of confidence in their natural abilities and in the competence of the coaching staff to develop a winning football program.

FIGURE 12–1

For this reason football coaches must develop and encourage a philosophy such as the one contained in figure 1–6 in Section 1. It identifies the athletic department's position regarding training rules, and it outlines reasonable consequences for violations. Like John Wooden's philosophy, the rules are clear and the penalties severe—if not severe, at least consistent and immediate.

THE NEED FOR REMINDERS

Even the best athletic code is useless if it is not communicated routinely to the people affected by it. In addition, it will not satisfy the requirements of substantive and procedural due process if legal action should result from a player's expulsion from the team. Parents as well as players, therefore, must be reminded recurrently of the code's provisions, not as a threat but as the school's commitment to the positive development of its athletes.

One of the best places and times to remind players is in the lockerroom after each game. Win or lose, most players make a beeline for a party somewhere following the game. A reminder at this time gives them something to think about and reaffirms the coach's responsibility to uphold the training rules. Again, the code should not be discussed to threaten players but to remind them of consequences, most of which are beyond the coach's control.

One very successful coach congratulates his team after the game, talks about the upcoming opponent, and concludes the post-game meeting by imploring the team "not to destroy everything you've worked so hard for by making a dumb mistake!" At that point, he reminds them that the consequences "are out of my hands" and that players who break the code may not be bad people—they just wont' be allowed by the school's administration to play football. His approach is non-confrontational, and it works.

The best way to remind parents is to refer to the code during group meetings with them. The meetings discussed in earlier chapters designed to address academics, the NCAA, and scholarships are also good times to refer to the code, perhaps to redistribute copies. The more frequent the reminders by school personnel, the more effective the code and the less likely parents will engage in legal response resulting from adverse action.

WORKING WITH THE COMMUNITY

Establishing a positive relationship with official organizations within the community has several benefits. One, as already discussed, the visibility of football coaches within the community, particularly at functions and places that are important to community members, improves recruiting and parental support for the football program. Two, coaches and persons who work with kids, such as police officers and youth officials, can complement each other's efforts by working together. A whole lot of trouble can be avoided when a police officer knows he can call a parent *and* a boy's coach rather than make legal charges when the boy gets a little out of hand.

Three, some communities are trying hard to eliminate teenage drug abuse. Their efforts should be applauded and enhanced by school personnnel, especially coaches who enjoy influential relationships with so many kids. Four, the media have had a good time recently spotlighting the few cheaters out there who seek to win at all costs. It's time for "the good guys" to counteract such media attention by increasing the visibility of the *routine* good they do.

Finally, the more parents within the community can identify the football coach as "one of us," the more willing they will be to work with him in the future. All coaches are members of the community, whether they live there or not. Providing parents and other community members the opportunity to get to know you is perhaps one of the wisest things you can do for your program.

GETTING KIDS TO TAKE A STAND

What better way to show parents and other community members your position on drug abuse and your relationships with your players then to have several of them accompany you to meetings or speaking engagements? When athletes speak to parents about drugs, they generally help sell the influence and the value of the football program. But when they speak to their younger counterparts about drugs, they genuinely influence them in the right direction. I've been hard-pressed over the years to find even one freshman football player who wasn't awed by a senior on the varsity.

The opportunity is good for the senior, who gets the chance to share his values and to learn speaking techniques in front of large groups. And it is good for the underclassmen, who receive the kind of peer pressure that we adults want for them. Parents, coaches, and school officials can talk until they're blue in the face about the dangers of drug abuse. Put one or two well-respected senior football players in front of a group of underclassmen, however, and the message is not only believed—it's *received*.

It is wise to bring players with you on certain occasions when you meet with or talk to selected community organizations, including not only drug committees and parent groups but fraternal and service organizations. It's also a good idea to encourage the athlete's involvement and leadership within these groups. The experience is good for them, and it is a highly visible and positive reflection on your football program.

Many schools have freshman orientation meetings with students and their parents early each fall. The general purpose is to introduce the family to the school's culture and personnel. It's also a good idea at such times to get all the freshmen athletes and their parents together to introduce the athletic code and get their signatures of acceptance.

Such a practice is a legal guarantee that parents are familiar with the code and that they have accepted its provisions. It's also a great time to have the senior varsity athletes make their pitch to the freshmen players. It affirms the leadership positions of the seniors within their respective programs and shows the freshmen that opposition to drug abuse is not only an adult postion.

Obviously, it's a good idea to select the seniors very carefully and prepare them for the experience. The unprepared All-State tackle who intimidates with his size may amuse with his speaking ability and be counterproductive to the objectives of the meeting. If coached beforehand, he may do an excellent job. He may even be able to memorize the few words he is expected to say. A few well-chosen words, well-delivered, often make a more lasting impression than lengthy speeches—a little something for all of us to keep in mind.

LET'S WRAP IT UP

Our society is fixated on appearance. Just a cursory glance at television commercials reveals a parade of deodorants, wrinkle reducers, shampoos, hair sprays, weight-loss supplements, cosmetics, perfumes, and dietary food products. At one time, maintaining a youthful appearance was the focus. More recently, youth is not enough; good-looking youth is the goal.

Closely related to appearance is the need to feel good. The remainder of the television commercials promise relief from upset stomachs, headaches, and cramps; the restoration of sleep and "regularity;" and "the right thing, baby!" It is not surprising, therefore, that young people seek the artificial pleasures our society has to offer, including steroids to look good and marijuana and alcohol to feel good.

Add a preoccupation with winning to the equation, and it becomes obvious that young people are only partially responsible for the harm they may be doing their bodies. We, too, must share some of the blame. The best way to purge ourselves is not to try to change all those television commercials. Television is called a medium because it presents nothing rare or well-done, but it is here to stay.

We can help by giving young people frequent experiences to channel their efforts in different directions, the directions that emphasize seeking good and doing good. Football is one of several excellent organized experiences for young men that proves every day that it's not what you have or what you look like that counts but what you do and what you are.

The more often you and I reflect such values in our behavior and expect them of our athletes, the less often Dianabol, stanozolol, anadrol, and Deca-Durabolin will be answers to the pressure they are experiencing as the inevitable consequence of growing up in our society.

Until the powers-that-be eliminate television coverage of high school athletics, focus their energies and attention on the development of well-organized intramural programs, and value coaches and players for what they are as opposed to how many games they win, football coaches will continue to have their work cut out for them combatting the kinds of values and pressures that sanction drug abuse. Fortunately, we have a sport on our side that provides "highs" far in excess of anything found in the drug culture, and we can make players feel good about themselves much more than anything found on television can.

THE HIGHLY RECRUITED ATHLETE

College recruiters are consumers in need of quality products, and high school coaches are one of their best suppliers. The players are the products, little more or little less. We all realize that college coaches operate in one of our society's most competitive and highly visible jobs and that their success is dependent upon the likelihood of their "products" getting the job done.

When college coaches begin their annual "shopping spree," therefore, players and their parents must recognize that a young man's interest in a career in civil engineering or television production is at best incidental to the product the recruiter is seeking. Recruiters want to buy football players. Such a comment seems quite obvious, but it suggests a range of considerations for the "suppliers."

George Kelly, my former coach at Nebraska, who is now an assistant coaching legend at Notre Dame, once told me, "Give me pre-med and engineering students with good football skills, and I won't lose a game." Well, you and I know that games are dependent on a whole lot more than that, but I understand what he meant. Good athletes who are also good students provide brain power that complements their physical skills.

Students who can't or won't perform in the classroom are also limited on the football field. More recruiters, therefore, seek players with physical as well as mental skills. What the player chooses to do with his mental skills off the football field is normally his business and is not a focus for the recruiter during the recruiting process. However, a high school players' mental skills must be one of the primary focuses of the athlete, his parents, and his coach.

I suspect an inverse relationship exists between the high school's focus on the needs of the athlete and the potential for abuse by college coaches. Intercollegiate abuses are not exclusively the fault of college coaches. Certainly a few have accepted heat from the media because their misuse of college athletes is most visible. Some university officials have also been blamed for not taking control of their respective schools' athletic programs.

To effectively prevent abuses or misuses on the college level, questions of control must be answered before the athlete selects a school. High school coaches, safe from the media spotlight, must share some of the blame of misuse of college athletes. The better the high school coach's job in the recruiting process, the less potential there is for abuse on the college level.

════════════ EXTENDING THE CONSUMER ANALOGY ════════════

A closer look at college recruiters as consumers sheds additional light on the responsibilities of coaches at both levels:

- *Quality*—All consumers seek quality. The consumer's job is to find it; the suppliers job—if he wants to sell his product—is to provide evidence of it. Most college recruiters, therefore, expect to see films and/or tapes that highlight player performance. They have infrequent opportunities to watch games because of their own schedules, so tapes become very important. See Section Seven for a review of this topic.

Because quality is such an important issue, high school coaches must be careful not to oversell certain players. Sometimes the high school coach's fondness for a player causes him to overestimate the player's potential for college football, even at the Division III level. A mediocre player who fails to meet the college coach's expectations damages the credibility of the high school coach and his ability to sell future players.

High school coaches, therefore, must be careful to accurately assess the abilities of players, then to display those skills in such a way as to attract the attention of principled recruiters. When coaches do this, they enhance their credibility and become a favorite "shopping place" for college coaches. At this point, they become very powerful people because recruiters need them. The recruiters are inclined *on that basis alone* to treat their players fairly.

- *No Hassle Buying*—When recruiters find quality, they want to buy quickly, or at least they want to know they can stay in the bidding. Any high school coach with one or more blue chippers knows that telephones can transform overnight into inconvenient conveniences. The coach is pestered in his office, the parents at home, and the athlete at school. Quality athletes receive immediate and numerous scholarship offers. Obviously, the sooner they make decisions, the less time is wasted by recruiters and players alike.

That's why the information in section one is so important. The greater the preparation before the recruiting process starts, the easier it will be to make a decision. Once the decision is made, everyone wins. The player can get on with his schoolwork, and the recruiter can either sign him or start looking elsewhere. The sooner the recruiter can expand his search, the better his chances to find the players he wants.

- *Bargains*—Someone once defined a bargain as a deal in which both parties think they've cheated the other. Perhaps the word cheating is a little extreme, but such a definition is not that far from the truth. We all like to be smart shoppers, especially when our finances are limited. Recruiters in all schools have a limited number of scholarships to offer and want the most for their money. Recruiters in NCAA Division Iaa and Division II schools want to get as many quality players as they can for the smallest partial scholarships they can offer.

It's not a matter of cheating, just of shopping intelligently. The same is true of dealing with walk-ons. A good walk-on is one of football's best bargains. He comes free, and he eliminates speculation for the recruiters. Mark Twain once indicated that there are two times in your life when you should not speculate: when you can't afford to—and when you can. Walk-ons don't involve either. Review chapter ten for ideas involving high school players who may want to walk on in college.

- *Using the Product*—To repeat, recruiters are not buying rocket scientists; they're buying football players: big, tough kids with the physical and, hopefully, the intellectual skills to contribute to a winning program. They're interested only incidentally in a young man's intellectual pursuits and career interests. Certainly the satisfaction of such interests can become an important issue, but only after the young man's physical skills have made him a "commodity."

It stands to reason, then, that someone other than recruiters must guarantee all the other factors that constitute a successful college experience for student-athletes. The large part of that responsibility falls to high school coaches. Their job is to assure the fair treatment of the "product"—or they don't deal with that recruiter again.

Recruiting Restrictions

The person to really worry about in the recruiting process is not the cheater but the college coach who doesn't know what he's doing. Cheaters know the rules; they just manipulate them. The coach who doesn't know what he's doing can cause all kinds of trouble—in the most well-intentioned ways. It's wise, therefore, for high school coaches, even athletes, to know the important recruiting restrictions, regardless of the qualifications or intentions of recruiters.

- *Contacts*—College coaches can contact high school students only after the completion of the player's junior year. A "contact" is any face-to-face meeting away from the coach's campus involving a simple hello. Players can meet with college coaches before the completion of the junior year if the player pays for all the expenses of the visit and if the visit occurs on the coach's campus. Additional restrictions govern the frequency of recruiting contacts; they can be found in *The NCAA Guide for the College-Bound Student Athlete*. A copy can be secured by writing the NCAA, 6201 College Boulevard, Overland Park, Kansas 66211, or by calling 913-339-1906.

- *College Visits*—During the senior year, an athlete may receive only one full-expense paid trip to a particular campus, and he may engage in only five such visits to different schools. He can visit a campus as often as he wants, but recruiters can pay for only one visit. Additional visits must be financed by the athlete, and there is no limit to how many campuses he may visit as long as he's paying the bill. This restriction applies even to athletes who are being recruited for more than one sport.

- *Entertainment*—During the visit, the athlete may receive housing and meals, and he may be entertained by someone from the college or university. The host may receive up to $20 for entertaining the athlete, but he may not use the money to purchase a college souvenir for the athlete.

- *Boosters*—Most highly recruited athletes and their parents realize that the athlete can receive no benefit or inducement to sign with a particular college or university. Less well-known is the fact that university alumni or boosters are not allowed to help recruit. High school coaches must be careful to advise their athletes accordingly.

- *Recruiter Drop-Ins*—Recruiters are permitted by the NCAA to visit athletes three times away from school and once per week at school during December 1 through the first day for signing the National Letter of Intent, excluding certain periods of time as specified by the NCAA. High school coaches are well advised to require college recruiters to check with them before contacting the athlete at school. Such a procedure will protect highly recruited athletes from a parade of coaches wanting to see them. Because this time of the school year usually involves final exams, athletes don't need to be bombarded by recruiters who are interested primarily, maybe exclusively, in the athlete's football ability. See figure 13–1 for a reproducible.

THE NEEDS OF THE ATHLETE

We already have discussed at length the academic and career needs of student-athletes. We have acknowledged that such needs are the student-athlete's primary reasons for selecting a particular school. There are other reasons as well. These additional reasons must be discussed with the athlete and his parents before and after he visits a college and begins to make preliminary decisions.

If you are being recruited or expect to be recruited by one or more colleges within the next several months, you and your parents require some special information. The coaching staff recommends that you learn the following information so that you don't jeopardize your future playing career by violating one or more of the regulations of the NCAA or the NAIA.

The following information explains how and when college recruiters can contact you regarding the possibility of attending their school:

What is a contact? A "contact" is any face-to-face meeting away from the coach's campus involving a simple hello. This is not to say that if you bump into him in a shopping mall and say "hi," you're going to be in hot water with the NCAA. It does mean that you cannot arrange to meet the coach, nor can he arrange to meet you, anywhere other than *his* campus before the completion of your junior year in high school. If you do meet him before the completion of your junior year on his campus, *you* must pay the expenses of the trip.

ADDITIONAL RESTRICTIONS

1. You may receive *one* full-expenses paid trip to a particular campus. Additional trips to that campus must be paid for by you. Altogether, you may receive full-expenses visits to a maximum of five campuses. You may visit other schools beyond the five permitted by the NCAA, but such visits have to be financed by you. This restriction applies even to athletes who are being recruited for more than one sport.

2. During each visit, you may receive housing and meals, and be entertained by a host from the college. Your host may receive up to $20 to cover expenses, but the money may not be used to buy you a souvenir.

3. You may not receive benefits or inducements to sign with a particular school, nor may alumni or boosters from that university help recruit you. Be very careful in this area. Many boosters and alumni aren't aware of this restriction and might unknowingly jeopardize your athletic future.

4. Recruiters are permitted by the NCAA to visit you three times away from school and once per week at school from Dec. 1 through the first day for signing the National Letter of Intent, which is your promise to play for a particular school. *I* will make arrangements for all recruiters to stop by my office first before they can see you in school. I'm sure your parents will agree that you should not be bothered during school hours.

Talk to me if you have additional questions.

FIGURE 13–1

======================== **DURING THE VISIT** ========================

Athletes must have several very important questions answered by recruiters and others during the campus visit or at some time during the recruiting process. Many of these questions can be answered by persons other than coaches, so one of the first pieces of advice to offer a recruited high school athlete making his first college visit is to TALK TO PEOPLE. He must aggressively seek answers to his questions, not simply allow the totality of the experience to overwhelm him. Figure 13–2 will help.

Because the recruiter/coach is the primary person in the process, most of the questions will start with him.

- *Ask the Recruiter*:
    —"What position do you want me to play, and how many other players are being recruited for the same position?" Generally, coaches will answer this question honestly, particularly if it is asked in the presence of the high school coach. It is such an important question, in fact, that I always ask it just before one of my players leaves for his visit. I call the football office and ask the recruiting coordinator several questions, the first two of which are always, "How many players are you recruiting in his position?" and "How many of your current players in that position are returning?"
    —"What is your philosophy of offense? Defense? Are you considering any changes?" College programs that are struggling to establish themselves will often vary their offensive attack to capitalize on the skills of their best players or simply to find something that works for them. High school players who have pronounced but limited skills—great throwers who can't run, for example—need to know this.
    —"Do you plan to red-shirt me?" Red-shirting generally works to the advantage of the player. He adjusts easier to a new environment, gets another year to grow, and receives a fifth year of financial aid to complete his education or to pursue graduate work. Some athletes, however, prefer to play immediately and to try to graduate in four years. Regardless of the player's preferences, the knowledge of whether or not he will be red-shirted will influence how he approaches the first few months of his college experience. For example, if red-shirted, he might assume a full academic load his first semester; if playing, he might take the minimum load—usually 12 semester hours—to lessen some of the academic stress during the season.
    —"If I need a fifth year, will you finance it?" More and more athletes every year require five years to earn their degrees. This, too, is one of the first questions I ask recruiters when they express interest in a player, particularly when the school is rebuilding its program. The more often recruiters are required to promise a five-year scholarship to players, the

Before you decide to make your first visit, it's a good idea to think carefully about the kind of information you are going to need to eventually make a decision. Once you do, you'll be able to ask the right kinds of questions. Following are some good ones to get you started.

ASK OF THE RECRUITER:

1. What position do you want me to play, and how many others are you recruiting for the same position?
2. What is your philosophy of offense? Defense? Are you considering any changes?
3. Will I be red-shirted?
4. If I need a fifth year, will you finance it?
5. What happens to my scholarship if I'm injured or ineligible?
6. Who do I see if I have academic problems?
7. Has drug use been an issue at your school?
8. Are all injuries handled by a team insurance policy?
9. If injured, can I use my family doctor? Who determines my fitness to play after an injury?
10. What is expected of players during the off-season?

ASK OF PLAYERS AT THE SCHOOL:

1. What does your typical daily schedule look like? In-season? Off-season?
2. Approximately how many hours a night do you study?
3. What generally are the attitudes of professors in different fields of study?
4. How do you like the living arrangements?
5. Do you have an academic advisor who helps you register for courses? Is he/she any good?
6. Are the coaches available to help if I have academic problems?

ASK OF NON-ATHLETES AT THE SCHOOL:

1. What do you think of the quality of the education you are receiving at this school?
2. If you had it to do all over again, would you choose this school to attend? Why or why not?
3. What is the general opinion of athletes on this campus?

ASK OF SCHOOL OFFICIALS/ADMISSIONS OFFICERS:

1. What is the graduation rate for football players?
2. About how long does it take a football player to earn a degree at this school?
3. What is the placement rate and the average starting salary for graduates in (your field of study)?
4. What is my eligibility for additional financial aid?

If you like any or all of these questions, let's talk about them before you visit a particular school. Let's include your parents in the discussion.

FIGURE 13–2

more likely they will deliver. They can't put such a promise in writing because of NCAA regulations, but they can commit orally.

—"What happens to my scholarship if I'm injured or academically ineligible?" The five-year commitment should cover both contingencies—within reason. A career-ending injury should not terminate the school's commitment to finance five years of education, particularly if it was the school's decision to red-shirt the player. The same is true of a player's academic ineligibility—unless the school drops him for academic or other reasons.

—"What academic assistance programs are offered/required by the team? Does the football program require academic study halls, advisement, built-in assistance? What about individual tutors? What do I do/who do I see if I have academic problems with one or more courses?" These questions are critically important, considering the demands on players' time, especially in-season.

—"What are the specifics of team discipline? What kinds of discipline problems have you responded to within the past few years? Is there a specific written code? Has steroid use been an issue at all? Do you require drug testing? What penalties are applied?" The answers to these questions provide insights into the kinds of players previously recruited. Drug-free athletes don't want to be competing with steroid users for a position on the team, nor do they want to associate with "bandits" who are not remotely interested in working toward a degree.

—"Are injuries handled by a team insurance policy? Will my parents be expected to use their policy to supplement the school's?" Answers to these questions can save parents a lot of money.

—"If injured, can I use my family doctor? Who determines my fitness to play again after an injury? The team doctor? Can I get a second opinion?" Stories of football and basketball players dying during games or at practice because of questionable medical treatment shock us. Fortunately, they are rare. Less rare and far less publicized are the stories of players who ended their careers because they played on an injury that should have sidelined them.

—"What is expected of players during the off-season?" Good conditioning has become a year-round proposition. Competition for positions has become so pronounced in many schools that players must commit to an almost daily regimen of running and weightlifting during the off-season. In addition, some schools expect players to assist with the recruiting of high school players, to escort them during their campus visits. Such commitments take time away from course work. It's wise to get these issues into the open before they become problems.

—"What are the chances of getting help to find summer jobs?" This may not be a pivotal question, but the answer can avoid a lot of trouble during the early summer months, and it's a fringe benefit that might as well be explored. The NCAA prohibits the involvement of boosters or alumni during the recruiting process, but it permits their involvement in such things as providing summer jobs after the Letter of Intent has been signed by the player.

* *Ask of Players at the School:*

   —"What does your typical daily schedule look like? In-season? Out-of-season?" Only a player can answer these questions. A coach's time perspective is substantially different. Meetings, meals, practice, taping, therapy for injuries, in-season conditioning, movies, and getting to and from these activities can add up to a whole lot more time than even coaches realize.

   —"Approximately how many hours a night do you study/work on assignments to be successful in (the player's program of study)?" The answer to this question relates to the players' daily schedules but provides more specific information about the demands of certain academic programs. Obviously, the recruit should talk to several players in his field of study in order to get a range of reactions. Some quick addition can reveal a total time commitment that tells the recruit if this particular school is right for him.

   —"What are the attitudes of the professors in (the recruit's field of study)?" Let's face it, the idea that small concessions have to be made occasionally for college football players may be bothersome to some non-athletes and much of the media, but the reality remains: football players' schedules require occasional flexibility from professors who understand the time demands being imposed on them by sources well beyond their control. That's not to say that professors must gift-wrap grades or abandon attendance requirements, but it is helpful if they provide make-up opportunities and reasonable extensions when players need them.

   —"How do you like the living arrangements?" The answer to this question is particularly important if players stay in an athletic dorm or share a room only with other football players. Growing numbers of coaches and university officials are asserting that athletes benefit considerably more from their total college experience if they room and associate with regular students as well as teammates. Certainly the college experience is more broadening if their range of acquaintances extends well beyond the football field.

   —"Do you have an academic advisor who helps you register for courses? Is the advisor a coach? Is he/she any good?" My experience has included several players who went to college and had real problems during their first year because of poor academic advice. Often they were overwhelmed by a first-semester schedule that included too many credits and too strong an academic emphasis. Sometimes they were even steered in the wrong direction. The quality of the counseling received on campus is often one of the biggest factors influencing the success athletes experience on and off the field.

—"Are the coaches available to help if I have academic problems?" Coaches may give one answer to this question, the players another. It's wise to ask both of them.

—"How involved are the players in off-season activities that are required by the coaches?" This also is a question to be asked of both coaches and players. Sometimes the answers are substantially different.

- *Ask of Non-Athletes*

—"What do you think of the quality of the education you are receiving at this school?" This question addresses the primary reason for selecting a particular school. It should be emphasized with the recruit before he leaves to visit schools.

—"If you had it to do all over again, would you choose this school to attend? Why or why not?" This question can provide very revealing information. Many students become adjusted to a particular routine, establish new friendships, and choose to remain on a campus that they might otherwise have left after the first year. Many of them will indicate as much if this question is phrased correctly.

—"What is the general opinion of athletes on this campus?" Answers to this question reveal far more than the biases of non-athletes. If the consensus opinion is that they are "irresponsible jerks," then the coaches are not doing their jobs to sign the right kinds of people or to emphasize the right values and behaviors in their players. If the opinion is that they are "OK" or "just like the rest of us," the school and the coaching staff have achieved a good balance between athletics and academics.

- *Ask of Admission Offices/University Officials:*

—"What is the graduation rate for football players and how does it compare to the general student population? NCAA Division I universities are now required to share such information. This is another question that probably is best asked by the high school coach before the recruit decides to visit a particular school. In some schools, answers to this question are shocking. For this reason it is wise to ask the question of university officials; their interests are not as biased as coaches.

—"About how long does it take a football player to earn a degree at this school?" The NCAA has made recent attempts to reduce the time demands on all college athletes. The adjustments have been helpful, but the average athlete's time commitment is still substantial, especially if he is dedicated to his sport. A five-year graduation rate has become prevalent within many major universities, especially with the red-shirting during the first year in many schools. Many athletes will play for four years and still not graduate. This, too, is a concern of the NCAA and should be a primary consideration for the recruited athlete.

—"What is the placement rate and the average starting salary for graduates with a degree in (the recruit's field of study)?" Four or five years of good times are not worth it if the player can't find a job after graduation.

Some schools have exceptionally high placement rates; others not so good. This is an important question to ask during the recruiting process, perhaps one of the most important.

—"What is the eligibility for additional financial aid?" This is an important question for athletes receiving partial scholarships, but it is equally appropriate for those receiving full scholarships. Athletic scholarships are confined to the cost of room, board, tuition, fees, and books at the institution. Other monies, such as Pell Grants, may be received up to the "cost of attendance" at the school. Parents may be especially interested in this information!

AFTER THE VISIT

This is another good time to activate the Coalition. The concern and the support from parents, the coach and the counselor provide the atmosphere a young man needs to think through the experiences he has had during his visits. The Coalition may decide to meet with him when he has completed all his visits or after each one. Obviously, time and scheduling availability are considerations. My experience has been that the Coalition should meet with the player when he has completed all his college visits. His parents and coach, however, should sit down with him to discuss his reactions after each one.

The kinds of questions asked during these meetings are very important if the player is to focus on the right issues. See figure 13-3 for a reproducible. Following are some examples:

—"Did any of the recruiters have bad things to say about the other schools that are recruiting you?" The job of a good recruiter in a classy school is to sell his school to potential athletes, not to bad-mouth everyone else. I become immediately suspicious of the college recruiter who starts blowing out everyone else's candles to make his own shine brighter.

—"Did any of the recruiters promise you a starting position during your visit?" This is an attractive and complimentary offer, but it is generally dishonest. The skill levels of most college football players are not differentiated enough to guarantee starting positions to incoming freshmen. Good seniors have a tough enough time holding down starting positions from one year to the next. Again, be suspicious of the recruiter who makes such comments. I've always believed that a promise is something that is easier said than done. Some college coaches prove it every year.

—"Would I attend this school if I had no intention of playing football?" This question forces the athlete to consider all the factors that don't relate to football. Such a focus is very important, particularly if the player's life revolves around the sport. Sometimes it's even a good idea to have him make a list of the factors that genuinely impress him about a particular school, *none* of which can relate to football. Injuries are commonplace in college football. A related question is, "If I get injured and cannot play, will I want to stay at this school?"

—"Do the coaches and players enjoy good relationships? Do they seem to care about each other?"

—"Will I be successful academically at this school? Athletically? In essence, will I develop as an athlete and as a person?" Sometimes a young man, even a gifted athlete, has to be encouraged to reach beyond his immediate grasp. His desire for quick success sometimes results in the course of least resistance. You and I realize that the course of optimal resistance results in the greatest growth. This again is where the Coalition plays an important role.

—"Were the people I met honest, available to me, friendly, genuinely interested, or were they basically disinterested and phony?" Young men, perhaps better than you and I, can spot a phony. All they need is a push in the right direction.

—"Were the coaches interested in academics? Did they talk about my educational and career interests?" An exclusive focus on football during the visit says a lot about the priorities of the coaching staff. Conversely, recognition of the "student" in student-athlete suggests something of the roles coaches will expect players to perform.

—"Will I fit in with the rest of the student body at this particular school?" Football will consume a lot of time, especially in-season, but most of the player's time will be in the classroom, his room, someone else's room, or any of several social settings on and off campus. The "football fraternity" has strong ties, but they're not the only ones on campus.

—"What happens if one or more of the coaches leave? Will I still be happy with the school? The football program?" This is an easily overlooked question but one of the most critical. I overlooked it with my daughter Peggy a few years ago. Recruited by a basketball program that had everything she wanted in a school, she accepted a scholarship offer. She discovered upon her arrival at school in the fall that the head coach, the coach who had recruited her, had resigned to accept a job elsewhere.

The program went steadily downhill: relationships suffered and losses piled up until finally the school decided to drop the women's basketball program. Rather than transfer to another school, however, my daughter decided to forego any more basketball because she was so happy with her current school. It all worked out well for her, but she lost an important element in her life when basketball was dropped. We might have avoided some of the problem with a well-directed question during the recruiting process.

The issue can be further complicated in football because of the influence of assistant coaches, many of whom leave quality programs to become head coaches elsewhere. A players' relationship with the assistant he works with each day is very important to that player's attitude about the game. The loss of such a relationship can cause adjustments that may affect his play.

On the other hand, the loss of a coach may have no effect on the player's performance. The point is, a recruited athlete may have selected one school over another because of one or more of the coaches. If the coach were to leave, the

QUESTIONS TO ASK AFTER THE VISIT

You will have to ask yourself several important questions *after* you have visited your schools in order to ultimately decide on the right school. These questions will get you started in the right direction:

1. Did any of the recruiters have bad things to say about the other schools that are recruiting me?

2. Did any of the recruiters promise me a starting position? If they did, they probably were being less than honest.

3. Would I attend this school if I had no intention of playing football?

4. Do the coaches and players seem to genuinely care about each other?

5. Will I be successful academically at this school? Athletically? How do I measure up to everyone else?

6. Were the coaches and players I met honest, available to me and others, friendly, genuinely interested, or did they seem phony?

7. Were the coaches interested in academics? Did they ask me about my educational and career interests?

8. Will I fit in with the rest of the student body at this particular school?

9. How will I feel if one or more of the coaches leaves? Will I still be happy with the school? The football program?

10. Does the school satisfy all the requirements that I identified earlier with my parents and counselor? This probably is the most important question. Give it a lot of thought.

Again, I am available to you and your parents if you want to discuss any or all of these questions.

FIGURE 13-3

school may suddenly be less desirable to the player. Such a problem can be avoided with a simple question during the recruiting process.

—"Does the school satisfy all the requirements I identified earlier with my counselor and parents?" This final question probably is the first to be asked when making a decision. It is mentioned last now because it brings the college selection process full cycle. The better the job done in the earlier college selection process, the easier the decision now.

FINANCIAL CONSIDERATIONS

Figure 13-4 provides important information about NCAA regulations regarding financial aid. The handout is not exhaustive, but it covers most of the important points for athletes and parents who are entering the recruiting process. It reminds them, for example, that athletic scholarships are one-year renewable and that other kinds of financial aid are available. It outlines the time limits of athletic aid and provides examples of proper and improper inducements to sign with a particular school. In conjunction with the other reproducibles in this section it provides very useful information for any recruited athlete.

LET'S WRAP IT UP

Studies indicate that high school athletes perceive geographical location and the reputation of the head coach as primary variables in the selection of a school. The graduation rate of athletes from the school is rarely mentioned as a reason for selecting a particular school. After a year or two in college, a sampling of athletes was asked to reassess their priorities and, in light of their recent experiences, indicate what their reasons should have been for selecting a school.

The college's curriculum jumped to the number one priority, and the graduation rate of athletes followed closely behind. Similarly, the athletic traditions of the school became more important, primarily as a reflection of the treatment of athletes and the school's balance between athletics and academics. Experience, it seems, gives athletes a whole new perspective on the important elements in the selection of the "right" school. Experience really is what you get when you're looking for something else!

Coaches and parents, therefore, must share their experience with recruited athletes through asking them the right questions. Such dialogue helps young players interpret their own experiences and identify their long-term goals in order to make intelligent decisions when selecting a school. It also reduces the possibility that unprincipled recruiters will take advantage of them.

In May of 1991, the Federal Trade Commission subpoenaed the 106 Division I football schools for records to support the FTC's claim that college sport is commercial—not educational. The FTC subsequently spent a lot of time re-

You'll need to have a general understanding of financial aid in college, especially the NCAA regulations. The following information should be helpful. Be sure to come to me with any questions you may have.

FINANCIAL AID

1. Athletic financial aid is awarded for only one year, but it is renewable. The school may inform you of institutional policies regarding automatic renewal, but it can't put it in writing.

2. Athletic financial aid may not exceed the cost of room, board, tuition, books, and fees at the institution. Other exempt aid such as Pell Grants (up to $1,400) may be received up to the "cost of attendance" at that particular school.

3. A school may award no more than five years of aid within a six-year period after the student enrolls.

4. A school must notify you of renewal or nonrenewal by July 1. If the aid is not renewed, you are entitled to a hearing.

5. Scholarships from outside sources for athletics must be administered through the school and may count against your athletic financial aid.

6. Aid may be limited by:
   6.1   The amount of aid permitted.
   6.2   The amount of aid countable in the sport limit, or
   6.3   The number of countable players in a sport.

IMPROPER INDUCEMENTS

You also should be aware of inducements determined by the NCAA as improper. Inducements such as the following will jeopardize your college career:

1. Employment for prospect's parents or relatives.
2. Loans to relatives or friends.
3. Cash
4. Free services or rentals.
6. Free or reduced-cost housing
7. Other inducements as determined improper by the NCAA.

You may have employment arranged for you only after the completion of your senior year. A booster from the school can help with employment only after you have signed a National Letter of Intent.

FIGURE 13–4

261

searching a fairly obvious answer. Of course intercollegiate football is commercial; it's also educational. I learned some of life's best lessons on the football field at the University of Nebraska. Players today are learning the same lessons: the value of hard work, a confidence in one's own ability, a willingness to battle adversity, and the importance of teamwork.

I also learned that college football is big business. Stand outside Nebraska's Memorial Stadium on a sunny Saturday afternoon; you can *hear* the cash flow. Is college football commercial? You bet it is. Do recruiters want the best athletes in order to win and keep the bucks flowing in the right direction? You bet they do. Do I blame them? Absolutely not—unless they *use* athletes to do it.

The job of the high school coach and his Coalition is to make sure that colleges don't use players and that everyone gets a good deal. If you become familiar with the rules, ask your players the right questions, help them find their own best answers, and oversee the recruiting process, you will do much to help your players find a successful college experience. The player and his college coach will be winners. There's nothing wrong with that.

SECTION 14

Legal Issues

Trying to be reasonable with some football players is like trying to wave down a team of runaway horses. You'll look good—right up to the moment they run over you. But it's a chance coaches have to take. "Reasonability" is the standard used within every court system in the country. It is the basis for most due process considerations and all questions of negligence.

Consider substantive due process. The rule of reasonability requires that all rules and expectations be within the athlete's ability to perform, that they be clearly understood by the athlete, and that they be consistently communicated to him. It would not be reasonable, therefore, to kick a player off the team for using smokeless tobacco if snuff and chewing tobacco were not mentioned in the training rules or if the training rules were not communicated consistently enough to guarantee that all players understood them.

Reasonability also applies to questions of negligence. In essence, a court may ask, "Would a reasonable man have done the same thing under similar circumstances?" Given the current volume of medical opinion regarding the need for water during practice, for example, it is *not* reasonable to deprive players of water in order to condition them or "toughen them up." A dehydrated football player purposely deprived of water could cost a coach his job—and then some. One recently died in an Arizona high school. The parents sued for $850,000—and won.

Consider one of high school sport's biggest examples, the NCAA's Bylaw 14.3. The school that fails to inform its athletes of Bylaw 14.3's provisions opens the door to possible litigation, particularly if one of its athletes fails to receive a scholarship because school personnel didn't inform him or his parents of NCAA regulations.

The issue of reasonability, therefore, is the underlying concept throughout the remainder of this section. It relates to everything we as coaches do with our players, in-season and out.

=========================== PRE-SEASON CONSIDERATIONS ===========================

Off-Season Conditioning

All the reproducibles found in Section Nine and several of the other references within the book that relate to conditioning and nutrition suggest consultation with the family doctor to develop a program that meets the special health needs of individual athletes. Such a qualifier accommodates athletes with specific health problems and provides written evidence of the coach's reasonable approach to conditioning and nutrition. Reasonability is further enhanced each time the coach emphasizes conditioning to prevent injuries as well as to enhance performance. He is most reasonable and least subject to litigation the more often and the more clearly he communicates all of his expectations.

Equipment

- Proper Maintenance—Football coaches are on solid ground legally if they have all player equipment checked and repaired annually. If this is not done with used and older equipment, especially with shoulder pads and helmets, the coach and school are open to litigation in the event of injury due to equipment failure.

- Documentation—Coaches should file all equipment invoices and guarantees in the event of player injury during practice or a game. They are written proof that the coach and school have exercised a reasonable standard of care of all player equipment. This includes the routine maintenance and repair of "blasters," two and seven-man sleds, ropes, and other training devices used during practice.

- Proper Fit—As many coaches as possible should be on hand during the distribution and fitting of player pads and helmets. Each player should be checked to see that equipment fits properly, even to the point of having each player acknowledge that it all "feels OK." Periodically during the first few days of practice some players will complain of headaches. Normally they are caused by the lack of familiarity with the helmet, but occasionally, some players may need a different sized helmet. It's wise to take the few moments to acknowledge each complaint.

- Player Care—It's also a good idea to tell the team during your first meeting in the fall that the school has spared no expense to get them the best equipment available and that you expect them to take care of it. Let them know that sitting on their helmets or throwing them is unacceptable and that they will be expected to tell a coach if any piece of equipment is missing or needs repair.

Permission Slips

It simply makes good sense to have appropriate permission slips on file at all times. The two most important are from the athlete's parents and his doctor. (See figure 3–1 in Section 3.) Some schools secure the athlete's signature as well and provide a reminder of the Athletic Code, including specific references to violations of training rules. The form also makes reference to insurance coverage, and it requests specific information in case of injury.

The original form should be kept on file in the athletic director's office, and a copy should be given to the school trainer and/or the football coach in the event of an emergency. Once the permission sheet has been given to the athletic director, he or she should give the player a permission slip to give the coach and/or the equipment manager to receive his equipment.

Information Sheet

Another important piece of information is the sheet which is distributed to incoming freshmen and transfer students. It simply lists the sports available in the school and provides yet another reminder about the school's requirements for student behavior during athletic competition. Again, remind athletes and their parents about school expectations at every opportunity. It makes for excellent communication and satisfies the provisions of substantive due process. See figure 14–1.

Special Needs Sheet

Finally, it's generally a good idea to identify athletes with special medical or physical needs. Coaches can distribute copies of figure 14–2 before the season starts and file them separately in order to have a complete record of special medical needs. Normally, only a few players have such needs. Their names and conditions should be shared with all coaches, the trainer, the school nurse, and the athletic director.

The Pre-Season Meeting

All football players—at all levels—and their parents should be encouraged to attend an evening meeting that is held during the first week of practice and that introduces everyone to the football program. This is the time to introduce the coaches, trainers, managers, booster club officers, and others who are in any way associated with the program. It is also the time to explain important

HIGH SCHOOL ATHLETICS

Fall Season

Boys Cross Country
Girls Cross Country
Field Hockey
Football
Boys Golf
Girls Golf
Boys Soccer
Girls Swimming
Girls Tennis
Girls Volleyball

Winter Season

Boys Basketball
Girls Basketball
Girls Gymnastics
Boys Swimming
Boys Indoor Track
Girls Indoor Track
Wrestling

Spring Season

Girls Badminton
Baseball
Girls Soccer
Softball
Boys Tennis
Boys Track
Girls Track
Boys Volleyball

Requirements of All Athletes:

1. Yearly physical

2. Attendance at one Athletic Code Meeting

3. Yearly parent permission

4. Passing work in 20 hours of classwork per week

FIGURE 14–1

SPECIAL MEDICAL ATTENTION

Please provide the following information if your son has a special medical condition of which his coaches should be aware.

Player's Name _____ Parents' Names _____

Home Address _____

Home Phone _____

Doctor's Name _____ Doctor's Phone _____

Please describe the condition and provide relevant information from the family doctor:

Special circumstances of which the coaches should be aware: (medication, physical limitations, and so forth)

Please feel free to share additional information with any member of the coaching staff.

FIGURE 14–2

procedures and to introduce—or re-introduce—information about the NCAA and the school's training rules.

- Training Rules—Training rules are not designed to trip up young athletes or "to catch 'em being bad." They are intended to emphasize the values that are important to the football team and its coaches, namely appropriate behavior and good mental and physical health. They should be presented as such to all athletes and their parents. Good training rules are not used to beat kids over the head but to give them something to hold on to. Remind parents of this every time the opportunity presents itself.

- Equipment—It's generally a good idea at this initial meeting to have one of the players model his uniform while a coach explains each piece of equipment to the parents. Parents find the information very interesting, mothers in particular. They also leave the meeting feeling more comfortable about junior's physical well-being.

- Regulatory Organizations—This meeting should involve yet another reminder about the provisions of the NCAA and the NAIA. The passouts that are normally distributed to the freshman athletes and their parents (See figure 10–3 and 10–6) can be redistributed at this time.

- Injury Procedures—This meeting also is a good time to discuss the team's injury procedures. You might even distribute copies of the school's accident report to inform parents of the process followed. See figure 14–3. I make a point of emphasizing the section entitled "Follow-Up." It allows the person who is documenting the injury to indicate when and if he informed the parents and/or the family doctor or hospital emergency room.

  It also gives the coach a chance to express his personal and professional reaction to injuries. Any injury that sidelines a player or that suggests the least possibility of permanent damage requires a doctor's OK for the athlete to continue playing. Even then, if the coach observes significant movement restrictions or signs of obvious pain during practice or a game, he should sideline the player. I withheld a star fullback from a critical game one year because of an ankle injury. It probably cost us a state championship, but he went on to start 33 games for Notre Dame and is now a well-respected heart surgeon. I'm sure I didn't have much to do with his later success, but I do know that we didn't waste him on a high school football field.

  Make it clear to parents that certain injuries require a doctor's OK and that all injuries require your OK. Parents feel better when their son is playing football for a coach who simply refuses to jeopardize a young man's present and future physical well-being for the sake of a football game. Again, proper perspective and reasonability are key characteristics of the genuinely successful football coach.

- "Football is a Tough Game"—Conclude the meeting with a word about "football being a tough game." The kids need to hear such a speech in the

TOWNSHIP HIGH SCHOOL DISTRICT

☐ HIGH SCHOOL **ACCIDENT REPORT** ☐ HIGH SCHOOL

Name: _____ School Year ☐ 1 ☐ 2 ☐ 3 ☐ 4

(Last)　　　　(First)　　　　(Middle)

Date of Injury: _____　Time of Injury: _____

Place of Accident: _____　Classroom: _____

Sport or Activity: _____　☐ Game　☐ Practice

LEVEL:

☐ Interscholastic;　☐ Intramural;　☐ Physical Ed.; If Football—Quarter ☐ 1 ☐ 2 ☐ 3 ☐ 4

Description of Injury: _____

_____

How It Happened: _____

_____

Follow-Up: _____

_____

_____　_____
Signature of Teacher in Charge　　　　Signature of Department Chairman

FIGURE 14–3

presence of their parents. Most coaches encourage their players to "baby" themselves when it comes to illness: get a lot of rest; take the proper medication; maintain the appropriate diet. They do not expect them to baby themselves when it comes to the minor injuries that are the reasonable consequences of bumping into your fellow man.

Bumps and bruises, cuts and scratches, sore muscles, strains, and assorted aches and pains "go with the badge." Football players disregard them on a daily basis. This, too, is a part of the game, and players and parents both have to realize it. They will be more inclined to accept this fact once they realize that the coaches will not allow players to compete with potentially serious injuries.

IN-SEASON CONSIDERATIONS

The principle of reasonability applies to a wide range of in-season activities. Football coaches assume a standard of care that involves responsibilities far in excess of what many of them realize. Just a cursory glance at a book on school law reveals possibilities of negligence that wait for coaches daily on the practice and game fields. We must remain alert to each possibility, not only to avoid litigation but to provide for the physical and emotional well-being of each young man entrusted to our care.

Overpractice

We've already discussed the important differences between aerobic and anaerobic activities as well as the negative effects of unnecessary repetition on memory. Poor attitudes provoked by overpractice can actually inhibit players from learning important skills and assignments. In essence, the harder and longer we work beyond an optimal period of time (usually 15 times for a drill and half an hour to 45 minutes for a scrimmage), the less the players learn and the more likely they are to tune out everything we try to teach them.

- Poor Performance—I knew a coach once who had a "hate day" on the first day of practice following a loss. He had his players bumping into each other for the entire practice, attempting somehow to teach them a lesson. All he did was subject them to needless injury, prove that losing was always unacceptable, bang up two or three players, and teach them that football isn't fun.

  I know another one who told his players after a string of losses that they were a bunch of sissies. His solution? He told them to pair off—and start fighting. He allowed, even encouraged, them to use their helmets to beat on each other. Fortunately, he lost his job after three seasons. So did the "hate day" coach. Both schools realized not only the harm the coaches were doing the players but the massive litigation that might have resulted.

- Unnecessarily Rough Drills—Sometimes even the most reasonable coach among us involves his players in a drill that is unnecessarily rough. It's generally too rough because we discover that players are getting a lot out of it, so we extend it to the point where they get tired. Let's admit it, some coaches, especially the older ones like me, remember our playing days with extravagant generosity. We were invariably a bit faster, a whole lot stronger, blessed with more talent, and generally tougher than today's breed. Such "creative recollection" causes us at times to expect more from our kids.

- Overmatching Players—If we're not careful during line tackling and blocking drills, we can end up with physical mismatches that can result in significant injury to certain players. The barely maturing youngster who put on the pads because he wants to be "one of the guys" can suffer embarrassment as well as injury if somehow he squares off with your All-State prospect who in a year or two will be starting for Notre Dame. Even if the All-Stater backs off—maybe especially if he does—the smaller player will be embarrassed.

Before such drills, then, tell the players to match up according to size and experience. They'll get more out of the drill, and the smaller, less experienced players will avoid needless injury. They, too, will get more out of the drill because they'll be able to execute the skill being practiced more correctly.

The Case for Water Breaks

Fortunately, football has come a long way from the time when it was thought that the deprivation of water made players tougher. The medical community is loud and clear in its demands for significant water intake during strenuous exercise, especially in hot weather. The issue has been discussed extensively in Section Nine. Review it as needed. Be reminded, however, that insufficient water during any kind of competition negatively affects the athlete's level of performance and, if the coach can be proven "unreasonable," opens the door to possible litigation.

Premature Scrimmaging

A colleague of mine found himself in deep trouble one year when one of his juniors broke his neck during the first scrimmage of the year. The coach had enjoyed an illustrious playing career and several years of outstanding service to his school. In a few short years he had established a solid football program and a fine reputation in the community. All of it was jeopardized because he had forgotten to drill the team on the fundamentals of tackling before he started the season's first scrimmage.

Fortunately, both the young man and the school survived the experience, but the coach learned an important lesson. The less we assume as coaches, the better off we are. When in doubt, drill. Always err on the side of too much rather than too little. That's what reasonable coaches do.

Injuries

Remember, first of all, that you're not a doctor. You may have had several courses in biology, human anatomy, and first aid, but your expertise involves motivation and strategy, not medical diagnosis. Reasonability demands that any serious or potentially serious injury be properly treated by the school trainer and/or the player's family doctor. Again, the less we assume, the closer we will be to the expectations of reasonability.

A final word: we've already discussed the school's injury forms and their disposition. It's important, however, to reemphasize the two cardinal principles regarding player injuries. One, if you have the least doubt about the nature or the seriousness of a player's injury, refer him to his family doctor and notify his parents of your recommendation. Simply telling the player to "get a picture of that ankle" may not be enough. In their zeal to play, some athletes can fabricate some mighty tall tales about their injuries.

The second cardinal principal involves the athlete's return to competition after the injury. Always require a doctor's written permission for him to play. On occasion, the suggestion that a player receive a second professional opinion may be necessary, particularly if the family doctor's prescription seems too extreme. As indicated already in this chapter, the coach might also reserve his own OK for players who do not seem completely recovered.

Transportation

Transportation to and from games always requires special diligence from coaches. Not only have players thrown things from buses, they have been known to "moon" opposing communities and even fall from bus windows. "Mooning" may not be an affront to our sensibilities, but it does reflect on our programs. And anything falling from a bus window, especially a player (!), suggests serious legal problems.

One coach per bus, therefore, is the bare minimum. The team manager and the team captains normally may be very responsible, but they are ill-equipped, particularly in the eyes of the legal community, to control a busload of football players. So is the cheerleader sponsor or a volunteer parent. Guaranteeing the appropriate behavior and the safety of a football team is the responsibility of the people hired for that job—the coaches.

Another consideration about transportation involves the starting and ending points of the coach's/school's responsibility. Many parents prefer to take their sons home after an away game, and some players like to say they are going home with their parents, then jump into a car full of kids and head for the nearest party. We have avoided both problems by redistributing the reproducible in figure 14–4 to parents early in the season, usually at the pre-season meeting.

It outlines the school's responsibility in a very positive way, and it establishes a reasonable position by the coaching staff. It also provides a process for parents who must seek exception to the policy—a process that gets the total burden of responsibility off the coach's shoulders. See figure 14–15 for the permission slip to be forwarded to the coaching staff. If parents have not pursued this process, and we feel relatively certain that we have communicated it well enough, we require that players travel to and from the contest with the team at all times.

Effective Supervision of Players

The easiest way to guarantee the reasonable supervision of players is to expect that they will never be unsupervised. This is a point that must be emphasized at the first coaches' meeting of the season. Coaches must be on the field first and off the field last, and at least one of them, probably on a rotating basis, should be in the lockerroom area until all the players are gone.

Temptations for players are everywhere. When leaving the practice field, they may pass gymnastic equipment in the school, nearby playground equipment, even park district or school pools. An unsupervised pool can be an invitation to disaster for overheated football players, particularly if the coach decides to reward their hard work with permission to take a quick dip. At the moment such a reward may sound like a good idea to the coach, but it can be an invitation to all kinds of trouble, not the least of which is a million-dollar lawsuit.

The coach and school can be in enough trouble if athletes are injured due to questionable supervision, but if the coach invites the athlete to engage in activity that results in serious injury, the school doesn't have a legal leg to stand on. One might argue that coaches should not be intimidated by "litigation-happy" communities, that we should not behave in accordance with people who get their kicks racing in and out of courtrooms. I agree, and so would all those courtrooms. We have nothing to worry about—if we are reasonable.

─────────────── **LET'S WRAP IT UP** ───────────────

The President's Commission, a group of 44 university presidents working under the aegis of the NCAA, has succeeded in modifying the provisions of Bylaw 14.3. By 1995, college-bound student-athletes will be expected to complete a core of

TRAVEL TO AND FROM CONTESTS

All members of the ____________________ High School football team are expected to travel with the team to and from all away games. As representatives of the school, the coaching staff has a responsibility for the well-being of each member of the team. We also use the time for pre-game and post-game meetings and as opportunities after games to reaffirm the training rules. We appreciate your helping the coaching staff to enforce this policy because it is in the best interests of our players.

Parents who have no alternative but to seek an exception to the policy are asked to contact the school's athletic director at least one week prior to the game in questions.

Thank you for your help.

FIGURE 14–4

TO: Head Football Coach

FR: Athletic Director

RE: (Name of Athlete)

This is to inform you that _____ has received permission

from me to be picked up by his parents at the conclusion of the _____

game on _____. Please be sure that you talk to at least one of
his parents before he leaves your custody. Thanks.

FIGURE 14–5

13 academic units instead of 11 and to earn a high school grade point average of 2.5 instead of 2.0. The Commission also plans to enact a sliding scale for ACT and SAT scores.

Such changes provoke a range of feelings in coaches at all levels. All these feelings notwithstanding, our legal responsibility remains clear. We share the task of communicating such significant information to the people most directly affected by it, the athletes and their parents. It is important for all of us, therefore, to develop the habit of calling the NCAA whenever we have a question, and also to check the organization's routine mailings. The failure to do so could result in a missed opportunity for one or more of our players as well as a direct hit on your school's pocketbook.

To summarize this section, always keep two principles in mind to maintain your responsibility regarding information. One, find it. Maintain open channels with the NCAA and other regulatory and informational organizations. Two, share it—preferably in writing. Face-to-face communication with athletes and their parents, including the distribution of printed information, avoids potential legal problems and provides great public relations value for your football program.

Finally, guarantee that your coaching colleagues share your interest in reasonability. Proper perspective invariably leads to reasonable behavior, and proper perspective starts with the head coach.

SECTION 15

Budgeting and Fund Raising

A professor friend of mine once defined a budget as a "mathematical confirmation of his suspicions." For most football coaches, it is confirmation of nothing less than our annual fears and expectations. Generally, we can count on having an inadequate supply of dollars, especially when the seven-man sled needs new pads and the equipment manager has given up trying to get the grass stains out of the game pants.

Good budgeting habits will help resolve some of these problems, but not that many. Coaches generally operate with a predictably finite amount of money, so they rely instead upon fund-raising efforts, some of which can be very successful. Both budgeting and fund-raising are the focus of this chapter.

THE COACH'S BUDGET

It's important for coaches to realize that the generosity of their budgets is directly proportional to the kinds of relationships they establish within the school and community. School administrators and influential members of the community react favorably not only to winners but to colleagues and friends. Successful coaches are often both, generally because such behavior comes naturally to them and because they realize the value and satisfaction of establishing such relationships.

School administrators will react favorably to budget requests and members of the community will help with fund-raising efforts if the coach sells himself as well as his program. This aspect of budgeting money is often overlooked and should be acknowledged before actual consideration of the nuts and bolts. Even the nuts and bolts, however, involve important insights that many coaches fail to consider.

The Document

It costs money to run an operation. Our job is to find that money. How successful we are with this search is often determined by the way we perceive the budgetary process. College coaches and high school coaches tend to look at it a bit differently. This book already has acknowledged the commercialism of intercollegiate football. It isn't a secret, and it isn't a sin. As far as I'm concerned, college football programs can make a ton of money, as long as they play by the rules and consider the best interests of their athletes.

Because of their commercialism, however, they look at the budgetary process differently from high school coaches. To a large extent, their budget is earned. In essence, the more successful the program, the more money they make. Such a situation is not inherently bad, but it does introduce the potential for abuse because of the focus on earning money.

High school coaches, on the other hand, usually operate with a deserved budget. In fact, most high schools are financed by their constituencies and increase their budgets primarily by keeping the local community happy. They may sell a service in the broadest sense of the word, but even if the service is relatively poor, they know that they will continue to be subsidized by the community.

Such predictability is an advantage to the school and to the football program, but a deserved budget has its disadvantages as well. It may reduce the potential for abuse, but it also increases the probability of marginal planning by the coaches and others in the building. In essence, the budget becomes a statement of expenses instead of a planning document.

This section focuses on the budget as both: an indication of where the money is going and an expression of its use in terms of future plans. The document itself must provide room for each. See figure 15–1 for a reproducible. Subsequent figures will provide examples of how the document is used. The procedure is purposely simple. We don't want to spend a lot of time filling out a form, but we do want to sell the football program and receive the support we need to maintain it.

Expenditures

The actual outlay of money is divided into two categories. The fixed costs, as illustrated in figure 15–2, are approximately the same from year to year. They may be influenced by inflation and the slightly changing costs of the products and services coaches require, but they remain relatively predictable. The variable costs are unpredictable because they are influenced by factors beyond our control. Fortunately, as evidenced in the following figures, most of the football coach's expenses are predictable.

The "Expected" and "Actual" columns were included to show the discrepancies between the coach's anticipated costs and his real costs. A sizeable increase in the "Actual" column, for example, might reflect the inability of a supplier to continue providing his service or product at a previously low cost. Or it might reflect the coach's ability to find a less expensive but equally effective service or product. Whichever is the case, the coach should explain the discrepancy in the "Comments" section of the document, on the one hand to seek additional money next year, on the other to pat himself on the back!

BUDGET STATEMENT
DHS FOOTBALL

For the School Year:

Expenditures	Expected	Actual
Fixed		
Variable		

Objectives for the Year

1.

2.

Comments:

Coach's signature _____

FIGURE 15–1

279

BUDGET STATEMENT
DHS FOOTBALL

For the School Year:

Expenditures	Expected	Actual
Fixed Costs of officials	$ 600	
Transportation (away games)	$ 375	
Equipment maintenance	$1,283	
Helmet decorations and awards	$ 213	
Maintenance and marking of fields	$ 720	
Teaching equipment (new air flates)	$2,000	
Video costs (game and practice)	$ 350	
Scouting expenses	$2,200	
Professional expenses	$1,200	
workshops, conventions, clinics		
Total:	$8,941	
Variable		
None		

Objectives for the Year

    1.

    2.

Comments:

Coach's signature _____

FIGURE 15–2

Following are brief explanations of selected expenditures:

- *Coaches' Salaries*—The salaries of assistant coaches normally are included in the school's budget, not the football program's, but salaries are a budgetary item and, as such, sometimes warrant mention in the head coach's annual objectives.

- *Costs of Officials*—Officials must be scheduled not only for game days but for other purposes as well. Some teams use officials for their game-like intrasquad scrimmages which conclude pre-season practice. It's also wise to have them meet with the team before the scrimmage to underscore rule changes and answer questions. Because the scrimmage is shorter than an actual game, the officials normally will include the meeting in their regular stipend.

- *Transportation*—This item will vary from year to year, as will meals and housing and cash guarantees for visiting teams. It's wise, therefore, to perceive the budget as a multi-year proposition and build it accordingly from one year to the next. Increased expenditures resulting from atypical scheduling should be anticipated by the coach and the athletic director.

- *Equipment Maintenance*—Coaches can cut costs but not in this area. As indicated in the previous chapter, the proper maintenance of equipment involves significant legal issues. Less expensive maintenance services, therefore, must provide comprehensive guarantees, including the legal pledge to stand behind their work.

- *Awards and Decorations*—Stars, helmet decorations, numerals, and letters are not a major expense but can significantly affect the program's success. Many schools, ours included, decided years ago to give letters to everyone on the team. The elitist idea of awarding letters only to players who competed during the season in a specific number of quarters disregards the essential contribution that prep teamers make to the team's success. The player who never gets in a game often works harder and takes a bigger beating in practice than the team's star. He deserves a letter. Give him one—and everyone else like him—then take notice of how many students want to play football for you next year.

- *Teaching Equipment*—Stand-up dummies and air flates wear out considerably faster than the blaster and the seven-man sled, but they are not an annual expense. Coaches are advised to develop a replacement schedule to attach to the annual budget in order to anticipate such costs and to prepare the athletic director for additional expenditures. Such schedules should reflect manufacturer's specifications whenever possible. See figure 15–3. It's also wise to have such requests on record to avoid personal liability in the event a player is injured due to faulty equipment.

REPLACEMENT SCHEDULE
FOOTBALL EQUIPMENT

EQUIPMENT	DATE OF PURCHASE	SCHEDULED REPLACEMENT

COMMENTS:

FIGURE 15–3

- *Scouting Expenses*—Assistant coaches sacrifice a lot of time away from their families on weekly scouting assignments. Depending upon the distance traveled and meals required, they should be compensated accordingly.
- *Professional Growth Expenses*—Coaches are certainly within their rights to request funding for all professional growth expenses, including the costs of clinics, books, magazines, workshops, and conventions to enhance their performance. Included in such costs should be travel and room and board expenses for extended trips. If such funding is not possible, coaches should negotiate for some kind of paid release time to permit such experiences.

Objectives

Objectives can be stated in annual or multi-year terms. See figure 15–4. Generally, a coach wants to have at least one objective per year to improve his program and to reflect his planning ability. The objectives must not be restricted to win-loss records but should relate to student participation in the program, attendance figures at games, or professional involvement in the community.

Notice that the objective as written in figure 15–4 is stated in measurable terms and specifies the conditions to be realized. It specifies what is to be accomplished, not how it is to be accomplished. The "how"—the detailed solution—may have been selected from many and is outlined in the "comments" section of the document.

Other solutions might have been possible, including:

- Free bus transportation for parents to and from home games—refreshments served.
- Free drinks with hot dogs at school-sponsored tailgate parties at home games.
- Door prizes for adults, the prizes donated by local business communities.
- Sideline seating for regular attendees.

A little brainstorming will identify other possible solutions, some of which will be better than others. The coach simply combines two or three of the options or chooses the best of them to realize the specifics of his objective. If the performance requirements of his objective are not realized, he either reassesses the workability of the objective or seeks alternative solutions for the next year. The important point is, he is using his budget not only as a statement of expenditures but as a planning document.

BUDGET STATEMENT
DHS FOOTBALL

For the School Year:

Expenditures	Expected	Actual
Fixed		
Variable		

Objectives for the Year

1.

2. By the end of the current school year and at an added expense of no more than $400, the average adult attendance at home games will increase by at least 20% over this past year. This should result in an additional $400 in attendance receipts per home game, or a total of $2,000. (See "Comments")

Comments: (Objective #2) The Student Council agreed in a recent meeting to co-sponsor a "School Spirit Drive" to increase community attendance at home athletic contests and other school-sponsored activities. They plan to coordinate a competition among the freshman through senior classes to sell season and activity tickets to adults in the community, with the winning class to have a pizza lunch during an extended lunch period. The proposal has been approved by the administration. I am requesting additional funds to help with the costs of the pizzas and to assist with the increased attendance at football games.

Coach's signature _____

FIGURE 15—4

========================= **FUND-RAISING** =========================

Most of us are only too aware of the fact that money doesn't grow on trees. We learned a long time ago that we have to beat the bushes for it. Fortunately, the bushes can yield more than many of us realize. Fund-raising doesn't have to be a chore. In fact, much of it can be quite simple.

Let's consider some examples. The foremost among them is the most reliable and probably the most widespread, the ever-popular Booster Club. Most schools have parent Booster Clubs as well as student Pep Clubs, Varsity Clubs, and so forth. Each of these organizations provides significant fundraising potential, particularly the Booster Club. Parent assistance is so important to many coaches that they organize Parent Advisory Councils to help with the operation of selected elements within their programs.

Unfortunately, some coaches see the involvement of parents as an intrusion, primarily because they don't know how to work with them. Coaches who are able to establish positive relationships create allies within the community who can provide considerable help, including financial support. Parent Advisory Councils can provide the conceptual and vocal support football coaches require to establish a solid power base within the community, and they can give the energy and the "personpower" needed to conduct a variety of fundraising activities. it's nice to have someone beat the bushes for you.

In addition to parent and student groups, a range of popular and effective options are available to the coach seeking ways to supplement budgetary funds:

- *Candy, citrus fruit, and pizza sales*—Several commercial organizations are available to supply the product and the process for selling items to raise money.

- *Auctions*—Footballs from championship seasons, old game jerseys and helmets, photographs of former players, and what we thought was junk lying in the corner of the equipment room can raise a lot of money at "fun-type" auctions, especially if they're conducted at related activities such as football picnics or post-season dinners.

- *Dances*—An old-fashioned "Sock Hop" with everyone dressed in '50s costumes can involve parents as well as students after one of the home games. Door prizes, donated by the local merchants, can be awarded during the evening.

- *T-Shirts*—The United States is enjoying an unashamed romance with T-shirts—all kinds of T-shirts: tie-dyed, cut-off, sleeveless, and over-sized. The right slogan, particularly one celebrating the team's accomplishments, can make them a hot item within the community.

- *Liftathons*—Weight-lifting contests for which players secure monetary pledges from people in the community are often very successful. A pledge of only five cents per pound can result in a donation of $15 for a 300-pound bench press. We outfitted our weightroom after only two annual "Lifta-thons." The players worked hard at not only securing pledges but improving their own strength training. The winners in each category got their pictures in the yearbook.

- *AV tapes*—The widespread use and convenience of videotapes open the door to a variety of fund-raising activities, some of which remain untapped in many schools. Some schools routinely take orders for old game films from alums attending reunions. They sell them for $10–$15 a copy not only to former players but to many fans who enjoy reliving the "good old days" at a high school game.

In addition, highlight tapes of the past season, particularly if they include early shots of the whole team doing calisthenics, are desirable to seniors, even some juniors, at the conclusion of a season. The tape can be displayed at the door as athletes and parents enter the post-season banquet, or it can be shown as a part of the program. Orders can be taken afterwards.

Most schools have the capability to videotape games, then to edit them, and to add graphics and some music. Students involved in an AV club can do much of the work. The thoughtful football coach might even share this idea with other coaches in the school. The girls' sports as well as the other boys' sports have the same fund-raising potential and might donate some of their proceeds to charitable school activities such as the School Chest. Such donations coming from the athletic department do much to cement good relationships within the school.

═══════════════════ LET'S WRAP IT UP ═══════════════════

The budgetary process outlined in this section is purposely uncomplicated. Different schools may require different kinds of forms and documentation. The forms included in this section, therefore, may or may not serve your purposes. The forms really are unimportant; the process is what counts. The listing of expenditures, the identification of cost discrepancies, the development of objectives, and the description of solutions provide a format that reflects the coach's planning ability and justifies the school's generous investment in his program.

Another important element in the section is the emphasis that successful fund-raising is a function more of community relationships than of creative activities. Parent allies will invest themselves and their money in a football program and coach that are assets to the community. In many instances, particularly if the parent group is appropriately organized, the simple awareness that the football program needs a new "whatever" will motivate group members to handle the fundraising activities themselves.

A final important consideration involves the use of videotapes. The relative ease of filming, editing, and duplicating videotapes makes them perfect for selling to students and parents. Complete games and season or game highlights provide the visual memories that most players and their parents want to save for the future. Many schools across the country are developing videotaped supplements for printed yearbooks. Football programs can do much the same thing to supplement their fund-raising efforts and assist with the school's charitable activities.

Recordkeeping

During my first few years in this adventure that I hoped would become a career, I decided to do myself a favor and get organized. After what I thought was a good attempt, I suddenly realized that I had done nothing more than develop the ability to lose things more systematically. Instead of being simply lost, most of my scores, scouting reports, and practice plans had a place where they should have been—but weren't. I discovered that I still needed to get organized.

My filing and recordkeeping systems weren't bad. It doesn't take a rocket scientist to organize files and records. But the best filing and recordkeeping system in the world is worthless if it's never used. So it didn't take long for me to realize that organization is, above all, a frame of mind. Once I refined the system and made the decision to use it, I discovered that it actually worked for me.

A good recordkeeping system requires the efficient use of an effective process. This section discusses how to do both. It considers what information to keep and how to keep it.

THE "HOW"

The simpler and the more useful the process, the more likely you and I are to use it. I found one that works for me. Several years ago I determined what I needed to be effective and efficient. Simplicity was a prerequisite, so I used it as a standard for every decision I made about the process.

I decided that I needed three fundamental elements. One, I needed a system for saving and having relatively quick access to information that might be useful to me in the future. Successful offensive and defensive strategies versus past opponents, particularly effective practice routines, successful drills, even inspirational pep talk themes were among the items in this file. They constituted a pool of information that would be available to me during planning sessions, particularly when I was searching for ideas.

Two, I needed a file for the information that related to that year's program, an intermediate file in my office to provide quick answers to questions—anyone's

289

questions. It was a file that included such information as that season's game statistics, equipment repair invoices, and all relevant correspondence. It contained the kind of information that would be either discarded or filed for future reference at the end of the season/school year.

And three, I needed immediate access to a file of information that involved current decisions. It was a file that had to be nearby at all times because it involved that week's game or the relevant information regarding all recruited players. It involved information that was immediately useful and that was either discarded or abstracted and filed elsewhere after being used—to be replaced by the next batch of critical information.

I referred to this latter batch of information as my Immediate File, the current season's information as the Intermediate File, and the information for future reference as the Indeterminate File. The names are important only as references throughout the chapter. They illustrate how the system was developed; what it includes is the next consideration.

THE "WHAT"

The Immediate File contains information that coaches may need at work, at home after dinner or the night before a game, or in the car en route to the game field. This kind of information is routinely stored in manila folders with appropriate headings. To assure immediate accessibility, it should be filed in one or two briefcases and carried to and from work. I even bring mine in the car on relatively long trips to wrap up loose ends—when my wife is kind enough to drive!

Depending upon the time of the year, the following information generally is stored in the Immediate File:

- *Addresses, Phone Numbers, "Extras"*—because the coach's briefcase has suddenly been transformed into a portable workplace as well as a file, he should be sure to have all important addresses and phone numbers on hand. He should also carry a pad of paper and extra pens and pencils.

- *Game Plans*—The "ready list" for any game evolves during the week—particularly when players are injured, scouting reports and game films are re-analyzed, or someone comes up with a good idea.

- *Personnel Adjustments*—Players get hurt or suddenly perform so poorly that they must be replaced. It's always wise to carry a current personnel chart to reflect changes and to provide something substantive to review when analyzing or discussing offensive or defensive personnel.

- *Scouting Report*—As indicated in Section 5, the scouting report should include all the opponent's offensive and defensive tendencies. A periodic review of the report is helpful to reaffirm the game plan and to use as a guide or quick reference when analyzing films/tapes during the week. Such an analysis is ongoing throughout the week. All good coaches try to "get into the opponent's head" by watching his games. Often such reviews occur in the wee hours of the morning when coaches suddenly find themselves staring at the bedroom ceiling. The scouting report comes in handy at such times.

- *Individual Player Stats*—College recruiters sometimes call at the strangest times, especially near the end of the season when interest is brewing about particular players. Coaches should have ready access—in the office or at home—to individual statistics of highly recruited athletes to answer questions or provide information. See figure 16–1 for examples.

- *Scouting Reports/Upcoming Games*—Available scouting reports of future games should be reviewed periodically to determine if offensive or defensive changes will have to be made several weeks in advance to prepare for a particularly tough opponent. Many coaches, for example, will introduce substantial offensive changes against weaker opponents to give future, tougher opponents something to think about.

We ran the wishbone one year during our first three games to force a future opponent to devote precious practice time to defending "the bone." It worked. We caught our toughest opponent of the year off guard with our usual Wing T offense. He even laughed about it after the game—we think.

========================= THE INTERMEDIATE FILE =========================

The Intermediate File usually is stored in a cabinet in the coach's office and consists largely of manila folders. Some of the information has been transferred from the Immediate File; most of it is material that relates to the activities of the current school year. Because it is mostly temporary information, it is either discarded or transferred to another file at the end of the school year.

- *Season Statistics*—We've discussed in earlier chapters the value of scouting yourself: determining your own tendencies and identifying the successful defensive strategies of some of your opponents. That kind of accumulated information is very helpful as you plan for upcoming games. Your opponents scout you as hard as you scout them. Certainly you want to discover about yourself the same things they do. You also want to review the reasons behind your past offensive and defensive successes.

The successful strategies you used against the 44 gap stack early in the season may be potentially just as successful two weeks from now. That's why it's a good idea to quickly review previous games. Notice in figure 16–2, for example, that DHS played RM twice, the second time in playoff competition. The total

CAREER SUMMARY
GEOFF

1,818 RUSHING YARDS ON 213 CARRIES FOR AN 8.5 YARDS PER CARRY AVERAGE.

32 TOUCHDOWNS IN A SINGLE SEASON BREAKS SCHOOL RECORD OF 30 SET

BY BILLY _____.

372 YARDS IN A SINGLE PLAYOFF GAME TO BREAK RECORD SET BY LARRY

_____ OF _____ IN 1975 PLAYOFF GAME.

2,433 ALL PURPOSE YARDS IN TWO SEASONS.

27 YARD PER RECEPTION AVERAGE THIS YEAR.

100 CAREER TACKLES.

MIKE

SET SCHOOL RECORD FOR TACKLES PREVIOUSLY HELD BY ALL STATE TACKLE

JOHN _____. CAREER TOTAL NOW STANDS AT 165.

MADE KEY DEFENSIVE PLAY IN GAME AGAINST _____ THAT PROPELLED HIS TEAM TO VICTORY.

LED OFFENSIVE AND DEFENSIVE LINE PLAY FOR AN UNDEFEATED TEAM THAT AVERAGES 29 POINTS A GAME AND ONLY ALLOWS 10 POINTS PER GAME. OFFENSE AVERAGING 365 YARDS PER GAME.

FIRST THREE YEAR STARTER AT DEFENSIVE TACKLE IN SCHOOL'S RICH FOOTBALL HISTORY.

CALLED BY _____ COACH JOHN _____ THE BEST LINEMAN HE HAS SEEN IN THIS PART OF THE STATE IN THE LAST THREE YEARS.

ROCKY

HAS PLAYED IN THE SHADOW OF GEOFF _____ ALL YEAR. DURABLE FULL-BACK WHO HAS RUSHED FOR 788 YARDS IN 10 GAMES. STARTING MIDDLE LINEBACKER WITH 40 CAREER TACKLES AND 1 INTERCEPTION.

FIGURE 16–1

GAME SCORES	TOTALS										
	DHS 36 RM 14	DHS 27 WY 0	DHS 29 NW 6	DHS 6 ETHS 0	DHS 39 ME 7	DHS 28 HP 23	DHS 33 GBN 7	DHS 20 W 14	DHS 29 MW 8	DHS 38 C 14	DHS 34 RM 20

OFFENSE

RUSHING

YARDAGE	351	283	293	140	209	208	255	229	186	381	413
ATTEMPTS	49	41	49	43	40	43	29	49	41	43	41
AVERAGE	7.2	6.9	6	3.3	5.2	4.8	8.8	4.7	4.5	8.9	10.1

PASSING

ATTEMPTS	7	4	7	4	8	5	10	6	12	6	4
CMPLTD	3	3	3	3	7	2	9	2	9	2	2
YARDAGE	103	78	70	47	244	44	220	52	126	34	43

TOTAL

OFFENSE	454	361	363	187	453	252	475	281	312	415	456

TIME OF

POSS.	29:20	31:18	27:01	26:16	27:29	25:25	24:09	26:57	29:35	19:14	23:01

FIRST

DOWNS	19	15	19	10	19	15	14	14	14	16	16
RUSHING	16	12	17	7	12	13	8	13	6	15	15
PASSING	3	2	2	3	7	2	6	1	8	1	1
PENALTY	0	1	0	0	0	0	0	0	0	0	0
TURNOVER	0	1	2	0	0	1	2	2	1	0	1
FUMBLES	1/0	1/1	2/2	1/0	1/0	0/0	3/2	1/1	2/1	2/0	3/1
INTERCEP	0	0	0	0	0	1	0	1	0	0	0

DEFENSE

STATS
RUSHING

YARDAGE	138	100	66	120	64	112	135	146	64	189	84
ATTEMPTS	13	22	31	30	24	23	28	21	12	28	22
AVERAGE	11	5	2	4	3	5	4.8	7	5.3	7.1	3.8

PASSING

ATTEMPTS	25	10	16	17	7	18	7	10	19	8	21
COMPLTD	12	2	5	3	2	10	1	4	7	2	11
YARDAGE	189	35	31	56	48	186	14	34	58	58	183

TOTAL

YARDAGE	327	135	97	176	110	298	149	180	122	247	267

TIME OF

POSS.	18:40	16:42	20:59	21:44	20:31	22:35	23:51	21:03	18:25	28:46	24:59

FIRST

DOWNS	12	5	9	10	8	14	9	8	5	9	10
RUSHING	4	4	7	7	6	8	7	7	3	7	5
PASSING	8	0	2	3	2	6	0	1	2	2	4
PENALTY	0	1	0	0	0	0	2	0	0	0	1
TURNOVER	2	2	3	3	3	2	1	2	1	3	2
FUMBLES	2/2	1/1	2/1	1/1	4/2	0/0	2/1	1/1	1/1	0/0	0/0
INTERCEP	0	1	2	2	1	2	0	1	0	3	2

FIGURE 16–2

offense for both games is almost identical. Probably not much had changed from one game to the next.

Notice as well that the early part of the season reflected relatively few passes. As the season wore on, the passing attack steadily increased, probably because defenses were starting to load up against the team's running game. The good coach obviously wants to anticipate such a defensive strategy—not be surprised by it. A review of previous games will help with such planning. Such information is also helpful when recruiters stop in, and when you want to recap the season for the media and for audiences at banquets.

- *Correspondence/Recruited Athletes*—The 6'10" freshman phenom in high school is on every basketball recruiter's list. This kind of thing doesn't happen very often in football, but it can happen, and sometimes does, with the big junior tackle who is starting on offense and defense for his second year. College coaches often will ask such athletes to visit their campuses near the end of the junior year—at the player's expense in order to stay within the provisions of the NCAA.

While all this is going on, the correspondence can pile up. We normally give such correspondence to the player during the off-season but file it in-season. Coach, player, and parents will have ample opportunity to deal with it when the season ends. It's a rare 17-year-old who can do justice to his schoolwork, play an entire football season, juggle a busy social schedule, and still survive the swelled head that results from scores of letters telling him how great he is.

It is advisable for the coach, however, to look at each letter and to forward appropriate requests to the registrar to mail transcripts to college coaches. Recruiters like to have them on file as soon as possible—and we like to provide them. No one wants to waste time trying to get an academically unqualified athlete into a school which is wrong for both him and the school.

It's a good idea, therefore, to have players, particularly those with college potential, sign the form in figure 16–3 for your files. Once signed, you can forward a copy to the school's registrar and keep the original. Mailing a transcript without such permission can result in legal problems. Obviously, the parent doesn't have to fill out each form, just sign the original; the coach can take care of the rest.

- *Weightlifting Progress Charts*—Because strength conditioning is ongoing throughout the season and school year, progress charts must be filed and reviewed periodically to evaluate player progress. Players who aren't making the gains expected of them require an occasional "conversation," particularly if they are being recruited. College coaches seek this kind of information when they make their first few contacts. That fact alone is motivating to most athletes.
- *Internal and External Memoranda*—I discovered a few years ago that if I dated memos when I responded to them and filed them for future ref-

RELEASE OF INFORMATION

I hereby request that _____ High School forward a copy

of _____'s transcript and test scores to:

_____

_____

_____

Date of original request: _____

Student's full name, including middle initial:

_____

Student's birth date: _____

Student's year of graduation: _____

Please make additional comments or requests:

Parent's signature: _____

Student's signature: _____

FIGURE 16–3

erence, I avoided a whole lot of trouble when "someone" eventually misplaced my response. Better yet, I routinely copy and file every memo and letter I write. There's nothing like documentation when someone swears "you never told me!"

- *All Correspondence*—The same is true of memos and letters you receive. Some folks have a way of writing one thing and remembering something else.

- *Budget Document and Goals*—The yearly discrepancy between expected and actual budget expenditures, particularly if it reflects positively on your planning, is useful for future budget discussions. It is wise to update the document as relevant information is received. It is also wise to document the accomplishment of yearly goal statements and to share such information with appropriate others. People in charge of the purse strings are usually more generous with good planners.

- *Game Films/Tapes*—Smart coaches put original tapes of games in a locked cabinet. They also arrange to have a few copies made of each tape to mail to recruiters who are interested in evaluating the performance of players. It is never wise to send recruiters the only copy of the tape. The originals should always remain in the coach's office. One tape can sometimes determine whether or not a young man plays for a particular college.

- *Letter to Incoming Freshmen*—The Intermediate File is the best place for the letter to eighth graders because the letter is sent in the spring of every school year. Coaches are well-advised to give copies of the letter to every feeder school for distribution to all eighth-grade boys. If finances permit, coaches might even mail them to the homes of each student, particularly to the outstanding athletes.

Coaches who are experiencing a declining student population which is affecting their player turnout are further advised to have senior players visit the homes of selected incoming freshmen to sell the high school football program and to answer questions. Such a procedure underscores the quality of the program and promotes the personal touch that can be so effective when recruiting players. See figure 16–4 for a reproducible. Space has been left at the top of the letter to enable you to copy it on your school's stationery.

- *Memo to Senior Players*—Earlier sections emphasized the need to plan early for the right college experience for student athletes. All senior football players may or may not have done such planning. It's a good idea, therefore, to have each one fill out a form such as the one in figure 16–5 to express their interest in college football and to identify the nature of their preliminary planning. The form also documents all that has been done or that should have been done by the athlete and his parents prior to initiating a process that a results in such an important decision.

Dear Incoming Freshman:

Please take a few moments to accept this invitation to join the _____ High School football team. We are proud of our athletic tradition and recognize that we will be unable to continue it without the involvement of young men like you. We know that you are about to graduate from a school that encourages the kinds of values that we consider so important: hard work, team commitment, individual excellence, and a positive outlook on life. Our football team embraces those values each year, and we have a good time doing it.

If you are interested in becoming a part of the football team's rich tradition and in doing your share to contribute to that tradition, check the box at the bottom of this letter, and we'll be sure to have someone contact you regarding important days and times. I can't think of a better way to introduce yourself to the high school environment and to expand your range of friends and acquaintances.

We hope you decide to join us, and we look forward to working with you during the next school year. Be sure to call if you have any questions.

See you next fall.

With warmest regards,

Head Football Coach

☐ Yes, I'd like to have more information.

Name: _____

Address: _____

FIGURE 16-4

FUTURE PLANS

TO: All Senior Football Players

Now that our season has concluded, you and your parents might be thinking about the possibility of your playing football in college. As the coaching staff has indicated so often in the past, we are always available to help you with any of your plans. In order to help with your plans for the future, especially if they include football, please fill out the bottom of this sheet. We will use the information during our discussions and when we begin the actual process of contacting schools. Recognize, however, that we may not see eye-to-eye regarding your ability to play for all the schools you have identified. You may be better than some, not good enough at others. This list is a starting point and will result in several schools that are just right for you.

Please list the schools that at this point in time you are interested in attending and playing for:

_____

_____

_____

_____

_____

Did you take an interest and/or career inventory to identify possible majors in college?

_____ Yes _____ No

Have you met with your counselor to discuss your college plans?

_____ Yes _____ No

Have you discussed the above list with your parents?

_____ Yes _____ No

Have you been contacted by any of the above schools?

_____ Yes _____ No

FIGURE 16–5

- *Reminder to Parents*—Figure 16–6 provides a reproducible memo to send to the parents of senior football players who are interested in playing in college. It refers to the coalition of coach, parent, player, counselor, and athletic director and reaffirms the importance of all the planning activities mentioned in earlier chapters.

- *Equipment Repairs/Invoices*—Be careful to save all invoices and guarantees regarding the purchase and the repair of equipment—all equipment, including pads, helmets, and uniforms as well as teaching equipment: air flates, stand-up dummies, blasters, sleds, and so forth.

- *Letters to College Coaches*—High school coaches should send letters, probably in the spring of the year, to the college coaches of former players to receive an update on how the players are doing. Such a letter maintains important relationships with college coaches and reminds them that the high school is interested in its graduates and in how they are being treated in college. See figure 16–7 for a reproducible.

- *Letter to Former Players*—It's also a good idea to send letters to each of your former players who are now juniors or seniors in college. A former player's reaction to his college experience provides the single most revealing insight into the quality of his school and its football program. See figure 16–8 for a reproducible. A file of such reactions, appropriately updated, can provide invaluable information for current high school players being recruited by such schools.

- *Maps*—Deerfield High School in Illinois provides a page of maps to parents each year to help them find game sites. I include such an item because of its significant public relations value as well as its encouragement of parent attendance at away games. Copies can be distributed at a pre-season meeting.

- *School Courses and Grading System*—One file should contain a printout of all the college prep courses offered by your school and another of the school's grading system if it is non-standard, i.e., other than A = 4.0, B = 3.0, etc. Such a printout shared with college recruiters clarifies the school's program in relation to NCAA Bylaw 14.3.

THE INDETERMINATE FILE

The Indeterminate File contains information that does not require immediate accessibility but that is potentially useful. Such information is best stored in a computer to save space and to facilitate changing and/or supplementing. Examples of information in the Indeterminate File are:

- *Game Tendencies Versus Regular Opponents*—A five-year accumulation of your own offensive and defensive tendencies versus conference/regular

Dear Mr. and Mrs. _____,

Your son has expressed an interest in playing football on the college level. Because this is such an important decision, I would like to invite you to meet with me at your convenience to discuss next steps. I am hopeful that your son has met with his counselor to discuss his college decisions and to take all the appropriate tests and inventories. If this has not been done, I would suggest that you have him meet with his counselor at his earliest convenience. Our counselors provide invaluable help in this whole process.

In the meantime, if you have any questions, please don't hesitate to contact me. I already have received a list of schools from your son that interest him. We will use that list as the starting point for our discussions.

Again, please don't hesitate to give me a call or to stop by my office if you should be in school.

I look forward to seeing you.

With warmest regards,

Head Football Coach

FIGURE 16–6

Dear Coach _____,

Just a quick note to see how things are going. We're hanging in there on this end and still graduating some pretty good football players. Because one of those players is in your program, I wanted to drop you this note to see how he's doing. I remember how excited he was when you and he came to an agreement; he's been excited ever since.

Have somebody drop me a short note to let me know how he's fitting into your plans and how his schoolwork is coming. If he's falling short of the mark anywhere, I can still exert a little influence on this end!

I hope all is going well for you and your program, and if I can help you in any way, please don't hesitate to give me a call.

I look forward to hearing from you.

With warmest regards,

Head Football Coach

FIGURE 16–7

© 1992 by Michael D. Koehler

301

Dear _____,

Now that you're winding down your college career, I thought you might be able to give your old coach some information. This won't take long, so sharpen one of your pencils and fill out the bottom of this letter at your convenience. I have even included a return envelope. Your convenience was always my first concern!

Are you happy with the educational program at your school?   Yes ____   No ____

What was your specific field of study? _____

Was the campus environment everything you expected?   Yes ____   No ____

From an academic standpoint, if you had the decision to make all over again, would you attend the same school?   Yes ____   No ____

Was your involvement in the football program generally satisfying?   Yes ____   No ____

Did the coaches treat you fairly?   Yes ____   No ____

Was your relationship with them positive?   Yes ____   No ____

From a football standpoint, if you had the decision to make all over again, would you attend the same school?   Yes ____   No ____

Please share any additional comments:

Thanks for taking the time to answer these questions. The information will be very helpful to my current and future players who may be interested in your school. If you have additional comments that you don't want to put in writing, give me a collect call. And don't be a stranger! Be sure to stop in when you next visit school.

With continuing warm regards,

FIGURE 16–8

opponents provides the self-scouting information you need to plan for future contests with them. Anything beyond five years may be useful but unnecessary.

- *Scouting Reports on Regular Opponents*—The five-year accumulation of opponent's tendencies is also very helpful when assessing what certain teams like to do best. If computerized, such information is readily accessible and very revealing.

- *Letters from Former Players*—It's wise at the end of each school year to transfer the insights provided by former players from the file cabinet in your office to the computer in order to develop and maintain cumulative information on each college. The routine cleaning of this file also provides the chance to erase outdated information.

- *Biographical Information*—The computer is the best place to store and, as needed, to update biographical information on the head coach and each of his assistants. Such information is appropriate for media releases, speeches, and publications.

- *History of Football Program*—A brief description of the history of the schools football program is appropriate for occasional media releases and local publications. It should be updated periodically to reflect recent win/loss records and the names of noteworthy players.

- *School Records: Team and Individual*—A comprehensive listing of "most season victories," "most consecutive victories," "most championships," and so forth documents the quality of the program and provides valuable supplementary information when requesting local, state, and national recognition for players.

  Individual records such as "most touchdowns," "most passes completed in a season/game," "most yardage gained in a season/game," "most unassisted tackles," and so on provide the targets for current players and the documentation of superior performance when recommendations are made for player recognition.

- *Effective Pep Talk Themes*—The Indeterminate File is even good for saving the essence of inspirational themes that were particularly successful for you. Sometimes the circumstances and the atmosphere of a particular game inspire us to new heights when we talk to the team before a game or at halftime. I discovered that my best moments occur during halftimes when the game and player performance have acted on me for a full half.

  Saying something at such times is never difficult, and once in a while I hit on a theme that really fires up the players. I like to jot down such themes for future reference. It's fun to resurrect one a couple years later to see if I can hit new heights!

===================================== **LET'S WRAP IT UP** =====================================

The items mentioned in this section were not intended to be exhaustive. Certainly, you will identify additional topics to include in your filing system. You may even use a different system. What is most important is not *what* you file or *how* you file it but *that* you file it. You can save yourself a lot of hassle, some of which is legal, if you maintain appropriate records.

You can also maintain the kind of long and short-term information that helps you prepare for games. As important, you will accumulate information on specific athletes that helps them earn not only recognition for their performance, but scholarships to college. Getting organized, therefore, involves doing yourself and everyone else in the football program a favor.